T0051750

Praise for *Witness*

"Lyle May has written a powerful, must-read book for those embedded in the struggle for freedom, justice, and abolition. Witness is essential reading."
—**MARIAME KABA**, author of *We Do This 'Til We Free Us*

"From death row, May not only presents a searing, unflinching and damning first-hand examination of North Carolina's death row, but also walks the reader through the decades of punitive policies that have built this house of hopelessness."
—**VICTORIA LAW**, journalist and author of *Sentenced to Covid*

"With fierce beauty, *Witness* brilliantly chronicles the everyday and intimate layers of life on death row in a US prison. May's detailed reporting—and, as powerfully, his critical analysis of the prison industrial complex—illuminates crucial pathways to strengthen our movements for healing and liberation for all."
—**ERICA R. MEINERS**, coeditor of *The Long Term* and coauthor of *Abolition. Feminism. Now.*

"Lyle May is a voice for the voiceless. He draws the reader into his experiences and perspectives as a man living with others condemned to death. Remarkably circumspect, he explores ineffective and deadening attempts to deal with crime and criminals that do not redeem the lost and forgotten. Whether or not you agree with him, it is important for us to listen to him. There are some passages in this book that may touch your soul."
—**ALICE LYND**, coauthor with Staughton Lynd of *Moral Injury and Nonviolent Resistance: Breaking the Cycle of Violence in the Military and Behind Bars*

WITNESS

AN INSIDER'S NARRATIVE
OF THE CARCERAL STATE

LYLE C. MAY

FOREWORD BY DANIELLE PURIFOY

Haymarket Books
Chicago, Illinois

© 2024 Lyle C. May

Published in 2024 by
Haymarket Books
P.O. Box 180165
Chicago, IL 60618
www.haymarketbooks.org

ISBN: 978-1-64259-971-8

Distributed to the trade in the US through Consortium Book Sales and Distribution (www.cbsd.com) and internationally through Ingram Publisher Services International (www.ingramcontent.com).

This book was published with the generous support of Lannan Foundation, Wallace Action Fund, and Marguerite Casey Foundation.

Special discounts are available for bulk purchases by organizations and institutions. Please email info@haymarketbooks.org for more information.

Cover artwork by Monica Randazzo.
Cover and interior design by Eric Kerl.

Printed in Canada by union labor.

Library of Congress Cataloging-in-Publication data is available.

10 9 8 7 6 5 4 3 2 1

This book is dedicated to the forsaken.
Our experience is our power.

Contents

Foreword

Danielle Purifoy

I didn't think about what prison does to memory until my uncle Ralph died of COVID-19 in February 2021, while incarcerated in Michigan. He was my dad's big—but not biggest—brother, he had a sweet face, and he could make basically anything with his hands.

I remember holidays and birthdays opening the mailbox to find greeting cards made for 4⅛ x 9½–inch letter envelopes. He folded the cardstock lengthwise, sketched beautifully intricate graphics on the front—candles and holly for the holidays, a cartoon just to say hello. His handwriting was a special slanted calligraphy, inked in straight rows across the paper he carefully pasted to line the card. Sometimes he would send copies of the family photos my dad sent to him back to us, with a cutout of his face pasted in. "Wish I were there!" he'd write. He wanted to share in our memories, but we never got to reciprocate.

The last memories my family has of Uncle Ralph outside of prison are of a man who had been scarred by war. He was the brother who went to Vietnam, who had unspeakable memories that they could not fathom. He was sentenced to life in prison in 1978. My dad was just headed to college. I was six years from being born. Uncle Ralph was only twenty-five years old.

He never wrote much about what happened to him afterwards. I've been trying to piece it together through what he left behind. The documentation of his life, public and private, is entangled with a system designed to throw him away. Every photo he took after 1978 was of a person circumscribed by the prison landscape, wrapped in the uniform of criminality—the jumpsuit, the brick walls, the sometimes weary and resigned face.

Besides the coverage of his crime and conviction, Uncle Ralph appeared in the news once, in *Detroit Free Press* in 1985. There's a picture of him seated casually in front of a US flag with two other men, under the headline "Incarcerated Vietnam Vets Seek Therapy." Despite their awareness of their own war trauma and years of advocating for group therapy and other wellness services at the Jackson prison, they were denied. My uncle wasn't able to process those memories, his past traumas, to get to the root of his harms so he could begin to heal, to be truly accountable to those he harmed. The prison system was only interested in punishment.

For forty-two years, including the day he died, my uncle's daily life was a mystery to most of us. If prison could be compared to a big house, we never got to visit his room. We never got to see how he arranged the photos we sent on his wall. How he sorted his books and magazines. How he got inspiration for his drawings, his cards. What he liked to do when he was outdoors. Who were his friends? What did they do together? What did it feel like when they got to leave, as many of them likely did over the course of four decades? Most of the intimate memories of his adult life, the moments that make you know a person, were contained in a space totally out of our reach.

The first time I got a better glimpse of what my uncle's life might've looked like was when I met Lyle C. May in 2016. Lyle was already a writer when I became his editor for what was then a brand-new magazine called *Scalawag*. I thought we might work on a few articles together and move on, like most relationships with freelance journalists. But Lyle invited me in.

Before the pandemic, every few months or so I'd take the forty-five-minute drive from my home in Durham, North Carolina, to Raleigh to visit Lyle at Central Prison. Every time, I'd have to leave everything but my keys and ID in my car. Despite the fact that I could only see Lyle through plate glass in a room the size of a cell, I was not even allowed to bring pencil and paper into the space. After passing through the metal

A collage by my uncle, Ralph Purifoy, his face layered over a cloudy blue sky.

detector, often more than once, I'd walk through an automatic door to a room that was empty except for a glass display case detailing a celebratory history of the prison and a wall lined with Central Prison T-shirts sold as souvenirs to tourists. The elevator took me to the row of cell rooms, and I'd always find Lyle in one of them, grinning, and ready for our two-hour conversation. We'd talk about everything: life inside, life outside, his writing projects, his classes, new technologies he'd never seen in person.

Lyle's stories helped me better understand what kind of place a prison is, and what those caught in its jaws do to make lives for themselves. I could imagine my Uncle Ralph—the handyman—in the tales Lyle told me about crafting useful objects from unusual scrap materials, in his musings about how fresh air feels after lockdown, in his recollections of random searches, arbitrary punishments, and finding loopholes of opportunity, however small.

In *Witness: An Insider's Narrative of the Carceral State*, Lyle extends his generous invitation to all of us not only into the memories of his life on North Carolina's death row but also into a view of the policies, laws, and procedures of the criminal legal system that are not reflected in the mainstream media. One of Lyle's many contributions to our media landscape is as a journalist on the inside, our witness beyond the prison system's public relations apparatus, beyond the state-controlled narrative. Lyle uses the power of his experience and his education—a rare accomplishment for anyone on death row—to shine a light on the lived realities of incarceration, on the cycles of policies and politics that bear on bodies and psyches and which reinforce daily our society's commitment to punishment over accountability, to disposability over transformation.

As an abolitionist on the "outside," my understandings of the prison-industrial complex are shaped more by ideology than lived experience. I could explain why our systems of policing and prisons should be abolished, but I could not perceive those reasons intimately. By inviting me in, Lyle allowed me to be one of his witnesses, to take in the breathtaking brutality of this system through his experience, and to understand not only how urgent abolition is for our futures, but just how possible it is for us to create a world where safety means systems of care, needs fulfillment, and a radical commitment to life and accountability, not to structures of punishment and disposability.

My uncle's life is over. I will sit forever with the weight of his disappearance from our lives without notice, without a chance for a phone call or even a vigil from my home several states away. Until I received the news of his death, I held tightly to the possibility the state might not swallow him whole, that it might release him to his family where we could make memories in a different landscape, under different conditions, with something other than sadness shaping our smiles. Uncle Ralph did not live to see the destruction of these death systems, but I am resolved that they will fall.

I am so thankful for Lyle's immense brilliance, courage, and strength as he takes risks to write the truth to the world, to tell us what we need to know to get us all free. I can't wait for the day we can take a walk in the Carolina sun together, no glass between us, no bars behind us.

PART I

STATE OF VIOLENCE

CAPITAL PUNISHMENT
AND DEATH ROW

Chapter 1

Learning to Die

Unit Three's pod reminded me of the Buncombe County Jail cell-blocks: L-shaped twelve-cell tiers, bright fluorescent lights that banish shadows, white walls, and steel tables amidst a light gray painted day-room floor. Except this was death row. Red lacquered paint coated the doors, rails, and stairs. Compared to the old death row blocks on Unit Two, Unit Three's pods were sterile, capacious, and vermin-free when they opened in June 2002.

Nearly two hundred death row prisoners were moved to Unit Three, and I knew a few dozen of them, mostly from the two blocks I had lived on before our exodus. The rest I heard about, saw once or twice, or did not know at all. When I arrived on the row in March '99, I did not have much opportunity to interact with people from other blocks. In the old building the only chance we had to intermingle between blocks occurred at bible study, and not many willingly suffered through an hour of biblical castiga-tion just to hang out. Unit Three's pods—four each on the two floors—sat adjacent to one another so we could wave through giant plexiglass win-dows, shout through cracks in the hallway doors, or stand in the hallway and talk when the pod doors opened for chow and outside recreation.

Assigned to Pod Eight, I only knew about half of the guys there. Settling in proved easy enough, because getting to know people in prison is only hard if you have never been there. Once in prison, if you're paying attention, you can get a feel for who you might be able to talk with and who should be avoided. It remains something of a process though, a tricky dance reminiscent of high school, but more dangerous.

When I met Eddie, he sat hunched over a dayroom table playing a card game my mother taught me as a child. From what I observed, Eddie seemed quiet and mild-mannered. No signs of sudden psychoticism or cruelty. No frothing at the mouth or telling twitches. For all intents and purposes, he appeared a normal middle-aged, pasty-faced white guy with a perpetual three-day beard. He didn't talk much or loudly (loud mouths, braggarts, and know-it-alls are the bane of every prison cellblock in America). Mainly, Eddie looked forlorn.

"You play cribbage?" he asked and gathered the cards. In jail and prison, playing cards or other table-top games has less to do with leisure and more to do with a shared medium through which people can communicate without any awkwardness or discomfort. Engaging in a game—any game—also gives people a chance to discover your character and provides you an opportunity to learn about theirs.

I hesitated before sitting. I didn't know this guy, and despite needing to learn more about who lived around me, caution was always necessary. Was he a predator? A bully? Or worse, somebody who would draw people like that? In my first few months on the row, I had to prove to others I would not be punked or bullied. Young white boys have it hard in prison if they lack a will to not only defend themselves, but live free of any future harassment. Thoughts of my first fight on death row ran through my mind: An older Black man named Fly tried to push me around, verbally disrespecting and otherwise letting me know what he thought of white people. When I asked him to cut it out he said, "Whatcha gonna do about it white boy?" So we fought and I earned my respect.

Eddie quickly dealt the cards as I set pegs in the cribbage board. The rules of the game returned with memories of rainy summers playing cards in a tent my siblings and I set up in the backyard. While we played, Eddie asked where I lived before becoming incarcerated. "Maine," I said, and his eyes widened a bit. "And I regret ever leaving."

"Maine? No shit? I should've stayed in Newport News or Virginia Beach."

"Hey! I've been to Virginia Beach. I took a Greyhound there in November of '96 thinking it would be crowded. The place was deserted."

"Yeah. You should've gone in August or earlier. The nightlife is amazing." We spoke knowing it had less to do with where we missed and more to do with a shared desire to be free from prison and the threat of execution.

Over the next few months Eddie told me he worked in a pawn shop and about the different things people from all walks of life sold there. I soon discovered the pawn shop stood central in Eddie's life. Whenever Dan, Tim, JJ, or I sat with Eddie at chow he would find a way to interject, "That reminds me of this one time at the pawn shop," and immediately launch into a story that lay on the shelf of his mind, marked at a discount: buy one, get three for free.

I always felt disadvantaged swapping stories about the outside. The amount of time I spent away from the sheltered world of my parents' house in Brunswick spanned three years. Between those ages of sixteen and nineteen my freedom was perforated by stints in a group home, rehab, hospital, and the Maine Youth Center. I knew more about life inside institutions than life on the outside. So I listened to certain older men like Harvey, Mule, Earl, and Roper to rid myself of any naivete. They stood in as uncles and mentors in a place with few role models. Eddie was more of a peer, so his stories about selling everything he owned as cocaine and alcohol addiction consumed his life were relatable.

"Man, I stayed high and drunk every day," he said. "Three- and four-day binges where I couldn't even remember my name or where I put my car. When I started shooting cocaine it was over. I'd wake up in a different zip code, in a strange house, struggling to remember anything." I nodded, glancing at the TV, overcome with kinship and discomfort because of the similarities to my own drug-hazed journey to death row. Beyond a shared addiction, Eddie and I held no expectations of each other aside from a quiet conversation about a book, movie, or song on the radio. Our conversations, like those with others I called "friend," were devoid of the posturing and lies typical in prison. And, of course, we discussed the executions.

In December of '02 Ernest Basden and Desmond Carter were put to death. Questions about Basden's innocence helped him get a few stays, but they were not enough to save him. Unit Three's atmosphere stayed the same as it had during an execution in the old building: tense, brittle, and oppressively quiet, as if too much noise would break loose a scream of terror trapped in all of us. We suspected the state would make up for the low number of executions in 2002. We were right; 2003 became the deadliest year for death row prisoners since North Carolina reinstated the death penalty in 1977.

An execution is scheduled by the warden ninety days in advance of the date, but the condemned is almost always notified forty-five days into that period, after the court, attorneys, and state receive notice. The condemned is summoned to the warden's office, informed an execution date has been set, and asked if he or she needs anyone contacted. About once a week, until the final twenty-four hours on death watch, the warden summons the condemned to his office—willing or not—to ask after his or her state of mind. Like with the warden, check-ins with a shrink are mandatory because a condemned prisoner has nothing left to lose, making them a significant security risk in the eyes of prison officials.

By the end of July 2003, William Quentin Jones was scheduled to die August 22; Henry Hunt, September 12; and Joseph Bates, September 26. As their dates approached, Eddie grew increasingly distracted and nervous. When I asked about it, he said, "I'm out of appeals and I think I'm next." I hadn't paid Eddie's appeal much attention, because Mule had already received a date. Also, Eddie seemed uncertain, as if he was guessing and had no official word from his attorneys.

Henry Hunt, or "Mule," as most of us knew him, was a good friend who taught me a lot. A full-blooded Tuscarora Indian from Robeson County and a devout Catholic, Mule and I received Catholic confirmation together in 2000 when Bishop Gossman came to Central Prison for the ceremony. Mule also introduced me to the resident stray cats in the old building, showed me how to make potato wine, fix a radio, and a host of other things only somebody who grew up in the country and prison would know. He was serious and funny, generous, and slightly wild. My favorite uncle in and out of prison, Mule liked teaching me things because I listened—especially when it came to "home remedies" and finessing limited resources in prison. Once, after playing with the cats, I noticed I caught a ring worm on my shoulder. Worried, I told Mule about filling out a sick call, but he stopped me.

"Boy," he said, "don't you know ring worm comes from animals? What you gonna tell them people? 'I got worms in the shower?' Come here." He took a rag, dipped it in bleach, and rubbed the infected spot until it burned. "If that don't fix it, fill out a sick call and tell 'em you been playin' with a mouse. Leave my cats out of it." Surprisingly, the bleach worked, leaving a light, ring-shaped scar on my shoulder.

Though Mule lived on another block when they gave him a date, I saw him at mass every Thursday and was present when Father Dan gave him viaticum—the last sacrament of a Christian. If Mule was worried, I never saw it. He seemed resigned to his fate, as if peace came with faith and understanding a new journey was about to begin.

A week before the state killed William Quentin Jones, a man I never met, Eddie received an October 3 execution date.

"What are your lawyers saying?" I asked, but Eddie just sighed.

"You know. Same bullshit they tell everyone. Clemency is my last best chance." My faith in clemency died after Harvey Green demonstrated rehabilitation through his Christian ministry, and Ronald Frye provided reams of documents detailing childhood abuse and was the poster child of abuse for the HHS.* Both were denied clemency by the governor and executed. But there was always a chance Eddie could get that golden ticket.

Mule's execution was a gut punch that left me numb and breathless, unable to think or know what to do. I tried to read but just stared at the page, waiting for the trapped feeling to pass. It never did. Since I lived on the pod with Joe Bates, seeing him withdraw as his time grew short was unnerving. Normally, Joe played poker, talked about sports, or religiously watched *The Young and the Restless*. All of that stopped after Mule's execution, and Joe sat on his bunk flipping through magazines, stood at a narrow window looking at the sky, or leaned against the wall, arms folded, frowning at the TV. He spoke little in the final days, and then only in terse statements. When the death squad came for him, Joe gave out some hugs and handshakes and, on his way out the door, said, "All right. Y'all be easy."

---

* Department of Health and Human Services

When the executions happened one after another, within two or three weeks of the next, it was too much to process. For the most part, we didn't. We were struggling to live, existing between the remorseless deaths carried out by the state and our own thoughts for the dark future. The people, our brothers and friends, who were escorted down the halls of the prison to be exterminated, disappeared from memory much like small-shelled creatures are buried by the pounding ocean surf. Here one moment. Then gone. We were the witnesses who remained, waiting for it to claim us too.

The day before they took Eddie to death watch for the final seventy-two hours of his life, we sat in his cell smoking cigarettes. Smoke streamed through a rectangle of sunlight, thick and poisonous with the things we avoided in idle conversation. His time on death watch would be spent visiting with attorneys, family, and friends, many of whom suddenly wanted to visit after years of silence. Eddie's time on death row had been harder than most since he rarely received visits or money for the canteen. What he had, he received from those of us kind enough to give it. People on the outside never give much thought to what prisoners do to get by, assuming meals provided at the chow hall are enough, but state food doesn't always relieve hunger and a little money for the canteen goes a long way. Without access to a job, Eddie went hungry for years.

I watched a curl of smoke roll up the cell wall and hit the ceiling as we sat in silence. Was it like this for all the condemned? This awkward time when you wait for the state to repossess your body. "Can I tell you something, man?" Eddie stared at the floor, hands on knees, his face slack and unshaven. "I'm scared. I don't want to die." He looked up. "Why does it have to be this way?"

How could I answer that, after seven people had been released from death row over the last nine months with their sentences reduced to life or less? Eddie was convicted and sentenced under the felony murder rule, the only difference between life and death, a robbery conviction with the murder. Hundreds of murder cases like his ended up with life sentences because the additional felony was dropped in exchange for a guilty plea. But Eddie refused to plead guilty and received a death sentence for exercising his right to a jury trial.

My faith in God was not strong enough to share with Eddie. Besides, we all prayed for deliverance from this nightmare only to awaken the next day, our lives ground into the concrete until only dust remained. Religion failed to comfort me, so how could I comfort him? Doubt and an overwhelming sense of helplessness made it hard to speak. "I don't know, Eddie. It just is." In my heart a voice spat bitterness: Our lot is based on luck of the draw.

When they came for Eddie, a sergeant pushed an empty hand cart onto the block; the warden, unit manager, and a shift captain walked in behind him. Eddie put a white plastic property bag on the cart: old pictures and letters to be collected by whoever came to pick up his body.

One by one, guys went over and gave Eddie a hug, dap, or handshake; a few saying nothing, others a brief word of encouragement.

"Keep your head up, Eddie."

"All right, my friend, I'm gonna miss you."

"Stay strong, my man."

When my turn came, I struggled to think of something profound and symbolic of our friendship, but words failed. "Take it easy. You're good people to me." I hugged him and turned away, not wanting to see him cry. Not wanting him to see me cry. The brass escorted him from the block and out of sight down the hallway.

In 2003, North Carolina's lethal injection was a three-drug cocktail that included sodium thiopental, which acts as an anesthetic; pancuronium bromide, a paralytic agent; and potassium chloride, which causes cardiac arrest. It has never been adequately explained why an overdose of some anesthetic is not an option. After the three-drug cocktail was administered, it took Edward Ernest Hartman nearly an hour to die. His attorney and other witnesses reported seeing him gasp and jerk against the gurney straps, his eyes fluttering open and shut despite being "sedated and paralyzed." The prosecutor who attended the execution—who could have just as easily given Eddie a life sentence—declared, "Justice has been served."

The day after an execution is like having a hangover; your head throbs and stomach turns; laughter grates on every nerve and the light seems too bright. That people are genuinely supportive of this misery makes it worse, but the state proved their intent to kill by scheduling three more executions after Eddie: Joseph Timothy Keel, November 7; John Daniels, November 14; and Robbie J. Lyons, December 5.

In the same period, four more prisoners had their death sentences overturned and were sentenced to life without parole. Reconciling the arbitrariness of who receives life and who is put to death is not something I have been able to do. In the meantime, I think about Mule, Harvey, Eddie, and all the rest who were executed. I try to overcome the bitterness, anger, and despair, and fail. Their faces rise up and engulf my thoughts in the quiet moments, leaving me to wonder which one of my friends will be next.

Chapter 2

Secrecy and the Death Penalty

When I told my mom I would be speaking about the death penalty with a group of students, she wanted to hear my talking points. I hesitated at first. Normally, we avoid discussing capital punishment because it upsets her. But she insisted.

I gave mom a synopsis of how secrecy laws allow state officials to hide their acquisition of lethal injection drugs. I told her that in the coming weeks my friend Jason would discuss his restorative justice efforts and how North Carolina laws prohibit prisoners from reaching out to the victims and their families, making atonement for a crime difficult. I told her how my friend JT would discuss his experience receiving an execution date, getting final visits from family, and then receiving an indefinite stay of execution, and the psychological toll this had on him. Finally, I talked about how life without parole (LWOP) is death by incarceration and the newest form of capital punishment—with none of its legal protections.

When I finished, Mom said, "What about the condemned's family? Nobody ever talks about what they suffer." She was right.

Family members of the condemned are victimized three times. First, by the alleged crimes their loved one has been convicted of and sentenced for, which brings horror, heartbreak, ostracism, and shame to the family. Unless family members publicly denounce the accused, they're thought to be complicit. Second, the family of the condemned—assuming they agree to help—is dragged through court proceedings, their backgrounds excoriated and their lives denigrated as if they were political candidates. Third, assuming the family sticks around after the trial—and many do not—they suffer in a way unique to blood bonds and unconditional love. My parents have suffered through my incarceration, day-for-day, for over twenty-six years.

The state does not provide victims' services for prisoner's families. What they do reserve are a few seats in a witness room attached to the execution chamber. They'll be in the same room as the victim's family, prosecutors, law enforcement, defense attorneys, and a single journalist to represent "the public." They will also be told not to speak to anyone or make a scene.

When my parents visited a number of years ago, we talked about the possibility of my execution being carried out. I did not want them to watch. No parent should have to experience the loss of a child, nor should they witness the manner of that death like some twisted sporting event, even if it is for moral support.

I knew enough about the lethal injection to recognize other reasons they should not watch. The three-drug cocktail used by North Carolina would not render me unconscious or unfeeling, just paralyzed and unable to vocalize being burned alive from the inside. I never told my parents about how Eddie and other friends of mine have taken a long time to die once given the lethal injection—and this was before the state ran out of sodium thiopental. I'll never tell them how my death certificate will read "homicide" as the official cause of death. My parents have suffered enough.

When talking with Mom about this class she asked a question that initially aggravated me, but I understood why she wanted to know. She said, "When the vet put Alex to sleep it only took a few minutes. Why don't they use those drugs in executions?" Alex was my dad's Great Dane.

My immediate response was to bristle—"Mom, we're not animals!" Then I took a breath and explained how the FDA* would never officially allow it, different doses would be needed, and secrecy laws prevent us from knowing what kinds of drugs are being used.

The lethal injection was created in 1977 by Oklahoma medical

_____

* Food and Drug Administration

examiner Dr. Jay Chapman. He designed the original three-drug cock-tail, variations of which are still in use today: sodium thiopental to sedate the prisoner, pancuronium bromide to paralyze and prevent any outward signs of suffering, and potassium chloride to stop the heart. Clean, ef-ficient, relatively quick, and modern. Chapman did not anticipate that other states would adopt his execution protocol, changing drugs without understanding their combined application. By medicalizing the death penalty, states hoped to further civilize the process and reduce public objections to its cruelty. If, after all, a convicted murderer drifts off to his or her final rest it's a win-win scenario: civilized, humane "justice"; painless, peaceful death.

There are several problems Chapman never accounted for. First, doc-tors and nurses swore an oath to "do no harm" and immediately balked at the use of their medical knowledge to kill. This left untrained prison guards to measure dosage, set up tubing, insert needles, and administer the injection—none of which is as easy as it sounds. Under the pressure of an audience, and with the ultimate goal of the cold and calculated killing of another human being, it becomes much harder. Small wonder human error is a common factor in the lethal injection.

Second, many drug suppliers demanded prison officials stop using their products in executions, filing lawsuits in federal courts to halt any execution using their particular chemical. As it became difficult for states to acquire sodium thiopental, they relied on compounding pharmacies to create the drug, which was almost always contaminated or inferior and caused the prisoner to be conscious during the execution.

Third, dwindling drug supplies led state officials to illegally import and otherwise smuggle execution drugs into the United States from other countries. While doing so circumvented litigation by US drug makers, this is illegal. Despite the fact DEA* agents and the FDA have caught and seized smuggled execution drugs, no state or prison official has ever been charged with a crime. The average citizen doing exactly the same thing can receive life imprisonment.

Finally, states turned to alternative drugs for the lethal injection.

---

* Drug Enforcement Administration

Because this requires guesswork, uncertainty, and creation of a new execution protocol—complicated by all the problems above—it allows for legal challenges to what is essentially human experimentation. New litigation also means greater expense to the state and longer delays for prisoners on death row. To avoid this, states began passing secrecy laws to hide where the drugs come from, what they are, how they're used, and who is responsible and involved in the process.

If the lethal injection was as quick and allegedly painless as euthanizing an animal, it's unlikely it would ever have faced the same level of scrutiny. The medicalized model implies an interest in killing people in a humane manner, but the evidence screams the opposite. It is an open secret that *your* elected officials in the legislature never cared *how* death row prisoners are put to death as long as the public acquiesces. Secrecy and the death penalty have an important historical context in North Carolina, one that is connected to the 2009 Racial Justice Act (RJA).[1]

North Carolina's death penalty grew from an effort by the state to curtail lynch mobs during Reconstruction and continue oppressing people of color. Legal lynchings, as the death penalty became known, did not give any more rights or protections to their primarily Black targets than did the ignorant, enraged mobs calling for their deaths. With the state firmly in control of very public executions, unruly crowds became willing spectators of the government's power over their lives. It wasn't until 1907 that the attorney general pushed the NC General Assembly to conduct executions behind closed doors. Although the reasoning had little to do with civilized society.

White supremacist observers and their ilk worried that the increasing racial diversity of the crowds at public hangings presented a social threat. Because the condemned were usually Black men and boys and were allowed final words to the crowd, concerns grew that they would become martyrs and incite unrest among the African American population. Those concerns arose in the late nineteenth and twentieth centuries because women of color had entered civic life in strength. Educated middle-class Black women formed suffrage and mutual-aid societies, developing networks that strengthened social and civic bonds while at the same time asserting their humanity. Public hangings became "surprising places of community building and political engagement."[2] Working-class Black women gathered to defend Black men and simultaneously developed their role in the Black community that so threatened Jim Crow society. Black women at public executions claimed enough civic space that it forced white supremacist state officials to conduct their legal lynchings in secret.

Over the years, execution methods may have changed—the amount of time between arrest and execution may have lengthened and more white people are sentenced to death—but the racist ideology governing capital punishment is the same; its fundamental flaws institutionalized. Now the death penalty impacts minorities, poor people of any race, and anyone who falls through the cracks of society. As 2016 exoneree Anthony Ray Hinton said, "Capital punishment means those without capital get punished."[3]

In an attempt to remove racial discrimination from North Carolina's death penalty and redress capital sentences gained through such prejudice, the NC General Assembly passed the Racial Justice Act in 2009. The RJA allowed death row prisoners of any race to challenge their sentence by using statewide statistics that show a pattern of discrimination. To be clear, racial bias relates to three specific elements of the death penalty: the race of the victim, the race of the defendant, and the racial makeup of the jury. Of the three, prosecutors are trained to remove potential Black jurors from consideration because they are less likely to vote for the death penalty, believe prosecutors, or trust law enforcement. Removing a potential juror from consideration on the basis of his or her race is unconstitutional and the core of the Batson doctrine, from *Batson v. Kentucky, 476 US 79* (1986).

Racial jury rigging in capital prosecutions affect every defendant, regardless of his or her race. Researchers were able to prove this by compiling a substantial amount of data that demonstrates routine prejudice during voir dire of capital trials. In other words, North Carolina's death penalty may originate from Jim Crow society, but the cancer of its racist past lives on in the twenty-first-century general assembly, the governor's office, judicial seats, district attorney's offices, and sheriff's departments.

In 2012 the Republican-controlled North Carolina General

Assembly removed many of the RJA's provisions, then repealed the law entirely in 2013 once they gained a supermajority in both chambers. The repeal was signed by Republican governor Pat McCrory. Four prisoners who received sentences of life without parole because of the RJA were returned to death row. It would not be until 2020 that the state Supreme Court concluded the RJA repeal and the amended RJA could not be applied to previously filed claims by people on death row. The court held that such alterations to the law violated ex post facto laws and cannot be constitutionally applied retroactively to defendants with pending RJA claims. This incensed the Republicans because nearly every death-sentenced prisoner (approximately 135) filed an RJA claim. The court, by restoring those claims, guaranteed at least a hearing for each individual to pursue "relief" from a death sentence in the form of LWOP. As of early 2023, only four of the original RJA claims have been processed by the courts and won relief.

Secrecy has no place in the criminal justice system, especially when the state makes life and death decisions as an extension of the public's "will." This is why it's *critical* to get educated about crime and punishment, the legal system, and who is elected to carry out "justice." Never think you are powerless to change the minds of the elected officials who represent you. Never think these laws and circumstances don't apply to you: plenty of innocent people have been put on death row.

As it stands in 2023, the majority of North Carolinians believe the death penalty is unnecessary, does not deter crime, puts innocent people at risk, and is fundamentally racist.[4] Yet Republican legislators and conservative southern Democrats continue to push for executions. They pass secrecy laws to restart medicalized, lethal experiments. They pretend there have not been twelve people exonerated from North Carolina's death row since 1973. Then they deny their responsibility for a criminal justice system that oppresses the poor and marginalized.

Lack of accountability among law enforcement officers (LEOs) and elected officials at the city, county, and state level enables the oppression of marginalized groups in the name of "justice" and morality. There was no justice or morality around when George Floyd was policed to death. John Neville faced the same fate while confined at the Forsyth County

Jail in 2019. About a month into his confinement Neville experienced a medical emergency. When deputies responded they placed Neville in the "prone restraint" position, the same that was used against Floyd. Neville went into cardiac arrest as a result of "compressional and positional suffocation." Unlike Floyd, when it became obvious Neville was dying, he was rushed to the hospital where the LEOs tried to wash their hands of it. Neville died. It would take some time before a tooth-and-nail litigatory battle waged by multiple media outlets gained video footage of the encounter between Neville and the LEOs. The truth outed, five former LEOs and a nurse were charged with involuntary manslaughter.[5] During all of this, the Republican-controlled general assembly, along with a number of Democrats, sought to pass a law that would prevent the release of any in-custody death records. Until the public protested it, Democratic Governor Roy Cooper, himself a former attorney general, was poised to sign the bill into law. Secrecy and state-sanctioned murder go hand-in-hand.

Chapter 3

A Confirmation of Faith

"If you believe and I believe
And we together pray
The Holy Spirit must come down
And set God's people free."

—Spiritual Hymn, author unknown

None who attend Catholic Mass on North Carolina's death row are especially pious or reverent. Washing hands prior to service, not cursing in front of the priest, and participating at all the appropriate moments proved challenging enough. Then there was the singing. I generally like to sing, and did my best to stay in tune, but most of the guys spoke or mumbled hymns through gritted teeth, as if the act of making a joyful noise in prison was painful. Sometimes it is.

Still, the ritual was often an oasis in the desolation of my confinement. When I first arrived on death row in '99 and began attending mass, there were eight of us: me, Angel, Elias, Eric, Jeff, Mule, Pat, and Terry. We were a small group in a prison dominated by Protestant Christians and Muslims. For decades, the Protestant chaplains refused to acknowledge Catholicism or provide services to anyone claiming the faith. When Angel got to death row in '96, he was so incensed upon discovering the anti-Catholic sentiment, that he wrote a letter to Pope John Paul II expressing his desire to practice Catholicism, receive communion, and give confession to a priest.

Though Angel never received a direct response from the Vatican, several months later the chaplain grudgingly announced that priests from the Church of St. Francis of Assisi in Raleigh would begin conducting Mass for us.

We met on Thursday afternoons for roughly an hour, seated at steel tables in the dayroom of the "church block," so designated because all religious services were held there. We sang, read, and discussed scripture, received the Holy Eucharist, and tried to develop our faith in God.

I wasn't new to Catholicism. My siblings and I had all been altar servers at two Catholic parishes in Maine. Mom taught Sunday school classes for children. She had strong opinions about other parishioners and, for a while, resisted what she saw as the falsity of their faith. Eventually then, it grew to be too much. She tried other churches in the area, but none seemed to fit. When she stopped attending, she gave us the chance to opt out, and as kids, we chose the free Sunday.

Jeff came from a similar background to mine—white, middle class—but his parents had been with St. Francis of Assisi Church since it was founded in Raleigh. Of our group, Jeff and Eric—a Costa Rican immigrant and Vietnam vet and former army captain, respectively—were the only members to have received the Sacrament of Confirmation prior to their incarceration. Our consistent attendance at mass prompted Fr. Dan to offer Angel, Pat, Terry, Elias, Henry, and me a chance to be confirmed, since we hadn't been as teens. We all accepted.

At first, I attended Mass on death row to escape the cigarette smoke and noise on my block, where people shouted to be heard over the TV, slammed dominoes on tables, squabbled, laughed, cursed, and made thinking impossible in the crowded space. Not that many people at the prison wanted us to think. Not the guards who carried out executions. Not the doctors who liberally prescribed opioids and toxic levels of psych meds. Not the nurses who gave out extra pills. And certainly not ourselves.

Catholic Mass became a respite in the way an Alcoholics Anonymous meeting in a church basement sobers some drunks. Knowing we had little time and not wanting to drive anyone away, the priests mainly cared that we were respectful and kept coming back. It didn't matter that

Pat grinned and made faces while we sang or that Terry was so heavily medicated he mixed pop culture with scripture or that Eric was ready to argue with everyone. Fr. Dan and Fr. Mark were patient, politely correcting our misunderstandings, and answering (most of the time) our obnoxious questions, even though we knew better: *No, Catholics don't worship Mary, they venerate her. Saints are not ghosts, and the Holy Spirit is not a saint or a ghost. Yes, even the people Mule called "heathens" could enter Heaven by the grace of God.*

We sat in a horseshoe around two tables, with the priest at the top, me on his left, then Elias, Angel, Jeff, Pat, Terry, Mule, and Eric. Fr. Dan gave the six of us who wanted to be confirmed a Rite of Christian Initiation of Adults (RCIA) study guide about choosing to convert to Catholicism as adults. I lived on the same block as Mule (who was only called "Henry" at mass; even guards called him Mule) and we studied together whenever there was a lull in the noise and we were both sober—neither of which was often. My questions continued, some of them earnest and genuine, others that would have embarrassed my mother. Jeff jumped in on the more philosophical discussions at mass, ready to argue about any secular or scientific point. Angel largely said nothing, only interjecting if some historical fact was in dispute. Sometimes we directed questions at each other, shared bits about our background in the Church, and got off topic, but the priests gently brought us back.

"Okay, guys. Let's profess our faith."

Though I attended Mass as a refuge, I remained defiant and angry inside. Faith in God was a question in my mind that would not be easily answered. I think Elias saw this in me. He mostly listened to our discussions, sometimes commenting, but always attentive. One day, after Mass, upon seeing me make the sign of the cross with my left hand, Elias pulled me aside.

"Lyle," he said, his Jordanian roots heavily accenting his English, "why you make the sign of the cross with left hand? This is bad. You should make it with the right." He demonstrated until I nodded. "Good. You seem a nice boy." Elias patted me on the shoulder, stern but pleasant.

I was one of the youngest people on death row at the time, turning twenty-one a month before being sentenced to death. This meant I got called "boy" a lot, especially by the older guys from the South. Elias acknowledged my youth, but he wasn't disrespectful, just kind.

Elias was generally quiet and unobtrusive. A machinist in the Jordanian Army before immigrating to America, he had a knack for finessing the few things we could have. He would, for example, sharpen a disposable razor purchased from the canteen for fifteen cents. Where I might use one a few times and throw it away, he reused the same one for months. Elias had a pair of black dress shoes he polished every day, only wearing them to Mass or visits. When the bottoms wore out, he resoled them with cutouts from a plastic-rubber trash can. After the prison banned personal shoes and he had to send them to a friend, Elias was disgusted.

"Why do they do this? These people—they have no mercy. Praise God I have learned better."

Elias was convicted and sentenced to death for killing his wife in the midst of a bitter argument over her cheating. He pled guilty, but the district attorney (DA) charged him with first-degree murder, which, in North Carolina until 2001, mandated a capital trial. The DA knew this when Elias pled guilty, and so did his attorney, but there was no offer of second-degree murder. Elias did not try to justify his actions, expressing only remorse and sorrow for his children, whom he prayed for at every mass.

After twelve weeks of study, Elias, Pat, Terry, Mule, Angel, and I received the Sacrament of Confirmation, the rite that sealed our entrance into the Catholic faith as adults. Bishop Gossman presided, wearing heavy robes and burgundy vestments, carrying an oak staff curled at the top like an unfurled fern, and greeting us like long lost sons, not grown men on death row. Fr. Dan and Fr. Mark served the bishop, one lighting incense in a brass censer while the other held a book containing the rite's liturgy, prayers, and vows.

We were allowed use of a small conference room for the occasion, barely big enough to contain eight death row prisoners, two priests, the bishop, the chaplain, and a guard. And it was nice to have a little privacy for what was a special moment in a place devoid of them. Elias looked harried and nervous. Pat cracked jokes about the bishop's garb and asked to borrow his staff. Terry talked quietly with Eric while struggling to stay awake. Mule and I stood in a corner watching everything get set up and laughing at Terry when he fell asleep as Eric talked about the military. Jeff and Angel watched the priests and spoke to each other in Spanish.

Pursuing faith in God while elected leaders and the courts invoked that same God to kill us was difficult at first. It's like digging into rocky soil for a place to plant a seed and only finding more rock, and then the shovel breaks and it refuses to rain. Part of the effort is desperation, a need that folds the body around it until ordinary thought becomes impossible.

Some people mock prisoners who experience come-to-Jesus moments, claiming it is a pretense—anything to save one's neck and gain compassion from a secular world. Maybe there are a handful of people who mistakenly believe that kind of thinking works, but they are usually the same people who learn about prison from TV shows and films. I returned to my Catholic upbringing, professing a faith I didn't completely feel, because I was suffering and needed answers from God.

Why have you allowed me to suffer? Why did you abandon me?

As a child, when I was an altar server, the priests often sent me on errands that required crossing before the altar. A giant crucifix hung suspended from the ceiling and every time, no matter how much of a hurry I was in or whether the church was empty, I genuflected and made the sign of the cross with my right hand. If I forgot, my feet stopped of their own accord and brought me back to kneel. This ingrained obedience and reverence to a God who often seemed absent had waned over time, but enough remained to continue seeking Him out. I knew no quick answers would be forthcoming, but at least I was not alone. Others searched for the same reason, digging in the rocky ground of our lives even when it seemed impenetrable. Elias, Mule, Terry, Pat, Angel, and I, in receiving the Sacrament of Confirmation as adults, affirmed our dedication to that struggle.

Growing faith in God, even faith the size of a mustard seed, is as much persistence with little obvious effect as it is an evolution in identity supported by action. The lessons the priests taught us were simple: Love one another. Love God. Forgive one another. Read the Word of God. Repeat. How we interpreted that in our daily lives varied: I listened, Pat laughed, Terry and Eric reminisced; Angel dispensed kindness, Jeff charity, Mule devotion, and Elias compassion. Together we prayed, learned, and shared our strengths while connecting both at mass and beyond.

Sometimes reality cuts so deeply and savagely that you feel the cold numbness of loss before any blood appears. It was like this the day of an execution. First, the executioner's meal appeared behind the large windows of a locked office. Two long tables laden with food for a picnic and a colorfully frosted sheet cake. Death row prisoners filed by the display on the way to and from the chow hall. Staff claimed they were snacks for guards serving the execution shift, but a sheet cake is a strange snack unless you're the executioner celebrating a job well done. I had already witnessed over a dozen such celebratory meals and knew enough to mentally prepare for what was to come.

Mule was put to death September 13, 2003.

The hardest discussions at mass were the ones that never took place. After Mule's execution, Fr. Dan's homily was short and fell into a bottomless silence. None of us wanted to be there and nothing was said for a few minutes. Being confirmed didn't alter our despair or make it less necessary to keep grief on a tight leash. More executions were scheduled for the year. In some ways it was easier to embrace fatalism, the inevitability of death. It made talking about an execution a frivolous exercise for the living. We were already dead.

Finally, Elias spoke. "Father, you know, it's hard to live in this place. They have no mercy. They kill us—young, old, Black, white, sick, healthy—then call it justice. Prison is enough, but still, they kill us. Where is the Church, Father?"

It may have been the hardest question any of us asked. Fr. Dan attempted to explain the disconnect between Vatican teaching and America's love affair with capital punishment. That devout Catholics could be totally against abortion, contraception, and embryonic stem cell treatment, yet support the death penalty was baffling. Diocesan bishops were too quiet on the matter, appearing more like bureaucrats than disciples of Jesus Christ. In the early 2000s, the loudest and most consistent voice cutting through Catholic hypocrisy and calling for the right-to-life from conception to natural death was not the Pope, cardinals, or bishops, but a nun from Louisiana. Sister Helen Prejean's advocacy for the men and women on death row forced anyone who kneels before the cross to answer a question: Can you really be a Christian, a follower of the Son of

God, and support the death of your neighbor? North Carolina Governor Mike Easley would have to answer this question when Elias received his November 18, 2005, execution date.

At his final Mass with us, before being taken to death watch for the final seventy-two hours of his life, Elias received the Sacrament of the Last Rite. When it came time to say prayers and intentions, my friend prayed for his children and asked for mercy, as he always had. Then he spoke to us.

"Thank you, brothers, for being with me. For accepting me. Peace be with all of you and your families." After the service we each gave Elias a hug and said our goodbyes.

I was naively hopeful that Governor Easley, who professed to be Catholic, would commute Elias's sentence. There was reason to believe he might—especially since Elias's adult children, who were also the victim's family, advocated for clemency. They met with the governor and begged him to spare their father, saying they didn't want to lose another parent to the same murder.

Elias's children also spoke with the local media, again pleading with the governor to show mercy. They pled with the DA who prosecuted Elias, rightly arguing that as victims of the crime, they should have a say in the punishment. Absent from their public pleas was any support from a victims' rights group.

Elias Syriani was put to death on November 18, 2005.

Pat had a fairly insouciant attitude about executions, including his own. "There's no need to get worked up over it. It's gonna happen whether I want it or not." Before he left for death watch, and after his final mass with us, Pat cracked jokes about going to see the big leprechaun in the sky. "I'm part Irish and they're executing me on St. Patrick's Day—that has to count for something."

Patrick Moody was put to death on March 17, 2006.

Celebrating the Last Supper often feels like a distant flourish of faith passed down over two thousand years. Connecting to its true meaning is a tenuous act made even more difficult by faulty institutions and flawed human beings. Early in my faith journey I thought the answers to my questions lay beyond my reach. But then I grew up on death row. In less than seven years I lived while thirty-three human beings, some of whom were friends and brothers, were exterminated. It changed how I understood life and death, a terrible knowledge that drew me closer to God. Slowly, I have come to realize we were never abandoned. The answer had been there all along in the Eucharistic Prayer.

On the day before he was to suffer,
He took bread and, giving thanks, broke it
And gave it to his disciples, saying:

"Take this all of you and eat of it, for this is
My body, which will be given up for you."

In a similar way, when supper was ended,
He took the chalice and once more giving thanks,
He gave it to his disciples, saying:

"Take this all of you, and drink from it,
For this is the chalice of my blood,
The blood of the new covenant,
Which will be poured out for you and for many
For the forgiveness of sins.

Do this in memory of me."

When I was a kid, as an altar server, I had to watch the priest during this prayer. As he raised the bread, then the wine, my task had been to ring a set of brass bells. "Ring them as hard as you can," one priest told me. "Make sure everyone hears them." Many years later, on death row, sitting at a table and watching the priest perform this rite, I still knew the exact moment the bells rang. Their clangor crashed into the bottomless silence, banishing despair and defeating death, if only we believed. That sound was not just an answer to our suffering, but an end to it. Clear in its reminder. Absolute in its purity. Certain in the promise of eternal life.

In memory of the Catholic Community of St. Francis of Assisi 2000 Confirmation Class, Central Prison, North Carolina.

Henry "Mule" Hunt

sentenced to death 1985;
executed September 13, 2003

Elias Syriani

sentenced to death 1991;
executed November 18, 2005

Patrick "Pat" Moody

sentenced to death 1995;
executed March 17, 2006

Terry Ball

sentenced to death 1996;
died of natural causes, October 18, 2017

Angel Guevara

sentenced to death 1996 . . .

Lyle C. May

sentenced to death 1999 . . .

Chapter 4

Death Row Phenomenon

Imagine this: there are people on death row who used to support the death penalty—a process dependent upon a complex appellate procedure that works against rather than for them—who would willingly drop their appeals and volunteer for execution. What would make them commit state-assisted suicide?

What if you are one of those people on death row, wrongly convicted of a crime and ignored by your attorneys because—let's face it—nobody believes you? Once a jury of random strangers says you're guilty, the rest of the world is convinced without any facts to support the opinion, only what has been repeated by the state in the media. How many years of due process do you deserve? Two years? Five? Ten? As long as it takes? What if it's your brother, cousin, sister, aunt, father, uncle, or mother? Maybe a friend of yours? Would you want the amount of time between sentence and execution shortened then?

Death row phenomenon is a conceptualization of the experience that is a death sentence. It's an idea that first appeared in the 1989 case of *Soering v. United Kingdom* as international recognition of the human right not to be tortured.[1] The European Court of Human Rights determined the German youth Jens Soering could not be extradited to the United States to stand capital trial because upon a sentence of death, he would "pass" a *very long period of time spent on death row*, in *extreme conditions*, under "mounting *anguish of awaiting execution*." These circumstances, declared the court, would breach the prohibition against torture, and inhuman or degrading treatment or punishment.[2]

Death row phenomenon became the international arbiter that capital punishment is inherently cruel and inhumane because of the three elements outlined in *Soering*: prolonged waiting on death row as a result of the process; harsh conditions, especially in solitary confinement; and psychological trauma that had recently been recognized as "death row syndrome."

The UN Convention against Torture and Other Cruel, Inhuman, or Degrading Treatment or Punishment, provides the most widely accepted definition of torture under international law. An act of torture qualifies as such if:

> The nature of the act, or omission of an act, inflicts severe mental or physical pain and suffering;
> That pain and suffering is intentionally inflicted;
> Public officials consent to the act or omission of an act in their official capacity.
> The specific purpose of the act or omission of an act is punishment, discrimination, or to obtain information.[3]

To put this in context, think of state officials who create secrecy laws to hide where, how, and from whom they procure drugs to carry out the lethal injection. They are acting in their official capacity to further an act of capital torture.

The major distinction between the international and American definitions of torture is that by US standards, any act carried out or omitted by a public official, in the capacity of that office, will not be viewed as cruel and inhumane unless a court rules said act violates the Eighth Amendment of the US Constitution. In other words, international treaties that expressly prohibit all forms of torture can be ignored unless US courts make the same finding. This includes the Vienna Convention, which prohibits the arrest, trial, and execution of foreign nationals;[4] the European Court of Human Rights, which prohibits capital punishment for member nations and will not extradite people to countries where they face capital punishment;[5] and until recently, the Geneva Convention, which prohibits the execution of people who were under eighteen at the time of the crime.[6]

According to Article VI, Clause 2 of the US Constitution, the "supreme law of the land" is based on the constitution, laws, and treaties of the United States. If so, US treaties should apply as much to the death penalty as any other major provision of US law.

Except, they don't.

For example, when America ratified the International Covenant on Civil and Political Rights in 1992, it stipulated that "cruel, inhuman, or degrading treatment or punishment" shall be defined by punishments acceptable under the US Constitution.[7] International rights be damned, the US would incarcerate and execute whomever and however it wanted. One could argue this nullifies America both as a signatory to any treaty regarding international standards of human rights and their claim to moral leadership.

US courts don't recognize death row phenomenon because doing so would acknowledge an evolving standard of decency outlined in the Marshall Hypothesis of the US Supreme Court in *Furman v. Georgia* (1972). It was an evolving standard of decency that led the court to abolish capital punishment, if only briefly. Unfortunately to reach that standard again, it will require crossing the progressive-conservative divide within the court. As it stands, a conservative court previously held that "American conceptions of decency . . . are dispositive in evolving standards of decency."[8] International standards need not apply. Sadly, American standards of decency on the issue of crime and punishment are far behind those of every other democratic nation in the world.

Lest you think the refusal of US courts to recognize death row phenomenon is a matter of not wanting to "coddle" people convicted of murder, let me describe what the experience actually entails.

The term "death row syndrome" came from psychiatrist Stuart Grassian's examination of solitary confinement. In a 1986 article, Grassian explained his findings that people in extended periods of solitary confinement develop panic attacks, anxiety, fear of impending death, clinical depression, and emotional flatness or blunting, which is the inability to have any "feelings," lethargy, and social withdrawal.[9]

The first time I experienced a panic attack was after my third execution. It felt like an earthquake shook my body and jerked me out of a sound sleep. Heart hammering, sweating, it was a sudden boost of terror and adrenaline, as real as anything I've ever felt. It didn't happen after every execution, but periodically over the years. The attacks always happen in my sleep—jerking me awake, sending my mind into overdrive as if at any moment the walls could collapse. Depression and lethargy are constant, so much so that I've learned mental gymnastics to power through the worst moments.

Many on the row can't say the same.

Grassian also described anger, rage, violence against others, cognitive disturbances, an inability to concentrate on mental tasks, memory lapses, disorientation, paranoia, psychosis, schizophrenia, hypersensitivity to noises and smells, hallucinations, and depersonalization as further symptoms of death row phenomenon.

Concentration is difficult for me. My mind wanders a lot. I live in a constant state of anxiety or anger, rarely able to relax. Conversations that are too loud, obnoxious smells, and inane prattle agitate me. Meditation, prayer, and long-term goals help me focus; prison journalism and community outreach give me purpose. Higher education has helped me become more aware of the psychological impact of a death sentence and resist the worst effects, but others are not so fortunate.

Kenny is fifty-five and has been on death row for twenty-five years. During that time, he has tried to commit suicide and now experiences early-onset dementia. He struggles to remember his name. Jerry is a few years older than me and has been on death row an equal amount of time. I've watched him deteriorate over the years, becoming severely schizophrenic and dissociative, hallucinating and holding conversations with people who don't exist. It's not a coincidence nearly half of those on North Carolina's death row take psychiatric medication.

Death row syndrome is not exclusive to solitary confinement. While socialization and some freedom of movement slows the impact of isolation, death row is still a prison within a prison—twice removed from society. Symptoms of death row syndrome are merely harder to identify and often get misattributed to other causes.

Self-mutilation and suicide are frequent on death row. In segregation, it's not atypical for prisoners to cut their flesh, swallow sharp or indigestible objects like razors or batteries, repeatedly smash their head against walls, and smear themselves in feces. Why, you ask? Because they have lost touch with civilization and have been tortured past the breaking point of their own humanity. Some studies propose that self-mutilation occurs as a means to "liberate the self from unbearable tension" as "the physical pain becomes a compensatory substitute for emotional pain or shame,"[10] or that it "asserts the prisoner is still alive."[11]

Many in the public hold the misguided belief that the long period of time between a death sentence and execution is caused by prisoners doing everything they can to delay the inevitable, as if exercising one's Fourteenth Amendment right to due process is somehow an affront to the victim's family. But, after all, who wouldn't try everything they could to save themselves?

In many cases, the reality is actually the opposite. A lot, if not most, of the time, decades-long delays are a product of apathetic courts and attorney generals. Capital case files often get pushed aside and lost. Civil litigation over execution protocols and various other elements further stretch out the process. All of this is out of the capital defendant's hands. We cannot command our attorneys to do anything, and unless you know enough about the law to file motions in court—or are willing to drop your appeals and volunteer for execution—you are sentenced to simply exist in a state of legal limbo.

Extending one's life on death row is an excruciating oxymoron. Some prisoners volunteer to be executed, not because they want to die per se, but because the alternative life is unbearable and torturous. Between the conditions of confinement, uncertainty of the future, and ever-present threat of death, they choose death because of its certain end to their suffering. In the state of Nevada for example, twelve people have been executed since 1976. All but one of those people—including one as young as twenty-five years old—waived their appeals and volunteered to be executed, rather than continue living under a sentence of capital torture.

Maybe you're thinking of ways to shorten the amount of time one spends on death row, streamline the appellate process, and reduce the likelihood of death row phenomenon. Some prisoners appear so guilty that there's no need to stretch out their appeals, right?

Right-wing conservatives led by Republican Bob Dole followed that same logic in the nineties. Since the Nixon administration, they sought to limit federal judicial oversight of state court decisions, thereby restricting a defendant's ability to file a federal habeas corpus petition. In the wake of the Oklahoma City bombing, Republicans used the fear and anger of the moment to pass the 1996 Antiterrorism and Effective Death Penalty Act (AEDPA). On its surface, the law appeared to reduce the amount of time people spent on death row. What actually took place however, was that after an initial spike in executions—especially in Texas—the average amount of time one spent on death row in fact *increased*, while noncapital defendants were largely blocked from federal judicial relief. AEDPA made it much more difficult for federal courts to overturn state court decisions and address issues like systemic racism, malicious prosecutions, and claims of innocence. Furthermore, it's important to remember that every innocent man and woman exonerated from death row or prison in general was thought to be "obviously guilty" and not deserving of due process.

As long as the death penalty exists, exercising one's Fourteenth Amendment right to due process cannot be divided from the amount of time spent on death row. Reducing attorney inactivity and improving conditions of confinement may limit lasting psychological trauma, but there is no way to completely avoid the psychological impact of a death sentence.

In 2006, several days before his scheduled execution, JT had visits with family members he hadn't seen in years. They brought his grandchildren to see him. Hours before he was to be escorted to death watch for the final seventy-two hours of his life, a court ordered an indefinite stay of execution. For weeks, then months, and then years afterward JT has lived in fear, anxiety, and utter exhaustion of a potential execution date being rescheduled. Alternating feelings of hope and despair emphasize the indefiniteness of his future. The depression can be overwhelming.

It is this feeling, stretched out over the years, coupled with the abandonment by family, a lack of communication with attorneys, and the legal limbo that is a moratorium of North Carolina's death penalty, that makes for the special kind of suffering called death row phenomenon. It's why most of the free world has abolished capital torture, and why it is past time for America to follow suit.

Chapter 5

A Tale of Two Henrys

Henry Bailey, a Black man, was one of the last prisoners publicly hanged by the state of North Carolina in 1906. Accused of killing a white person, Bailey lamented that were the roles reversed, the state wouldn't even consider the murder a crime. Moments before his death, he spoke about the inequality of his jury, on which none of his Black peers sat. His truth telling stirred the large crowd, where many Black people gathered to support him in his last moments. They knew that with little provocation or due process, it could be them on the scaffold.

Over a century after Bailey's "legal lynching," after working-class women of color defended Black men in a campaign to stop the state from lynching them, and after the state medicalized its executions and removed them from public view, the 2009 Democrat-controlled North Carolina General Assembly attempted to amend death sentences gained through racist tactics. They enacted the Racial Justice Act (RJA), which granted death row prisoners the right to challenge their sentence if it was "sought or obtained on the basis of race," including by the systematic removal of Black people from juries.

Prisoners who win RJA cases are granted life sentences instead of the death penalty.

But in 2010, Republicans won a supermajority in the North Carolina General Assembly. They immediately worked on first diluting, and then ultimately repealing the RJA in 2013. The repeal applied *retroactively*, condemning prisoners recently removed from death row back to death row. Litigation over the retroactive application of the repeal continued for seven years.

As a death row prisoner, I've watched the fight over the RJA slowly take shape over the last decade. Despite being celebrated as a progressive beacon, the RJA was presented to my peers, 54 percent of whom are Black, as their only real option for leaving death row. This happened even when other options, like exoneration, might be possible. Many attorneys operate under the belief that any relief from a potential execution is good relief. This "shut up and accept it" attitude is so pervasive that it fuels a lot of cynicism and apathy toward the legal system. As a result, the RJA is viewed by many of us on death row as another attempt by attorneys to avoid the hard work of freeing their clients from prison.

In June 2020, in the midst of global uprisings against the murder of George Floyd by Minneapolis police, the RJA was partially salvaged by the North Carolina Supreme Court, thanks in large part to Chief Justice Cheri Beasley, the first Black woman to hold the court's top position in the state's history. In *State v. Ramseur*, the court ruled that the RJA repeal could not be applied retroactively to death row prisoners who filed their claims back in 2009. This ruling does not restore the RJA as current law, but rather allows death row prisoners who filed RJA appeals before the repeal to proceed with their cases.

Over 130 death row prisoners (about 90 percent of North Carolina's death row prisoners) are now entitled to a hearing to prove race was a significant factor in their capital prosecution. If successful, these death row prisoners will receive a revised sentence of life without parole (LWOP).

At best, LWOP masquerades as leniency. The reality is a silent execution.

Some prisoners reject the idea of the RJA because they believe accepting its relief will end their right to claim innocence. At a minimum, LWOP could mean losing legal representation because noncapital defendants have no right to an attorney beyond appealing their case after trial. This is especially damning for prisoners who are fighting to prove they are not guilty of first-degree murder.

North Carolina prisoners only recently (2021) gained access to a digital law library, but this does not equate with legal training, and jailhouse lawyers are rare. The North Carolina Prisoner Legal Services is under-staffed and underfunded, and spread thin among thousands of prisoners seeking relief. Dying of illness or age-related causes after decades in prison often evokes as much fear as being executed.

For those on death row who admit guilt, can no longer appeal their sentence, and have no other options, the RJA may feel like an extension of life away from the depressing confines of death row. Though it's often hailed as merciful by anti–death penalty advocates, LWOP is anything but.

Choosing between dying on a gurney or in a prison infirmary is not an alternative, it's death masquerading as leniency.

I asked my friend Mac, who has been on death row since the mid-1990s and is one of the 130 people eligible for a hearing, what he thought of the June 2020 RJA ruling. "Praise God," he said. "I'm ready to give these people back their death sentence and get away from this place. I don't want no life without parole, but if that's what they give me—so be it."

But another friend, a fifty-five-year-old Black man who hadn't heard from his attorney in two years, recently got a letter from the lawyer about his RJA claim. Before his murder trial, he was offered a twenty-year plea deal. Winning under the RJA wouldn't restore that plea deal. "So I get death either way for going to trial?" he said. "I've done over twenty years in prison already. My kids have kids. The RJA won't help me be with them."

My other peers on death row told stories of racism so explicit there was no need for statistics: white bailiffs intimidating Black witnesses; white jury foreman belittling Black jurors who question state evidence.

"Cuz, you think they care about fair?" Chief* asked me. "The [district attorney] in my county wore a gold pin of a noose. Like a badge of honor for hanging another person from a tree."

That prosecutor was former Union County district attorney Kenneth Honeycutt, who awarded similar pins to assistant prosecutors who won death penalty cases. As of 2023, all current death row prisoners from Union County were people of color.

Just as bitterly ironic as RJA's "remedy" is the story of how the law was repealed. In the run-up to the 2010 midterm election, which resulted

---

* This is a pseudonym.

in a Republican supermajority in the state legislature, the North Carolina Republican Executive Committee used Democratic Representative
Hugh Holliman's vote for the RJA against him politically. The committee sent mailers to every resident in Holliman's district, threatening the
release of death row prisoners who win RJA relief. The mailer featured
two prisoners who "could leave prison early and move in next door."
One of the prisoners, Henry McCollum, was a Black man convicted and
sentenced to death for the 1985 rape and murder of Sabrina Buie, an
eleven-year-old Black girl.

The mailers read, "Holliman voted to allow activist judges to weaken
the sentence of death row inmates . . . making some eligible for parole
immediately" and "Keep Death Row Inmates Where They Belong and
Get Rid of Criminal Coddler Hugh Holliman."

The fear mongering worked, and Holliman was defeated by Republican Rayne Brown. One of the RJA's principal opponents, Representative Phil Berger, became speaker of the house. By 2012, the legislature
amended the 2009 RJA, eliminating mandatory hearings, restricting use
of statistics, and requiring claimants waive any objection to LWOP even
if they would have otherwise been eligible for parole, and forcing previous claimants to file under the amended RJA.

Even despite these new hurdles, four death row prisoners still won
their RJA cases, receiving LWOP sentences and paving the way for every
other claimant on death row. Opponents of the RJA in the legislature,
realizing that even the amended RJA could potentially empty death row,
quickly repealed the law in its entirety in 2013. The four prisoners who
won LWOP were returned to death row, beginning the seven-year-long
litigation battle over retroactive application of the repeal.

A year after the RJA repeal, Henry McCollum was exonerated by
the North Carolina Innocence Inquiry Commission after thirty years
of wrongful imprisonment on death row. When McCollum was nineteen, he and his fifteen-year-old brother Leon Brown were misidentified
as suspects, and coerced by detectives into confessing. DNA evidence
that had been hidden by the Red Springs Police Department eventually cleared both men. The man who actually committed those crimes,
Roscoe Artis, had already been a suspect. Artis was sentenced to death

for another rape and murder, and then had his sentence converted to LWOP while McCollum remained on death row. Had it not been for the Innocence Inquiry Commission, McCollum would still be on death row while his attorneys try to persuade him to accept his lot under the RJA.

Republican Governor Pat McCrory, who signed the RJA repeal, was publicly pressured into pardoning McCollum and Brown, who had been serving LWOP. There was no public response by US Supreme Court Justice Antonin Scalia, who referred to their case as continued justification for the death penalty. No public apology was ever made for using McCollum, a wrongfully convicted and falsely imprisoned Black man, as a Republican scapegoat to repeal the RJA.

Between the RJA repeal in 2013 and the court's ruling in June 2020, the RJA litigation effectively stopped other types of death penalty appeals. Instead of serving the interests of justice based on the facts of each prisoner's case, attorneys and judges took a "wait and see" approach to death row cases, tying everyone's fate to the reinstatement of an inactive law with a minimal remedy. When several prisoners sought to withdraw their RJA claims to pursue other appeals, one judge left the withdrawal decision to their attorneys.

Rather than a clear victory, the reinstatement of the RJA for previous claimants means that death row prisoners will have to wait even more years to see if they "win" LWOP or if they can move on to seek justice in some other, likely more preferable, way. The arbitrary and racist state court system (and many attorneys) have made it clear defendants on death row do not get to choose how, when, or what kind of relief they receive.

Henry Bailey died like so many other Black people in the United States—in full knowledge of a state system unwilling to uphold "equal justice under the law." Eighty years later, Henry McCollum experienced the evolution of that injustice, the victim of a racist criminal legal system. The harm caused cannot be remedied by an easily repealed law that provides dubious relief to a small group of people on death row. If George Floyd's murder has taught us anything, it's that the time for accepting half-measures is over. No justice. No peace.

Chapter 6

Qualified Immunity

How "Ordinary Police Work" Tramples Civil Rights

On September 28, 1983, fifteen-year-old Leon Brown and his nineteen-year-old half-brother Henry McCollum were detained for interrogation about the gruesome assault, rape, and murder of eleven-year-old Sabrina Buie in Red Springs, North Carolina. For hours, Robeson County sheriff's deputies simultaneously cajoled, bullied, threatened, yelled at, and lied to the two Black intellectually disabled teenagers while feeding them information about a crime they didn't commit. Police told them that they could go home if they signed a piece of paper. Wanting it to be over, and not understanding that they were being coerced, the two teenagers signed false confessions. But Henry and Leon wouldn't go home for thirty-one years.

Only after they signed the fabricated documents did the deputies read them their Miranda rights. A year later, they were sentenced to death.[1] The same night as the brothers' detainment, police ran into a man named Roscoe Artis, who just weeks later would lead police to the scene of another identical rape-murder he confessed to committing—in the same soybean field, in the town of four thousand people. He lived a block away from where Buie's body was found.

Investigators didn't bother to run a background check on Artis the night of the murder. If they had, they would have seen both his history of committing violent sexual attacks dating back to 1957 and the active warrant for his arrest in yet another rape-murder in which the victim was

39

asphyxiated and left wearing only a bra—just as Buie was.

But Artis was never mentioned in relation to the Buie case. In the decades to follow, as all three sat on death row, he repeatedly told attorneys that Henry and Leon had nothing to do with the murder, expressed guilt for Buie's death, and revealed new details about the crime.

Artis wasn't listed as a suspect in the case until 2014, when the North Carolina Innocence Inquiry Commission, a neutral state agency, developed exculpatory DNA evidence indicating Artis, and not the brothers—as all signs should have from the start. Still, Sheriff Kenneth Sealy, deputy Joel Locklear, and State Bureau of Investigation (SBI) agents Leroy Allen and Kenneth Snead ignored him as a suspect, both on the night of the brothers' detainment and for the next thirty-one years.

In 2015 in response to petitions and advocacy on the outside, Republican Governor Pat McCrory pardoned the brothers following an additional nine-month personal review of the case. Henry and Leon filed a federal civil suit against the Town of Red Springs, the SBI, and the Robeson County Sheriff's Department for their wrongful imprisonment. Red Springs settled with the brothers out of court after their release, but law enforcement held out.

The SBI and the sheriff's department, represented by the attorney general's office, claimed that what happened to Henry and Leon was a product of "ordinary police work," and that the doctrine of qualified immunity kept the officers from liability.

Qualified immunity, based on the assumption that the officers were working in "good faith" and with integrity throughout the investigation, protects law enforcement officers' rights above those whose lives they ruin. "Good faith" is what sustains wrongful convictions like Henry's and Leon's to the exclusion of facts, exculpatory evidence, or any other due diligence reasonable law enforcement officers are supposedly obligated to perform during the investigation of a crime.[2] "Good faith" put the innocent teenagers behind bars and allowed Roscoe Artis to commit another rape and murder.

It wasn't until 2021[3] that a jury in Raleigh determined that SBI Agents Allen and Snead violated Henry and Leon's constitutional rights by coercing them into confessing to a crime they did not commit. Henry and Leon were awarded $31 million each in compensatory damages—$1 million for each year they spent wrongfully imprisoned—plus a total of $13 million in punitive damages. The payout represents the largest combined settlement in a wrongful conviction case in US history.[4]

This is a precedent-setting case for people who experience police brutality behind closed doors.[5] But the fact remains that it took more than three decades to correctly assign guilt and prove the obvious—that these teenagers were not involved in this crime.

Hard-fought exonerations like these are not a sign that the system works, but a snapshot of who maintains it and what facilitates injustice, as well as who it impacts the most: racial minorities, the impoverished, and those people society is willing to throw away. It's just as much a measure of who it works for: the ruling class and the law enforcement charged with upholding power.

Foundational to our criminal justice system is an obvious truth: state authority trumps civil rights.[6] Law enforcement testimony is accepted against the word of the accused, no matter what takes place behind closed doors.

I know this because I have been incarcerated for over twenty-six years as a consequence of such conduct.

At the age of nineteen, homeless and suffering from mental illness, law enforcement detained me in the early morning hours of July 10, 1997, as a suspect in a double homicide. The officer who took me into custody did not read me my Miranda rights, stating only that I was wanted for questioning.[7] Heavily intoxicated on Valium, alcohol, and a psychotropic medication prescribed during a recent hospital stay, I was held and isolated while, in another room, detectives interviewed a "witness" to the crime. An attendant officer kept prodding me awake until 6:00 a.m.[8]

When the detectives finally interrogated me, I was sleep-deprived, intoxicated, and mentally ill—all at an age when cognitive reasoning is not fully developed.[9] During my interrogation, I was incapable of comprehending what the detectives were saying or asking of me. I was not cognizant of the fact that they were feeding me information about a crime I did not commit, obtained from another suspect—their sole "witness."

In my case, officers used what's called the Reid technique, which relies on psychological tactics to overcome a person's will during an interrogation. Law enforcement officers will isolate a suspect in a room, falsely claim overwhelming evidence or cooperation from a nonexistent witness, and then cajole, bully, threaten, yell, and lie about a lesser punishment for cooperation. Interrogators also feed the person information about the crime, details known only to law enforcement and the perpetrator, and use the suspect's memory of those facts in the course of a confession as proof of its validity.[10]

The Reid technique increases the chances of false confessions and wrongful convictions. In a 2004 Northwestern University study, researchers identified at least 125 cases[11] in which false confessions were obtained using the Reid technique, including high-profile cases in which convictions were eventually overturned, like the Norfolk Four, Central Park Five, and Beatrice Six.[12]

This high likelihood of producing false confessions with the Reid technique even prompted North Carolina to become the sixth state to pass a law in 2007 requiring the complete electronic recording of interrogations in homicide cases that happen behind closed doors. The law is not retroactive, and even audio-video recordings can fail to prevent false confessions.[13] In the absence of any electronic recording of my own interrogation, proving that it was a false confession may be difficult, but not impossible.[14]

Still, my own false confession to a crime I did not commit was a routine matter for interrogators. Law enforcement officers have a long history of physically torturing suspects, applying what is colloquially called the "third degree" to obtain a confession. Fists or phone books, burning cigarettes or wielding batons, these examinations are not about whether or not the person subjected to their brutality provides accurate information. The goal has always been to score a conviction.

This was true during the infamous Burge torture cases in Chicago, which showed that between 1972 and 1991, Police Commander Jon Burge and fellow officers beat, suffocated, electrocuted, and generally tortured over 118 African American citizens, coercing them into false confessions and wrongful imprisonment for decades.[15] The press, political class, and most of the public were largely apathetic about Burge's "house of screams" until an FBI investigation revealed the allegations of torture were true.[16]

Jon Burge was prosecuted in 2010 and received a laughable three years on house arrest. Legislation for a Reparations Fund for Burge Torture Victims passed in 2015.[17]

But investigations like these are the exception rather than the rule. Besides, modern interrogations involve more subtle coercion than that of the third degree, the nuances of which seldom become public knowledge. Last year, at the height of antipolice brutality protests, the FBI launched a national database on law enforcement's use of force. Only 40 percent of police participated.

Qualified immunity, on principle, severely undermines Section 1983 of the Civil Rights Act of 1871 (42 U.S. Code § 1983), which allows for the right to file a lawsuit against public officials, including in cases of excessive police force. Passage of the section came by way of the Reconstruction Congress as part of the Ku Klux Klan Act, a piece of legislation designed to help combat lawlessness and civil rights violators in the postwar South.[18] Intended to protect Black voters, it was enacted a few years after the Fourteenth Amendment of the US Constitution to "give teeth to the promise of liberty and equality enshrined in the amendment's provisions."[19]

Nearly a century later, in reaction to civil rights legislation, the US Supreme Court, in *Pierson v. Ray* (1967), developed the doctrine of qualified immunity to limit the impact of liability to state actors who violate someone's federally protected rights "in good faith."[20]

In 1982 the court made that standard even harder to prove. With the addition of the standard of "clearly established law" in *Harlow v. Fitzgerald*, plaintiffs also had to demonstrate a case with "functionally identical facts" to their own mistreatment for a shot to prove if their civil rights were indeed violated.[21]

In so doing, the court created the ultimate catch-22, making it all the more unlikely that law enforcement would be held accountable for civil rights violations. To even get before a jury, civil rights plaintiffs must essentially first win two prior cases in a row: once before the district court and again before the court of appeals. This precedent continues to govern qualified immunity today.

For Henry and Leon, coerced just a year after the *Harlow v.*

Fitzgerald decision, this meant that their case required proof that RCS deputies and SBI agents violated both standards during their investigation. Since *Brady v. Maryland* requires the release of exculpatory evidence—and because no reasonable law enforcement officer would have ignored Roscoe Artis as a suspect—one would assume that was an easy point to prove.

But the letter of the law is not that simple. The brothers were tasked with more than just proving their innocence: They had to demonstrate not only an instance in which law enforcement withheld exculpatory evidence, coerced innocent defendants into confessing, and lied to cover it all up but also one in which the officers were held liable for it. The list of law enforcement's self-preserving internal protections only piles up against them from there.

In 2005 the Center for Death Penalty Litigation had a cigarette butt from the 1983 Buie crime scene tested for DNA. It excluded Henry and Leon as a match. It wasn't until 2014 that the state crime lab finally upload the DNA profile into its database and they found that it matched Artis. When the results reached Robeson County District Attorney Johnson Britt, he said: "Oh my god, the same [rape-murder], a mile apart . . . Why didn't somebody figure this thing out?"[22] The question was false, asked by a career prosecutor who benefits from absolute immunity just like his predecessor, Joe Freeman Britt, who maliciously prosecuted the teens. It's a question as disingenuous as the answer is obvious: There is little to no accountability behind the closed doors of police work.

It was later revealed that other evidence sat buried for decades too. After Artis's conviction, the Red Springs Police Department asked the SBI to test fingerprints on a beer from the crime scene for a match, three days before Henry and Leon's 1984 trial. That detail alone should have raised suspicion for the district attorney, but the test went unchecked.

But prosecutors often accept shoddy work, tenuous theories, falsified evidence, or maintain the same biases and tunnel vision as the officers they oversee. Moreover, bad actors rely on the institutionalized cronyism of police unions to protect them. Those unions, in turn, campaign against reformist agendas that attempt to remove barriers to greater scrutiny and accountability of law enforcement officers. As a result, police crime and misconduct take on a protected status.

Official misconduct, which includes law enforcement, prosecutors, judges, and other government officials who abuse their power, is the primary reason why wrongful convictions stand for as long as they do. According to the University of Michigan Law School's National Registry of Exonerations, between 1989 and 2015, nearly half (47 percent) of 1,740 noncapital exonerations were due to official misconduct. Of the 116 recorded death row exonerations, 76 percent were due to official misconduct.[23]

This small sampling does not include those people who had a conviction or sentence overturned but were not exonerated, nor does it include the many people in prison who struggle to get their cases heard. There is no database that tracks official misconduct in the criminal legal system. We only know it happens because older cases sometimes make it through entitites like the North Carolina Innocence Inquiry Commission, which has exposed corruption in the case of nearly every person it helped exonerate.

Maybe the worst of it all, the insult to injury, is how law enforcement and prosecutors typically continue to view exonerees as criminals who escaped punishment. By law, exonerees are not viewed as crime victims. This is reflected in the state's refusal to publicly acknowledge wrongful convictions, and manifests in their disqualification from state victims' services.

In a just world, state agencies would discipline or fire bad actors for misconduct, and improve transparency during the investigation of a crime. In a just world, the state would hold law enforcement to a higher standard than they do ordinary citizens, not a lower one. In a just world, "accountability" in the mouths of the oppressed would not be a curse against public officials, or a hammer in the hands of the state. Transparency throughout the criminal legal system would be a good thing that enables justice for all, not a thing resisted by public officials trying to control the narrative and hide their own crimes.

In a just world, Henry and Leon's precedent-setting case would not be a rarity, nor would it be ignored by the legislators who continue to support half-measures that don't even scratch the surface of what is offered by task forces seeking to retroactively overturn false convictions.

In a just world, the courts would see the burden put on the brothers as motivation to do better.

Henry and Leon may have received millions, but other exonerees don't even qualify for reentry programs post-prison. After release, some are lucky to get forty-five dollars for a bus ticket. Not all exonerees— or even most of them—receive compensation from the state, which in North Carolina is capped at $750,000 no matter how many decades are spent wrongfully imprisoned.

"Fair? What's fair?" recent exoneree Ronnie Long said when asked if he thought $750,000 was adequate compensation after spending forty-four years in prison for a crime he did not commit, the third-longest imprisonment in US history for an exonerated defendant. "Ask yourself that question when these people took away your twenties, your thirties, your forties, your fifties, and they started on your sixties."[24]

Equal protection means everyone is accountable to the same laws in the same ways, that no special treatment or punishment is affected because of status, class, or race. That was the intended design behind the 1871 laws—to work toward a more just world.

But much like the numerous Confederate monuments erected in the wake of the 1965 Civil Rights Act, qualified immunity is a memorial to division and injustice in the face of past progress. And just like those monuments, as long as qualified immunity stands, there can be no real justice.

Pull it down.

Chapter 7

The Economics
of Capital Punishment

An Abolitionist Argument

How much would you pay to execute someone guilty of killing a family member, friend, or neighbor? Anything? Maybe you support retributive punishment in general—would you trade clean drinking water, a functioning power grid, expanded broadband internet service in rural areas, or stable bridges for it? Would you rather fund the death penalty in your state than provide resources and fair wages to teachers in public schools?

Let's say you support the death penalty and would gladly keep it in exchange for higher income taxes, crumbling infrastructure, and a public school system that doesn't even rank in the top twenty-five countries of the world. Oh, wait, that's already the case.

So, let's carry it a step further. Not only do you support the death penalty and any elected official who does too, but maybe you think prison is the answer to crime. If this is so, then you should understand why the United States incarcerates more people than any other nation on earth, with 40 percent of the world's prisoners and only 5 percent of the world's population.

But I digress.

The death penalty is expensive and ineffective, but any rational criminologist or economist can tell you this as well as I can. Support of the death penalty presumes you can prove, through a flawed criminal legal system, not only that the person in custody actually committed the crime but also that a prosecutor filed the appropriate charge against them. Under our adversarial legal system, neither of these things is always the case. Truth is a relative term—the only facts that matter are those paraded before a jury. Even then, the facts don't always matter. That's the drawback to having emotionally driven laypeople judge legal facts and complex laws. The term "justice" in this sense has nothing to do with crime and punishment or the economics of the death penalty. In the end, your ignorance of how the criminal legal system works and your desire for vengeance are used to leverage money into the pockets of those who care little about public safety and a lot about staying in power.

Economist Dave McCord once wrote that if capital punishment were subject to consumer protection laws it would be recognized as a "lemon" in light of the fact that, among numerous deficiencies, so few of those sentenced to death actually end up executed.[1] That number hovers around 13 percent nationwide and slowly decreases as fewer people are executed, more are sentenced to death, and still more are removed from death row after a successful appeal.

Spending valuable resources to fund capital punishment for a 13 percent return is a poor investment. It's like getting robbed for the principal and paid a portion of the interest. When you also consider the death penalty doesn't deter crime, but instead has a brutalization effect that correlates with increased violent crime, this should cause worry.

Maybe I'm being too abstract about how much money is wasted on capital punishment. First, it's important to know not every capital trial ends in a death sentence—but don't worry, the odds are stacked against defendants, which puts them in your favor. Ahem, I mean the state's favor. You're just the silent partner sanctioning and funding this business. Regardless of the outcome, the defense and prosecution of a single capital trial costs between $350,000 and $750,000.

In some states, like Texas, total costs are paid by the county where a case occurs, which partly explains why counties with a higher population send more people to death row, and poorer counties opt out.

There are exceptions of course. Robeson County, North Carolina, is the poorest in the state, yet it was home to Joe Freeman Britt, hailed by the *New York Times* in his obituary as the nation's "deadliest D.A."[2] for his success at winning death sentences. Britt sent more people—guilty and innocent alike—to death row than anyone else.

This happens because prosecutors are never held accountable. While you may support the "any cost" approach, the real-world consequences belong to every taxpayer. Punishment at any cost is wasteful and irresponsible.

Waste is a common theme in capital postconviction proceedings. Remember that, despite the desire to harm those who have harmed your loved ones, the US Supreme Court mandated automatic appeals for people sentenced to death. These may last decades and be extremely expensive, but procedural safeguards on capital punishment are intended to prevent innocent people from being executed. Most of the time, anyway.

The average direct appeal costs between $15,000 and $340,000 per death sentence. Postconviction hearings at the state level cost between $43,000 and $300,000 per death sentence. Some cases, like my friend Scott's, require multiple hearings at the state level. One of his recent hearings was valued at $48,000. A brief filed by his attorneys a year later cost $55,000.

The cost of capital appeals at the federal level range between $96,000 and $1.1 million per death sentence. The 13 percent of those who are sentenced to death and executed might seem like it's worth the $2.5 to $4 million per person price tag, but that number fails to account for the 87 percent who serve expensive life sentences on death row, those who receive numbered terms, and those found innocent.

California, for example, has executed only thirteen people since 1976, yet has spent over $4 billion on death sentences. With more people on death row than any other state, that's an average prorated cost of $250 million per execution. Despite budget shortfalls and more unhoused people than any state in the US, California has resisted efforts to end the death penalty.

If that's not enough to illustrate the waste, in North Carolina capital prosecutions cost an average of $500,000 more than comparable cases where death is not sought. Between 1977 and 2014, of the 249 finalized death sentences, approximately 71% were reversed on appeal. Since 1973, there have been twelve exonerations from North Carolina's death row. Upon their release, the most recent exonerees, Henry McCollum and Leon Brown, sought damages from the State Bureau of Investigation and Robeson County Sheriff's Department to the tune of $75 million for the police misconduct that sent them to death row. This is in addition to what the state paid to defend the qualified immunity of its corrupt law enforcement, the ordinary costs of capital prosecution, and thirty-one years of wrongful imprisonment for each brother; the estimated loss of $130 million in state and federal money can be chalked up to vengeance at any cost. No one ever said retributive punishment is accurate. Between 1973 and 2015, over 190 people were exonerated from death row throughout the US. In other words: for every eight people executed, one person on death row has been exonerated.

Maybe now you're thinking of alternatives, like that other death penalty. You know, life without parole (LWOP)—aka death by incarceration. Life imprisonment is marginally cheaper than an execution, averaging $1 million per person, with costs for health care rising significantly after age fifty-five. But where there are just over 2,400 people on death row in the US, as of 2021, there were over 203,000 men, women, and teenagers serving some type of life sentence—more than the country's entire prison population in 1970. Keep in mind that death by incarceration includes LWOP, life with parole, and virtual life sentences of more than fifty years. This is the potential punishment for murder of different degrees, rape, arson, armed robbery, robbery, conspiracy, accessory to murder, drug trafficking, possession of a controlled substance, repeat offenses, property crimes, some white-collar crimes, and more. That's an estimated total of $206 billion for an aging demographic that will grow, become infirm, and drain limited county, state, and federal resources to satisfy the need to revenge punish at any cost.

The economics of capital punishment are only the tip of the ugly iceberg known as the prison-industrial complex. To fully understand the costs, one needs to first understand who is impacted by it—and who benefits from it the most.

In 2016 Anthony Ray Hinton was exonerated from Alabama's death row after thirty years of wrongful imprisonment. In his book, *The Sun Does Shine,* Hinton relates truisms about the death penalty, but one, in particular, stands out: capital punishment means those "without capital get punished."[3]

There are no rich people on death row, and very few people with middle-class backgrounds. Just because you're guaranteed legal representation at trial does not mean it's effective legal representation. Those who end up on death row are primarily poor, uneducated, mentally ill, intellectually disabled, disproportionately Black and brown, and a product of the school-to-prison pipeline. These people are from the poorest communities, which law enforcement overpolices and prosecutors target with discrimination. They are products of domestic abuse, underfunded school systems, deinstitutionalized mental health services, inadequate social services, and a system of punishment that exacerbates the cycles of racism and classism.

Who benefits from capital punishment? Crime affects everyone, and draconian policies neither deter crime nor bring back loved ones nor make neighborhoods safer. Those governing the system—judges and prosecutors—gain money and job security, but mainly they reap the reward of a power dynamic skewed in their favor.

The true costs of capital punishment cannot be measured in taxpayer dollars wasted on ineffective criminal justice policies. You'll discover this during the next teacher strike or rise in the percentage of adults who lack a college degree. You may awaken to a sense of guilt and disgust, like the buyer's remorse felt after some regrettable purchase you can't really afford and discover you don't really want. You might finally see that the cost of vengeance impacts more than the person you want it to. The question should never be how much would you pay to avenge the death of a loved one, rather, what will you do to prevent it?

Resources
Courting Death: The Supreme Court and Capital Punishment by Carol S. Steiker and Jordan M. Steiker. 2016.

Deadly Justice: A Statistical Portrait of the Death Penalty by Frank Baumgartner et al. 2016.

Let the Lord Sort Them: The Rise and Fall of the Death Penalty by Maurice Chammah. 2021.

The Sun Does Shine by Anthony Ray Hinton, with Lara Love: *Prisoners of Politics: Breaking the Cycle of Mass Incarceration* by Rachel Elise Barkow. 2017.

Chapter 8

On Death Row, Eating to Live

Last Meals

Out of all the meals consumed on death row, most people on the outside only know about the "last meal" requested by the condemned, provided out of some sense of dignity and humanity as window dressing for state-sponsored killing. They imagine lavish meals savored by hardened killers—and the invectives hurled by politicians as they pander to constituents about the extravagant cost.

But the public never hears about the executioner's meal.

I was not sentenced to death until March 18, 1999. Prior to that, as a "safekeeper"* at Central Prison awaiting my capital trial in 1998, I experienced two executions. The first being North Carolina's last use of the gas chamber, though I didn't know it at the time. I just knew the state was putting people to death. My first execution on death row occurred a mere eight days after I got there. The feeling was different since I had been sentenced to death. It was exponentially heavier. I would feel that enormous weight and grinding pressure thirty-three times before executions stopped in 2006.

---

* A *safekeeper* is a pretrial detainee whose confinement is contracted out to state prisons for reasons such as medical treatment, protective custody, mental health treatment, to ease overcrowding, or because the individual presents an increased security risk. Most capital defendants are placed in safekeepinig.

We heard talk about the executioner's meal before on Unit Two, the old death row, but no one saw it. The idea of it spurred vicious imaginings.

However, between 2002 and 2006, after death row had been moved to the new Unit Three, we witnessed something no one facing death should: a party the night of the execution.

The most galling part was the sheet cake.

At the time, the prison-staff break room was located in the main hallway of Unit Three. Two large plexiglass windows made it a sort of fishbowl: anyone could look in, whether the lights were on or off. On the day of an execution, the break room door was locked, and two long tables appeared, hugging the walls. Stacks of paper plates, napkins, Solo cups, and plastic utensils anchored one table, while a mess of food spread out over the other. Usually, there would be a half dozen two-liter bottles of soda, oversized family bags of chips, dips, cheeses, crackers, jars of cocktail sausages, trays of cookies, and that enormous sheet cake covered in colorful swirls of frosting. I know because I could see it. The meal was, for those of us shuffling back and forth from the chow hall, on full display. In 2003 there were seven such feasts.

Wide-eyed, and with barely concealed smiles, prison staff would deny that this was a celebration of any kind. No, they told us, on the night of an execution, extra staff were called in, just in case they had to quell a riot. And all those guards and executioners, well, they had to eat *something*. Execution nights are long nights, they insisted. Their denials were clearly lies, always delivered lightly with a guilty child's *who me?* impudence.

Birthday cake is an odd requirement for a supposedly utilitarian staff meal, but there it was, served on execution night. We prisoners began to think of it as the executioner's last meal, and one year, it was.

As of 2023, no one has been put to death in North Carolina since 2006. Executions were initially stopped because doctors refused to participate in them, and the European makers of one of the drugs used in lethal injections refused to export it to US prisons. Ongoing litigation over North Carolina's Racial Justice Act, which allows death row prisoners to challenge their sentence if it was "sought or obtained on the basis of race," has kept the de facto moratorium in place. Given the evolving standards of decency in the criminal justice system, the decline in capital sentences and executions, a high rate of death sentences reversed on appeal, and the increasing number of innocent people exonerated from death row, North Carolina may never put another prisoner to death. But until the state abolishes capital punishment, my friends and I know that our "last meal" may come much earlier than we hope.

What would you eat for your last meal? Would you even have an appetite, knowing that, in a matter of hours, after hugging and kissing your loved ones goodbye, your life would end? On death row, we rarely discuss last meals.

In 2006 the day before he would have been put onto death watch—the final seventy-two hours of isolation before the lethal injection—my friend JT received a stay of execution. I asked him about the last meal. "Eating?" He shook his head. "Who can think of food when you're preparing to die? I probably would have refused it." Newspapers report the condemned's last meal in the same paragraph as their final words, how long it took for the death to occur (and whether any step was "botched"), who attended the execution, and whether the prosecutor and victims' families made a statement. Lumping that information all together furthers the misconception that the last meal is eaten in smug satisfaction, at expense of the victims and the public.

For all the handwringing about extravagant last meals, those of us who know executions know that the gustatory requests of the condemned are seldom, if ever, met. Those awaiting death frequently refuse a last meal; others find that their facility allows them only to choose from what's on the standard chow hall menu that day. Visions of delivery drivers lining up with steaks from one place and milkshakes from another are almost laughably false. So, no, prisoners don't sit around drooling over what we would request, because we have no illusions that it would ever be provided. Discussions like that would just be feeding a fantasy, contrasting bitterly with the bleak food-as-required-calories system we actually live in (and may eventually die in).

The Usual

Early in the COVID-19 pandemic, the North Carolina division of prisons food and nutrition management director decided, as a "morale-boosting measure," to "make adjustments and enhance meals." The memo, posted in chow halls and cellblocks throughout North Carolina's fifity-five prisons, read:

> Food and Nutrition Management has recently changed the menus to provide new and different recipes to offer more variety. In addition, we will be adding food items to improve morale as we navigate through a difficult time for everyone. Food and Nutrition Management will continue to offer balanced meals in a safe environment as we have always done.

Apparently, under ordinary circumstances, food and nutrition management (FNM) recognizes that liquified pasta, straight-from-the-can collard greens, undercooked beans with molasses, and last year's apples (preserved in a deep freezer) being served until rotten is bad for morale. But at least something new and improved was coming. Or not. The "new and different recipes" changed nothing but the arrangement and labeling of our meals. The promise of variety could not mask the indifference of those tasked with food prep and cooking in Central Prison's (CP) kitchen. Like other memos posted on cell-block bulletin boards, the administration's promises were ludicrous. Chicken patties are fried chicken. Rotten is fresh. Hunger is satiation.

Maybe other prisons provide better food. Toast for breakfast with a dash of margarine, condiments with each meal, properly seasoned and cooked proteins, ripe fruit that doesn't appear diseased. Meals at CP, coronavirus or otherwise, are lusterless and so unremarkable that lunch is forgotten by dinner. The food varies only in its description on a menu, usually placed in a highly visible spot for inspecting prison officials who would never sit down and eat what comes out of this kitchen. After a while, eating becomes a mechanical process devoid of pleasure, an act of bare sustenance around which the day is structured. Pavlov should have studied prisoners.

Whether conditioned anticipation or incessant hunger, the most hated ritual in prison is standing in the chow line. Three times a day, seven days a week, we spend fifteen to twenty minutes lining up for a tray. Years of confinement threaded with thousands of hours standing in line while conversations wax inane and vitriolic, silent impatience shuffles the feet, and fantasies of flavorful cuisine go unfulfilled. By the time a tray slides through the serving window, you've lost your appetite. The chow hall is noisy, unpleasant tones ricocheting off hard surfaces under fluorescent lights. It smells of sour mop water. Flies congregate at the juice coolers, and the tables are encrusted with traces of what we hope was once food. But eating is a matter of survival, and going hungry is a hard way to do time. So, you line up, grab a tray, sit for the precisely allotted ten minutes, and try to choke down some fuel. Three times a day, seven days a week, you will be neither hungry nor particularly interested, but most likely, you will eat.

CP's four chow halls seat nearly four hundred prisoners at four-person steel tables. Like school cafeterias, there are cliques, though the social pecking orders here are mapped by gang affiliation, reason for incarceration, and race. It's a bit different among the death row population; most of us have known each other for decades, and we have few internal divisions. Executions are the great equalizer, and so our chow-hall seating first hinges on the types of table etiquette and conversation you can tolerate, then is established into a habitual seating chart. Prison is all about ruts.

With so many people and so little room to maneuver, accidents happen. People bump into each other, arguments flare, sometimes there's a fight—it will be brief, though, because the guards are quick to spray mace, which drifts, spreads, and chokes, ruining every tray of food (to the extent that it wasn't ruined before this unceremonious seasoning). Thankfully, fights are rare. Most of the arguments actually erupt in the chow line, between food servers and prisoners lining up to eat. All the CP kitchen workers are regular population prisoners with sentences as varied as five years to life without parole. They are overseen by kitchen stewards, who are prison guards with aprons, and the custody staff standing as a token force ready to radio for backup if there's any trouble—because prisoners serving food to other prisoners creates a power dynamic.

Kitchen workers in our facility are split between two shifts, with prisoner-cooks earning one dollar a day and dishwashers and janitors forty cents per day. Skill has nothing to do with this job assignment; it's all about kitchen stewards' favoritism and taste for pitting prisoners against one another for special foods and assignments. In practice, the stewards are so powerful that they, not the menus or FNM, determine what the prisoner-cooks prepare and what goes out on the trays. Sometimes the stewards abide by the menu. Mostly they do not. Every prisoner not under the protective umbrella of their favor hates the kitchen stewards.

The serving windows in CP's chow hall are narrow, waist-high, two-by-one-foot holes in a concrete wall, supervised on one side by custody staff and cameras, and on the other, the kitchen steward. Under this surveillance, the pass-through windows remain conduits for contraband, messages, stolen food, shorted trays, barbed comments, and threats.

Before David,* a friend in the cell beside me, received a death sentence, he worked in the kitchen. He recalls pushing hundreds of trays out of the serving window at every meal. "You'd not believe the abuse we get from people," he told me. "Bad enough I got a steward treating me like her personal servant. Then I gotta hear, 'Man, gimme a bigger scoop of eggs. Gimme another cookie. Gimme some more peanut butter.' And a lot of the time I would. But the first time I don't? They cuss and threaten me. The whole time a guard or steward is standing there smirking, daring me to give out something extra so they can throw me in the hole. The most ridiculous part is how much food we throw away because they don't want us to give it out. We're talking about roughly two thirty-two-gallon trash cans full of wasted food each meal. It took two of us just to move one of those cans."

With the capacity to confine over one thousand prisoners, only regular population and death row eat in CP's chow halls. the nearly four hundred prisoners in the hospital, mental health unit (MHU), and solitary confinement are fed in-cell. David worked preparing the meals for

---

* This is a pseudonym.

therapeutic diets—the medically necessary food for those in the hospital or MHU—as well. He remembered these trays, devoid of salt, sugar, seasoning, or fat; vegetarian; liquid; and Kosher meals. The diet-line menu is tailored by doctors and tweaked by custodial staff. David said, "Sometimes I'd get weird orders to debone a chicken leg or shell eggs for a tray. But one time I put a plastic spork with it, like every tray. A guard came back, mad, saying, 'You gotta leave sharp objects off this tray. No bones. No eggshells. No utensils. Write it down somewhere.'"

The officer explained to David that some MHU prisoners swallowed sharp objects or cut themselves just to leave their cells for medical treatment—a tactic to have another human being touch them. "After that, I really thought about who received these trays," David said. "It made me think of them more as people, not just another tray." He didn't learn that from the kitchen stewards or from serving on the chow line; in prison, granting others' humanity was the exception rather than the rule.

Creating Rituals and Makeshift Meals

Considering the toxic social environment of chow hall and the equally toxic "food" ejected from its serving window, junk food from the canteen makes up a large portion of the prisoner's diet. Ramen noodles are a forty-three-cent staple that fills burritos or makes a passable goulash with canned vegetables and, if you're lucky, a turkey thigh stolen from the kitchen.

Variations on the humble-yet-endlessly-adaptable burrito can involve everything from freeze-dried rice and beans to cheese, pickles, ranch dressing, canned fish, et cetera. It's an exercise in motivated improvisation.

For the twenty years Gilby and Squirrel have been friends on death row, they have pooled their resources to make burritos together on Sundays. The ritual is always the same, filled with good-natured bickering. On any given Sunday, Squirrel delegates food prep to Gilby, who usually cuts the sausage or pickle too big or forgets to heat the water. Squirrel fusses at Gilby to do it right while Gilby claims he did. Gilby forgets to warm the chili packet in the bucket of now-hot water, causing Squirrel to fuss some more, then take over the process. Gilby rolls his eyes like a teenager, rather than the fifty-five-year-old Appalachian hillbilly he is, but Squirrel is only satisfied when he does everything—berating Gilby in a Panamanian-Brooklyn patois while they eat and watch football or basketball.

A lot of prisoners prepare and share special meals for birthdays, Christmas, or major sporting events. These meals combine canteen staples with food purchased from the quarterly Union Supply Direct package program. It's nothing that couldn't be found in any neighborhood convenience store or gas station: prepackaged, freeze-dried, sodium-stocked, carb-heavy, ready-to-eat. But these simple meals taste better than anything from the chow hall. Without the stench of poor cleaning practices and the aggravation of standing in line, we can, in these moments, enjoy the ways food brings people together. The care that goes into preparing the meal and the joy and camaraderie it is shared among friends with, these makeshift banquets are indescribably special. Inside these walls, rare moments like these must be savored.

Peanut Burritos (serves 10)

Ingredients:
10 flour tortillas
1 4-ounce package freeze-dried rice and beans
1 11-ounce packet of chili with beans
2 ramen noodle packs (with chili flavoring)
2 dill pickles, diced
2 5-ounce summer sausages, chopped
3 2-ounce packs of salted peanuts, crushed
2 1-ounce cheddar cheese squeeze packets

Instructions:

1. Heat chili packet and sausages in boiling water. In a separate container, add 1 cup boiling water to freeze-dried rice and beans, stirring until water is fully absorbed. Add 2 cups boiling water to the ramen noodles (once cooked, drain and add seasoning

packets). Combine chili, rice and beans, and seasoned ramen noodles; set aside.
2. Evenly spread filling mixture across 10 tortillas, then top each with diced pickles, chopped sausages, and crushed peanuts. Spread a line of cheese on each burrito.
3. Roll, serve, and eat.

Banana Pudding (serves 5)

Ingredients:
10 packs of vanilla sandwich cookies (60 total cookies)
20 packs of nondairy coffee creamer
2 bananas
4 ounces milk

Instructions:

1. Split cookies, setting frosting filling aside. Line a large bowl with a single layer of cookies.
2. In a large cup, mix the frosting from the cookies with the coffee creamer and milk. Stir vigorously until mixture has the consistency of pudding.
3. Peel and slice bananas.
4. Layer "pudding," cookies, and bananas, continuing until all ingredients are used.
5. Let sit for two hours, then serve and eat.

First Meals

Those of us on death row don't fantasize about our last meals; instead, we focus on what our first meal would be on the outside, our first tastes of freedom. Like a pinprick of light, shining through a keyhole, it buoys hope. Whenever my mom asks, "What do you want to eat when you get home?" she emphasizes the word *home*. She knows my favorite meal is curried chicken over rice with almonds, saffron, and raisins. Oh, and a side of chutney. Our conversations provide a moment in which my mom can gain a sense of control, rather than feeling helpless to do anything for me in prison. Cooking meals for our family is how she shows her love for all of us.

It's a different conversation with my friend K. "We'll go out and celebrate!" she says. "What would you want to eat?" We discuss the kinds of meals she can prepare, for instance, or I'll prompt, "Breakfast!" and we'll brainstorm. We know it's hypothetical, but those fantasies let me temporarily forget the long road before I'll reach that spread. It's just a delicious symbol of love and belonging.

Capital postconviction appeals are notoriously protracted. I have been fighting my wrongful conviction for over twenty-six years, dreaming about that first meal, and avoiding thoughts of the last.

Maybe that's why our time in the chow hall is about *fuel*, about the basic arithmetic of keeping a human body alive, rather than *meals*, which revive and amplify our humanity, nourish us.

Frontline Snapshots
of Activism

There are many ways to resist the carceral state and drastically reduce the number of people impacted by the criminal legal system. Whether one is new to the fight, has a personal interest, or has a professional role in some nonprofit organization, we need individuals who can pursue justice for everyone, even when it seems inconvenient or impossible.

The people I have interviewed here are advocates, activists, fighters, and decent human beings who made it their mission to help those unfortunate enough to be caught within the criminal legal system. Where the idea of "criminal justice" has become a front for police brutality, overincarceration, and draconian responses to social ills, as well as a rhetorical phrase that expands the prison-industrial complex, these activists strive to reclaim the word "justice." Their pursuit is not adversarial or retributive or empty of logic, rather they seek to address harm in a restorative and balanced manner. Most importantly, they demonstrate mercy in action.

The following Q and A sessions occurred over a number of fifteen-minute phone calls from a phone in a dayroom on Central Prison's death row. These are not verbatim transcripts, but rather shorthand notes written by the author as the activist talked. Some of the answers have been paraphrased but are otherwise true accounts of the interview.

Interview with Ben Finholt

April 2022

Ben Finholt is an attorney who worked for North Carolina Prisoner Legal Services, a state-funded entity that provides limited postconviction legal aid to people in prison. While researching data on juvenile life without parole and virtual life sentences, Ben posed a question to the Vital Project Funds: What if I do this full time? From that proposal came funding to develop the Just Sentencing Project at Duke University Law School's Wilson Center for Science and Justice.

Lyle May (LM): What is the Just Sentencing Project and how does it attempt to counter specific policies of mass incarceration?

Ben Finholt (BF): The Just Sentencing Project is a data-driven approach to reducing the number of people serving really long sentences in North Carolina by finding out who those people are using a categorical review. Juveniles are the main focus right now, because we're still having a hard time gaining relief for them.

LM: What is the resistance to granting relief to people convicted and sentenced for crimes that occurred when they were juveniles?

BF: Mainly, it's the punitive attitude in the US. My understanding of humanity is so far from the idea that if someone gets convicted of a crime it means they should be left in prison to rot. It's cognitively easy to be merciless, and society has become increasingly cognitively lazy. It is much harder to think about the circumstances around crime, to put yourself in somebody's shoes. Then there are the politics of crime and how people in elected office have to appear tough just to stay in office.

LM: Why is there genuine disinterest among some prosecutors, judges, and lawmakers to accept that because juveniles' brain[s are] not fully developed, this reduces their culpability for a crime? Neuroscience on adolescent brain development is not as old as DNA testing [DNA testing made its debut in the early to mid-1980s, whereas neuroscience of adolescent brain development didn't have a major impact until the early to mid-2000s], but it is just as proven. Why do you think junk science such as blood patterning, bite mark evidence, and ballistics have greater weight in upholding a wrongful conviction than neuroscience that would merely reduce the harshness of an excessive prison term? Does this underline a fundamental failing of the criminal legal system that the state and judiciary pursues convictions and punishment—not justice?

BF: People and the courts value finality above correctness. I don't know why that takes precedence over getting it right. Going back to review faulty or overly harsh decisions would mean endlessly litigating cases. The average person also cannot imagine themselves committing crimes as a result of their circumstances, environment, peers, or other causes. All of it is a matter of cognitive discomfort. People do what causes the least amount of discomfort. Imagining oneself in a mental state or circumstances where commission of a horrible crime is possible is discomforting. So people don't. Instead, they respond with "I would never do that," and are unwilling to extend the idea of mercy.

LM: How much does misinformation or disinformation complicate the work you do at the Just Sentencing Project? How do you counter it?

BF: It's not as bad for me. That happens more at the political level. I have to deal more with micro-misinformation when people in prison write to me with an incomplete understanding of what we do or how a particular policy does or does not apply to them.

LM: How much do you think micro-PACs—fundraising at the local level to influence who becomes sheriff, judge, [district attorney], county commissioner, or schoolboard member—can impact a state's carceral footprint?

BF: They could have a big effect at the district attorney level for sentencing. In general, maybe the sheriff in terms of arrests and enforcement. Real reform happens at the legislative level. Durham has been very forward-thinking about sentencing.

LM: What does the Just Sentencing Project do with the data it collects? How does it carry out its mission when, like NC Prison Legal Services, it needs greater funding?

BF: We—mainly I—find people who are serving long sentences [who] don't need to be in prison anymore. The data is also a way of remembering exactly who is in prison, and how long they have been there. That data is used to inform policy. The Juvenile Sentence Review Board came out of that data. I've also worked with the ACLU to inform the governor's position on clemency requests based on the data. North Carolina is famous for data collected about incarceration. A lot of researchers use theses about policies. The NCDPS and state archives contain all of this information about people in prison. I just wish more hardcore data scientists would go through that information to understand charging and conviction trends. Fortunately, the Duke University Wilson Center has data scientists who are going to work this angle with the Just Sentencing Project.

Regarding funding—we definitely need more. I'm working toward a point where we will apply for more grants and accept donations.

LM: As an executive action, how can the Juvenile Sentence Review Board be maintained across administrations, especially if the next governor is a Republican?

BF: To ensure continuity of the Juvenile Sentence Review Board and similar efforts in government, we have to develop buy-in from other parts of the system—law enforcement, the judiciary, the Department of Public Safety, Postrelease Supervision, Probation and Parole, and others. We have to build holistic systems founded on good data and science. The JSRB's continued success means robust reentry development, coordination with [North Carolina Department of Public Safety] officials and buy-in from the parole commission.

LM: How can you protect the Just Sentencing Project against that one person who, despite your best efforts to determine will not reoffend, gets out and does so, creating a "Willie Horton effect" that has politicians ready to end a program that is 99 percent effective in every other case?

BF: You have to anticipate the Willie Horton effect on a program like this and hope you've built up a track record of success to buffer public backlash when it comes.

LM: Do you consider your work at the Just Sentencing Project as a type of activism?

BF: Yes. I'm trying to reverse things that were done incorrectly in the past. I can't sit here and allow people to suffer in prison, to turn my back on them and say, "Not my problem," while they serve out unnecessarily long sentences because of misguided politics from the 1980s and 1990s.

LM: What role do you think restorative justice has in the criminal legal system?

BF: I think restorative justice is a great tool to begin the process of accountability. Crime causes pain. Restorative justice programs can force people who commit crimes to deal with that pain. It all comes back to resolving cognitive discomfort. Even if a person must still go to prison, restorative justice should be a program where a parole commission or clemency board can check in every five years or so to see where he or she is on the road to accountability.

PART II

CARCERAL STATE

LIFE IMPRISONMENT

Chapter 9

Life without Parole
Is a Silent Execution

In 2011 four North Carolina prisoners serving parole-eligible life sentences for murder were nearing the minimum time needed to earn release. Three of the four were engaged in work release programs that allowed them to leave the prison to work within the community. One woman was a stylist at a hair salon, well-liked and thought of as a valuable employee. They were beneficiaries of a time when the state was still invested in rehabilitating inmates. Up until 1994, the Fair Sentencing Act equated life sentences to eighty years. Participation in programs, counseling, education, and work reduced the sentence by half. At that point, prisoners were considered for release.

The 1994 North Carolina Structured Sentencing Act eliminated parole, good time, and gain time for any A-E felony. Parole incentives were replaced with mandatory minimums and life without parole. But the law was not retroactive, and lifers sentenced under the Fair Sentencing Act could still pursue parole through the North Carolina Parole Commission. Or so they thought.

When then-governor Beverly Perdue discovered four lifers would soon be paroled after completing the standard minimum of forty years, she did the politically expedient thing and blocked their release. Ignoring the law and evidence of rehabilitation, the governor declared, "Life should mean life."

As of November 30, 2016, 1,733 people in North Carolina were serving parole-eligible life sentences. One of them was recently witnessed eating lunch with her prison-approved sponsor at a local Raleigh restaurant, a first step in the Community Leave Program that prepares parolees for release. A friend of the woman's victim complained to the director of prisons.

"It just seems so bizarre to me that our society supports a first-degree murderer going out to nice lunches and being treated to that . . . This defies logic . . . It is more than enough that [she] gets to live out her natural life [in prison]."[1]

Life without parole (LWOP) is no different from a death sentence that ends with the lethal injection. Whether one dies of natural causes in a prison infirmary or on a gurney in front of witnesses—both forms of punishment are life in prison with death as the only possibility of release. At their core is the belief that a prisoner is not worthy of freedom, that redemption is improbable and irrelevant to the overall purpose of the sentence: vengeance.

Yet the public believes LWOP is a mercy compared to an execution, as if decades on death row or decades in the regular prison population are much different. Neither changes the fact you will never again be a part of society. Tough-on-crime platforms tout "a life for a life" as the best brand of justice, turning Old Testament laws into modern criminal justice. That strategy, paired with mandatory minimums and a lack of judicial discretion, is a large part of why there are 2.2 million people incarcerated in prisons and jails in the United States, the highest rate of imprisonment, per capita, in the world.[2] Though there has been a slow downward shift in rates as the state realizes its unsustainability, the system's policies regarding LWOP remain stagnant.

While the increase in LWOP sentences correlates with mass incarceration, there is a valid argument that the punishment has its own trajectory. Abolition of the death penalty in 1972, then its reinstatement in 1976 had a significant influence, but is not the only explanation for the rise in LWOP. Before the US Supreme Court's ruling in *Furman v. Georgia* (1972), prisoners with "natural life" terms (the LWOP equivalent) had a reasonable chance at receiving a commuted sentence through clemency. This was also true of people on death row who had their sentence reduced to life imprisonment. However, when the court reinstated the death penalty in *Gregg v. Georgia* (1976) more states enacted LWOP statutes and usage of the punishment surged. Other causes of growth in LWOP can be attributed to abolitionists who argued that LWOP is a kinder, gentler death sentence than one by execution. At the same time a change in sentencing was occurring as indeterminate sentencing practices and judicial discretion were under fire for being too lenient, shifting sentencing schemes to longer fixed terms. LWOP became a "capital net widening mechanism" that expanded the range and number of people sent to die in prison. As of 2020 perpetual confinement has impacted over 210,000 people serving LWOP, parole-eligible life, and virtual life (over fifty years) terms.[3]

Life without parole is a conceit held by those who dislike the idea of executing anyone for any reason, yet believe it is okay to warehouse and forget those same prisoners. For others, it is their last best hope for rendering an ultimate punishment that forever incapacitates killers. Prosecutors use it as a bargaining tool in potential death penalty cases with great effect, scaring defendants into plea deals that eliminate further appeals. And defense attorneys settle on LWOP as the best chance their client has of avoiding execution, even though the "lesser" of the justice system's most punitive sentences is the difference between suffering fifty years as an exception to the Thirteenth Amendment and for fifty minutes as an exception to the Eighth.

All would rather wash their hands of and ignore the deeper societal problems rooted in crime—racism, poverty, and mental illness—maintaining that there are some prisoners who deserve no mercy. At best, this is a slippery slope that ignores evidence in favor of emotion. Crime is not simplistic, nor can it be addressed with one-size-fits-all mandatory sentences. In accepting heavy-handed justice that ignores important elements of crime and punishment, one supports institutionalized racism, classism, mass incarceration, and a prison-industrial complex that feeds on human beings.

LWOP obscures the more insidious issues of prosecutorial, judicial, jury, and police misconduct, as well as ineffective counsel. Beyond a cursory direct appeal, there is no appellate counsel assigned to noncapital cases after the direct appeal. Without the in-depth case analyses made by appellate defenders as there are in capital cases, many appealable issues are never discovered or developed, including innocence.[4]

The lack of legal aid in noncapital appeals makes it easy to see why a lower percentage of sentences and convictions are overturned when compared to capital cases. Where capital appeals seem to go on until the prisoner is put to death, the "legal window" for those serving LWOP is much more limited and time-sensitive. Despite the relative "safety" of being alive and in prison for the rest of your life, once that window closes all legal claims die. It bears repeating that, of the 8,466 prisoners who were sentenced to death between 1973 and 2013, 42 percent (3,619) had their sentence or conviction reversed. Since 1977, nearly three-quarters of all death sentences in North Carolina were reversed on appeal.[5] How much appealable information would have been developed in these capital cases without the aid of a legal team and the "immediate" threat of execution? How many people will die in prison because that same legal scrutiny is not provided in LWOP cases?

In a 2014 case, Federal District Court Judge Cormac Carney held that California's inability to carry out executions "has rendered the state's death penalty unconstitutional," referring to the punishment as "life in prison, with the remote possibility of death."[6] If the threat of death while in an isolated setting for decades at a time—regardless of whether the execution is carried out—creates debilitating psychosis and is said to be inhumane, how much worse is the oppressive nature of LWOP?

When a prison sentence is not balanced by at least a small chance to engage in and demonstrate rehabilitation, it is as cruel and unusual as a death sentence. LWOP is already where hope for legal aid dies, but so too does any real incentive to improve. Educational programs, work release, and vocational training are barred to prisoners who have no release dates. No parole board will revisit these cases and gubernatorial clemency is unlikely. Nationwide, governors "have denied virtually all clemency requests over the last three decades."[7]

There is not much help for the prisoner serving LWOP, because many of the nonprofits that strive to end the death penalty fully support

LWOP as an alternative. For first-degree murder, LWOP has become a foregone conclusion. Even among those who have parole-eligible life sentences for violent and nonviolent offenses, parole boards are unwilling to grant parole even when it has been earned through rehabilitative efforts.[8]

Mandatory LWOP means prosecutors, jurors, and the public never see defendants for who they might be after twenty-five or thirty years of incarceration. Instead, "crime" becomes this monolithic entity that overshadows and devalues the humanity of the prisoner. No longer the same person who may have committed the crime, once convicted, their life is cast off and forgotten. Whoever they used to be or struggled to become is lost in an existence identified by a number in a prison file with a description of the crime. There are no incentives or any hope of freedom beyond death.

LWOP is death by incarceration and must be abolished alongside capital punishment. A life sentence with parole eligibility after twenty-five years is certainly harsh, but it gives the offender something to hope for and work toward. In those cases where it is not considered harsh enough, or a person presents a continued public safety risk, parole boards have consistently denied release without the help of public sentiment, political pressure, or mandatory sentencing. Release must be a possibility for the person society wants the offender to be: one who can return to the community and contribute in a valuable and redeeming way. This is especially imperative for the nearly 3,300 prisoners serving LWOP for nonviolent drug offenses,[9] and the nearly 2,300 offenders sentenced to LWOP as juveniles.[10] Even though the US Supreme Court abolished mandatory LWOP for offenders who were juveniles at the time of the crime, many states are resistant to their potential for release.

There is a seemingly legitimate fear associated with people convicted of violent crimes receiving parole eligibility on a life sentence. However, even without rehabilitative programs, the very nature of confinement, while punitive, induces change. Maybe because of this, parole-eligible lifers who found release after fifteen to twenty years have the lowest recidivism rate of any reentering citizen. At the request of the Criminal Justice Policy Coalition, the Massachusetts Parole Board undertook a study of 151 second-degree-murder lifers who were released under supervision from 2000 to 2006. Of these parolees, 116 (72 percent) were not reincarcerated. Their average age was forty-eight. Of the forty-five who recidivated, it was for technical parole violations such as failing a drug test or minor felony offenses.[11]

There has long been evidence that lengthy prison sentences, like the death penalty, are not associated with less crime or enhanced safety. Quite the opposite. Public outrage over sensationalized crimes and political scare tactics drive the use of excessive prison terms. These same forces also cut funding to rehabilitative programs and education in prison, restrict the flexibility of parole boards, change laws to limit clemency requests, and scare away any electable public official who might even consider helping prisoners serving LWOP. In a heavy-handed inexpert attempt to hold offenders accountable for their crimes, the public and politicians prevent the criminal justice system from working as anything other than a hole in the ground. Lost in the retributive push to punish is the reason for that accountability: the victims.

Survivors of violent crimes and their families would likely prefer to forget the person who harmed them and move on. In their estimation, suffering in prison is a small price to pay, since they, too, suffer the pain, anger, and heartache of loss. While the court recognizes this in allowing for victim impact statements during sentencing, this does not go far enough. The responsible party needs to recognize that loss, and an effective way of doing this without trading a life for a life is through restorative justice.

Authentic restorative justice seeks to repair relationships within the community and hold offenders accountable by helping them to understand the loss of the victim. It helps to define rehabilitation for the offender, making it proximate to those he or she harmed. In the Vera Institute of Justice report *Accounting for Violence*, Danielle Sered discusses the powerful results of restorative justice programs at work in other Western nations and within the fringes of the US criminal justice system:

> By bringing people who commit harm face-to-face with those affected by their actions and giving survivors a central voice in the process, these programs give those who are responsible a chance to acknowledge the impact of their actions and make things as

right as possible. As such they do what prisons typically fail to do: they hold people accountable in a meaningful way.[12]

Though not all victims' families or violent crime survivors will be interested in restorative justice, this is the kind of accountability people who commit crimes need. While suffering is an integral aspect of criminal justice for the offender—and they should do so with the "difficulty of that reckoning and even the fear and pain it may cause"—they also deserve an opportunity to repair the damage they are responsible for.

LWOP does not provide such an opportunity, and our adversarial legal system is not designed for it. Prison does not hold the incarcerated accountable—it merely punishes them to the extreme extent of the law. Incarceration has become a bludgeon incapable of attending to the needs of victims and their families, those who harm them, or the communities where crimes occur. "No one in prison is required to face the human impact of what they have done," writes Sered, "to come face-to-face with the people whose lives are changed as a result of their decision; to take responsibility for that decision; and to do the extraordinarily hard work of answering for that pain and becoming someone who will not ever commit that harm again."[13]

There are viable alternatives to LWOP that worked well prior to 1994 and the inception of mandatory sentencing. Indeterminate sentences of twenty-five years to life granted access to a parole board or judicial review, but not necessarily parole itself. The lifer would have to convince a body of trained professionals, or a judge in court, at a public hearing that release is warranted and the community can benefit from his or her return. It is at such a hearing that a risk assessment of the incarcerated person would be conducted, taking into consideration his or her age, progress in restorative justice programming, and likelihood of success in society. Most of Europe, China, and Pakistan allow for similar reviews of life sentences; it's time for the United States to return to a sentencing policy that works toward reducing mass incarceration and is more humane than death or LWOP sentences.

If the public is to be engaged in this process it should be in a conversation on sensible reforms forwarded by penal experts. It should be about equal and equitable justice that restores balance to crime in society—not just retribution and incapacitation. The criminal justice system can function better than it has in decades and the current national conversation suggests most people agree on this point.

However, if there is to be lasting change in the justice system, like the people it imprisons, there must be an opportunity for everyone to do so.

Chapter 10

Beyond the Wall

The injury occurred during a basketball game on the yard. I went up for a rebound and came down on the side of my foot, driving my ankle to the ground until there was an audible pop. Down I went, holding my quivering leg and inventing new ways to curse.

When a guard later wheeled me into the prison ER, I expected to be told my ankle was broken, since it listed to the left without any effort on my part. I thought they might put a cast on it, give me a set of crutches and some ibuprofen, then return me to the block to deal with it. Reasonable medical care isn't something you expect in a place where they prefer "natural death" to intervention—where what is considered negligence on the outside passes for adequate treatment on the inside.

It was Saturday, and with no X-ray technicians available the doctor made some calls, then told me I would be going to an outside hospital. He gave me a pain pill (crushed and mixed with water to avoid abuse), put my ankle in a temporary splint, and left me to wait.

A couple of guards muttered incredulous comments about the cost of an ambulance while I stared at the splint, trying to keep my face neutral. Rattling in my head like a pair of carelessly tossed dice were two words: outside, hospital. Then one: outside. Through the haze of oxycodone, I focused on the waves of pain instead of what "outside" meant, but this failed as a long-forgotten beacon lanced through it all. Outside. Outside. Outside.

I had not been beyond the wall of Central Prison in seventeen years. For my entire adult life, I've existed in the same two hundred yards of dust and cement. Prison is so ingrained in my thoughts, that it is simply an extension of my headspace—impossible to step out of except in death. Even my dreams are tainted with fragments of this waking nightmare. It takes more time to brush and floss my teeth than to walk to the chow hall, the rec yard, or the canteen. I've become so accustomed to the lack of space and movement that an empty seven-by-nine-foot cell feels voluminous. Many of the people around me are so familiar, that what they say or do can be counted on like a drip from a leaky faucet.

This microcosm of life is so removed from the outside world that newspapers, magazines, and television provide glimpses of a reality too distant to touch, smell, or feel. Even on the yard, a craggy wall surrounds our dirt lot and cracked concrete basketball court, hiding freedom from hungry eyes and erasing memories of a different world that existed before . . . this.

Narrow slit windows blur a landscape in miniature—buildingstrees-birdsroadstrain—as untouchable as the Earth from the moon.

It is difficult to picture something you've forgotten. Then, when you've been reintroduced, it's impossible to understand how you forgot.

Not until we passed the checkpoint in front of the prison did it strike me that we were beyond the wall. As the last recognizable barrier of my concrete world dwindled, there was no doubt in my mind I remained incarcerated. Hands cuffed and chained at the waist, I sat on a motorized gurney with one leg shackled to the other over the temporary splint. To my left sat a transport officer whose hands were gripping the neck of her bulletproof vest. Two more officers followed in a pursuit vehicle. I noted these things, along with all of the storage compartments in the back of the ambulance, as enthralled with them as the pavement unfolding behind us at a rapid pace.

So, so many trees and leaves, tall trunks towering over paved roads with cars glittering in the sun. So much space expanding and filling the square windows before me. Engines hummed. A car honked and I jumped, laughing at the sound. The officer looked at me and I stared ahead, wide-eyed, then at her as the full significance of this trip became something I couldn't keep to myself.

"I haven't been out of that prison in seventeen years."

She looked at me—in disbelief, incomprehension, curiosity—then resumed talking to the EMT.

Street signs so vividly punctuated roads into neighborhoods both welcoming and alien that it made my eyes water. Colors glittered. Even rundown houses with their rusted oil tanks and peeling paint, overgrown weeds, and shuttered windows were perfect. My eyes jumped to cars I didn't recognize and a few I remembered from TV ads. They were real! Futuristic and fantastic—and me grinning like an idiot. Gloriously green leaves sprouted in lush bursts from branches shifting, swaying, waving, and living out moments of creation as happily as they could.

We pulled into the hospital emergency entrance where I was wheeled to a bed, x-rayed, told nothing was broken, and put in a tiny waiting room. Up to this point, I had received some curious glances from hospital staff, but most of it was reserved for the three pistol-toting transport officers in their vests. They paced and got in the way and gave serious looks, warding off conversation. As a result, eyes seemed to skip over me as I sat there, bemused and unable to shift without grimacing in pain or the cuffs sliding up my skinny arms.

Finally, three nurses arrived with more temporary cast materials in their arms. There wasn't enough space in the room for six people, so two officers stepped out while the nurses got to work. There was a friendly conversation between the female transport officer and a nurse about what my foot would smell like in six weeks and what a pain in the ass showering would be, with periodic instructions for me to breathe when they moved my leg. The friendly banter died when the male nurse asked an officer what my red jumpsuit meant.

"Death row."

Up to that point, despite the chains and the guards, I had adapted to the otherness of the hospital, and my thoughts were entirely in the moment. This was how I became aware of the major difference between the "outside" and the "inside." Silence. This preternatural quiet was the emptying of thought into space, where before it simply bounced and reverberated from the walls of my confinement. The "moment" in prison is full of hatred, bitterness, regret, and emotional pain. It never goes away, and being at peace with it simply means you've grown accustomed to its oppressive weight on your back.

People who like to say you can be free in mind but not in body while incarcerated have never experienced long-term confinement or been labeled "state property." There is no real freedom—just the ability to do mental gymnastics to convince yourself everything will be okay when in your heart of hearts you know there is nothing natural or okay or freeing about prison, and it is not necessarily a lesser evil than death. This weight is always present inside. Always nagging in the corner of the mind. Always reminding you of the utter wrongness of confinement.

Maybe it was the air and vibrant colors that hypnotized me into a false sense of well-being, but at the mention of death row, the noise came roaring back. I sank into the hospital bed beneath its pressure.

The nurse holding my leg up yelped as if pinched. At the same time the nurse in charge blurted "What?!" and snapped her attention to the guard who volunteered the information. Nobody moved or said anything until the silence embarrassed even the transport officers.

"Wow, that's incredibly sad," she said.

The other nurse looked like he wanted to hide his face, had his hands not been full.

The familiar sense of ostracism and isolation that has echoed through the years since the trial came back to me, and I found myself wanting to leave the hospital and return . . . Then I stopped the thought as soon as it occurred.

What did she mean? Was it "sad" because they were wasting resources on a condemned man, or "sad" because their profession is about preserving life and administering to those in need? Maybe she was commenting on her realization that a normal human being in need of care sat before her, rather than the sensationalized, deceptive image of a monster unfit for life and liberty? The last seemed the most plausible.

My physical presence reminded her there are real people on death row—living, thinking, feeling people who will be put to death because the law says, "Die."

In the disquiet that followed, the nurse in charge gave a few instructions on wrapping my ankle and left without another word. The other female nurse patted my knee with a small smile and left the molding of the cast to the male nurse. He was apologetic.

"It will hurt. Push foot against my chest." I moved, breathing hard into the pain. "You know," he said, "No one ever put foot on me. Ever. You first." He looked at me, serious, his Russian accent making me imagine him as some mobster trying to escape an ugly past. More than anything I appreciated his attempt to put me at ease.

I pushed hard and only moved an inch, my face breaking into a cold sweat. "It's a good habit, not letting people put their feet on you," I said. "They might think you're a doormat."

He smiled as the material hardened around my ankle, tapped it with a knuckle, then eased it to the bed. "All done," he said, and left to get a wheelchair.

Thirty minutes later, exhausted and ready to leave, they wheeled me out of the hospital and into the warm air and light of the parking lot. We were on a slight rise so I could see above the trees. In the wavering heat, leaves fluttered and branches waved. A car revved its engine. My ankle a distant ache, my eyes jumped from trees to cars and buildings and people, then locked on the vermillion brilliance of the setting sun. The light hurt to look upon, but I stared and struggled to inhale this achingly beautiful life on earth, holding on to the awe it inspired.

For the briefest moment, I remembered another life, where sunsets were normal and I didn't drink from this world as though dying of thirst. Then it was gone, lost in the gathering shadows and sound of clinking chains.

Chapter 11

Death by Incarceration

- By 2016, over 206,268 people were serving some type of life sentence in US prisons.
- Over 53,000 people were serving life without the possibility of parole (LWOP) sentences.
- Noncapital prisoners receive no legal representation on their appeals.
- More than 100 people sentenced to LWOP have been exonerated since 2013.
- Lifers account for approximately 12 percent of North Carolina's prison population; forty times the number of life-sentenced prisoners in the United Kingdom.

It is scary to think lawmakers and death penalty abolitionists alike believe LWOP is a more humane alternative to executions. It seems unlikely they really understand what living the rest of your life in prison is like. If they did, LWOP wouldn't exist. I don't want to die in prison, yet whether I am executed or receive LWOP, that's exactly what will happen. For many people on death row, LWOP is the only form of "relief" they may receive from a court. In many ways it's worse than being executed. You watch all your family and friends die or drift away as the world leaves you behind. You work fifty to sixty hours a week earning forty cents a day, unable to afford a stamp let alone a tube of toothpaste. Refuse to work and get you put in solitary confinement. If you get sick, you suffer. Medical care in prison is a joke and the only people laughing live in the free world. Prison can be a violent place, and no one escapes that threat if they spend their whole life here. Some might try to argue LWOP offers a better quality of life than death row—I'm pretty sure those people don't live in prison or know how degrading it can be. Sure, under some circumstances, a lifer has access to a limited number of programs, but that often doesn't include higher education, just GED and basic adult education—not the kind of stuff that stimulates growth.

Let's not forget about the gangs. Imagine being over sixty years old and needing to call home or use a tablet to communicate with your family, but a given gang's new recruits decide to take your tablet. Maybe they charge you "rent" to stay safe in their territory. What happens when you can't pay? Protective custody is solitary confinement until death. Imagine being eighteen or nineteen and trying to resist that recruitment. Imagine being forty and failing to resist. Imagine what happens to those who *do* resist. There are many gangs in prison. Resisting all of them is the hardest road of all; now imagine doing it for the rest of your life.

And then there are the rigors of aging in prison. Nurses care little and doctors even less. Imagine being seventy years old and relying on another prisoner to push your wheelchair, wipe your butt, wash you, and provide any care you need. Assuming you reach the age of seventy in prison and you haven't been crippled by years of kitchen or janitorial work and you don't have a chronic disease, you're probably either begging God to take you in your sleep or contemplating doing it yourself. What if your family is long-lived and you have another thirty years to go after that?

What if you committed a nonviolent drug or financial crime? Does that warrant death by incarceration? Or worse, what if you're innocent?

Conservative US Supreme Court Justice Antonin Scalia once said that an innocent person is "infinitely better off" challenging a death sentence than a life sentence. Wrongful convictions exist regardless of whether a capital case is converted into life without parole. However, a death sentence generates greater judicial scrutiny, so innocent life sentenced prisoners are more likely to "languish unnoticed behind bars."[1]

More than one hundred people sentenced to LWOP have been exonerated since 2013, but there are likely hundreds, if not thousands, more waiting for their chance in court. Pursuing a claim of innocence under a life sentence is much more difficult than has been implied by those who say, "At least with a life sentence you're alive to pursue justice."

Maybe. Maybe not.

In August 2019, the North Carolina Innocence Inquiry Commission overturned the wrongful murder conviction of sixty-six-year-old James Blackmon. An intellectually disabled Black man committed to Dorothea Dix Hospital, Blackmon had actually been in another state when Helena Payton was murdered in 1979. Police narrowed down the description of the perpetrator and decided it must have been Blackmon. With no other evidence, detectives obtained a false, coerced confession from a man wearing a Superman cape in a mental hospital who had an IQ of sixty-nine. It would be over *three decades* before Blackmon was exonerated. He left prison in a wheelchair.

Unless one has an airtight alibi, physical proof, or other incontrovertible evidence, most innocence projects will refuse a prisoner's claim or drag out the process for many years. Lifers who are not guilty of the crime they were convicted for, but instead a lesser crime, are virtually helpless. Without legal representation, LWOP is a certain death sentence.

Think of the death penalty as an icy peak thrust above the dark waters of America's criminal justice system. Judicial scrutiny and a warming national climate have shrunk capital punishment until only a tiny, arbitrary percentage of those convicted of murder end up on death row. This focus ignores the rising tide of LWOP sentences, which as of 2016, has put the lives of over 53,000 men, women, and children in a perpetual state of suffering and oppression, followed by an ignoble death. In the modern era of executions 530 people have been put to death; LWOP is one hundred times more deadly than the lethal injection, firing squad, electric chair, gas chamber, or hanging.

As of a 2016 Sentencing Project Report, the combined number of lifers in America's prisons, which includes LWOP (53,290), life with parole (108,667), and virtual life sentences of fifty or more years (44,311) was over 206,268.[2] As this population ages and begins dying, the costs will cripple state penal budgets and what medical care is provided to them will be so inadequate as to be inhumane.

I understand what some of you may be thinking: What about the worst of the worst? The truly horrific murderers, rapists, and habitual offenders? Surely out of the 2,700 or so people on death row, and over 206,000 lifers, there are people who should die in prison?

First, when has this country ever proven capable of reserving the most severe punishments for the most deserving? Over 175 innocent people have been exonerated from death row since 1976; before their exoneration they were all considered "deserving." Second, there is no exact criteria for the "worst" because LWOP and the death penalty are arbitrarily applied. Among the 206,268 lifers: 59 percent were convicted of homicide; 17 percent rape or sexual assault; 15 percent aggravated assault, robbery, or kidnapping; and 8 percent nonviolent crimes. Who is really guilty? Who is innocent? Can you, sitting at home watching the news, make such a judgment without knowing all the facts, circumstances, and players? That it is considered acceptable to punish lesser crimes the same way as murder, effectively circumventing the US Supreme Court's ban on capital punishment for crimes other than first-degree murder, is beyond draconian.

The United States is alone in its prolific use of death by incarceration. A 2016 comprehensive international analysis of life imprisonment by Dirk van Zyl Smit and Catherine Appleton found that the number of people serving life sentences in the US is higher than the combined total of 113 other countries. With the highest incarceration rate in the world, America accounts for 40 percent of the world's life-sentenced prisoners.[3] Canada, Mexico, France, Italy, and Germany don't have LWOP. The international criminal court, which tries dictators and generals for war crimes, genocide, and crimes against humanity, does not impose LWOP.[4] The European Court of Human Rights ruled that denying the possibility of parole is "inhumane and degrading treatment" in violation of the European Convention on Human Rights.

By contrast, as of 2016, North Carolina held 1,387 prisoners serving LWOP; 1,858 parole-eligible lifers; and 887 virtual lifers. A number that only increases with time, as lifers account for roughly 11 percent of North Carolina's prison population. This is nearly forty times the number of life-sentenced prisoners in the United Kingdom.

If there is a benefit to capital punishment, it's that it brings greater attention to the fundamental miscarriages of justice in the criminal legal system. The death penalty acts as a microcosm of racist, classist, politically misguided, anti-intellectualist ideas that masquerade as "justice" while pitting unlimited state and federal government resources against the poor and marginalized.

For example, the law provides defendants with an opportunity to plead guilty to a crime, and in return for admitting responsibility, the maximum charge and penalty are reduced. Most criminal cases plead out. This includes many capital cases, but the only "lesser" sentence available is LWOP. The catch with plea bargaining is that prosecutors overcharge a defendant knowing they might lose at trial because of circumstances in the case or a lack of evidence. Prosecutors then rely on both a defendant's fear of the most punitive outcome and ignorance of the law, and overwhelmed public defenders, to secure a plea arrangement and forgo trial. Fear and ignorance used as leverage over the poor.

Wake County District Attorney Lorrin Freeman often uses fear and ignorance as leverage over capital defendants, but in a more diabolical way. By pursuing the death penalty, Freeman gains death-qualified juries* who are more likely to return a guilty verdict. Even if the jury returns an LWOP sentence, she will have avoided the political optics of showing mercy as a prosecutor. This was demonstrated in eight consecutive cases where Freeman charged a defendant with first-degree murder and sought the death penalty. Eight juries returned guilty verdicts with LWOP. In defense of her choices, Freeman claimed capital punishment is a tool she uses to go after the "worst of the worst." Eight juries disagreed and may have opted for a sentence less than LWOP had it been available. Viewed another way, nearly one hundred citizens believed the DA was too harsh. Considering how capital juries are chosen, this also indicates declining support for capital punishment even among citizens

---

* A trial jury deemed fit to decide a death-penalty case because they have no absolute ideological bias against capital punishment. However, jurors are more likely to return guilty verdicts and death sentences because they are death qualified. If they were selected without death qualification, as every other type of jury, there would likely be fewer death sentences and more acquittals.

who would ordinarily support executions.

If LWOP is replacing executions, then defendants should receive capital defenders and postconviction counsel. You should not be subjected to LWOP as part of a plea deal. LWOP should be restricted just like the death penalty. The US Supreme Court seems inclined to agree.

In *Miller v. Alabama* (2012), the court banned mandatory LWOP for people under eighteen. In *Montgomery v. Louisiana* (2016), the court made the ban retroactive, forcing every state to provide juvenile lifers with what are now referred to as "*Miller* hearings." These hearings determine if the offender meets certain criteria that reduce his or her culpability at the time of the crime and thereby earn release. In her ruling, Justice Elena Kagan outlined such factors as level of maturity, impetuosity, common failure to evaluate risks, home environment, circumstances of the offense that include peer influence and codefendants, the youth's lack of sophistication relative to an adult, and the possibility for rehabilitation. *Miller* hearings, like parole hearings, do not guarantee release, merely the opportunity once a prisoner has served a significant amount of time.

The court's *Miller* ruling doesn't go far enough. MRI studies by neurologists show the prefrontal cortex, which controls risky decisions and impulsive behavior, is not fully developed until the age of twenty-five. The American Bar Association even cited some of these studies in a 2018 report to the House of Delegates urging that the imposition of capital punishment be restricted to people twenty-one and older. No such change has been made yet.

You would think if you have to be twenty-one to buy alcohol or a pack of cigarettes, then you should be twenty-one to receive LWOP or a death sentence.

If not LWOP, then what? The solution is already practiced in every other democratic country in the world, and was practiced in the US before tough-on-crime fear mongering proliferated LWOP laws in the mid-eighties and nineties: after a life-sentenced prisoner serves twenty years, a mandatory review should occur each year thereafter. If a parole commission finds in favor of the prisoner, then they earn release. Parole is a critical opportunity for the rehabilitation of prisoners, an incentive

for good behavior, and a check against over incarceration. North Carolina's abolition of parole in 1994 was an improvident decision that can
easily be reversed by the General Assembly, but it will require the right
kind of leadership, and the voters to put them there.

Chapter 12

The Myth of Deterrence

I wanted to begin with a brief description of the roots of deterrence theory, from the classical school of criminology. However, the reality is a bit different from the "facts" that compose the theory. You and I both know that people are often irrational and unpredictable, despite the best efforts of social scientists to anticipate behavioral responses. People may be generally rational, but they often experience momentary losses in reason, mistake-prone behavior, and breaks with sanity. In other words, people make bad decisions as often as they make rational ones.

Crime is more typically rooted in irrational, impulsive, and desperate behaviors than the progenitors of criminology, Cesare Beccaria and Jeremy Bentham, theorized in the eighteenth century. But they were somewhat blind, maybe intentionally so, to the bloodlust that infused gladiator arenas and punishment parades where "criminals" and slaves were tortured and killed in public spectacles. Intertwined with the evolution of slavery after abolition, it was this public bloodlust for retributive punishment that became the bedrock of the American criminal legal system, radiating vengeance through the false face of civilization, all of this obscured by the euphemism of "justice."

"Deterrence" is a civilized word, as false as the idea of equal justice for the marginalized. Roman arenas didn't make sport of the rich and educated any more than twenty-first-century prisons incarcerate them. These spaces are filled with minorities, poor white trash, the mentally ill, and the ne'er-do-wells of society who, for one reason or another, are uneducated outcasts. Men. Women. Children.

I earned a GED in a youth reformatory because it was forced on me. I was spending time in solitary confinement while other kids my age went to junior prom. The concept of deterrence never crossed my mind. Nor did the "rational thought" process of the classical school of criminology. My thoughts were occupied by hanging out with friends, partying, and being free. I would venture that these are the thoughts of most teenagers. Youth detention and solitary confinement might have been scary in the moment, but when compared to the urges of addiction in the midst of peer influence, that moment is separate from rational decisions. Or good ones, for that matter.

Imagine deterrence as an electric fence. Its shock deters cows from leaving the pasture. The pain from the shock is sharp, swift, and certain enough to stop the cow. The pain outweighs the desire to eat grass on the other side. This is the felicific calculus Bentham proposed in the rationale of crime. Cows are rational animals. People are not. Cows can be conditioned without much trouble—after a few shocks, they'll never go near the fence again. If people were that docile, deterrence would work.

But humans are irrational creatures and most crime is spur of the moment. Psychologists have spent centuries developing theories to predict and explain human behavior, only to discover they came close in the same way a sieve holds water. There are always anomalies or exceptions that turn theories into guesses based on some facts. As a criminological theory, deterrence is no different. Unfortunately, despite this fundamental flaw, criminal justice policy and punishment are based on deterrence theory.

There are two types of deterrence: general and specific. You can deter an individual who steals by imprisoning them, but their action or inaction remains limited to the duration of the sentence or the "moment." It doesn't address the cause of the theft—that is to say, the thief's thinking goes unchallenged and remains disconnected from the harm caused by the crime. Imprisonment neither addresses the economic disadvantage that is likely why the person stole nor teaches a better, more lawful way to earn a living wage.

Few people commit crimes believing they'll get caught. The premise behind premeditation and deliberation—rationalization of the behavior—is faulty if the person who commits a crime doesn't consider the consequences. The point here is that general deterrence is unlikely if no one thinks they will be caught or thinks beyond the criminal act itself. The reality is that most crimes occur while a person is in an emotional state, influenced by peers, mentally ill, or under situational factors like being in the wrong place at the wrong time. The sad irony of twenty-first-century criminal punishment in America is that irrational, ill-informed legislators continue to pass laws that disproportionately impact marginalized citizens, disregard equal justice (equal justice is actually part of the classical school of criminology), then falsely claim that draconian measures actually deter crime.

What draconian punishment really does create is a brutalization effect. Much like public executions and punishment parades of the pre–Industrial Revolution era, vulgar displays of state power make people angry and rebellious. This is part of the reason post-Reconstruction legal lynchings were removed from public view. You don't have to look any further than the recent curbside, extralegal execution of unarmed Black and brown citizens by law enforcement. Draconian force—whether from the end of a rope, in a gas chamber, or beneath a cop's knee—generates violent crime. Think of the rioters who tried to usurp peaceful protests. Think of the rise in hate crimes. Now, remember the law-and-order rhetoric behind it all.

You could say I support a more deterministic view of crime and punishment—external factors matter a great deal—but no single theory or perspective can simplify our understanding of crime or the effects of punishment. In other words, no theory is a pair of sweatpants—one size does not fit all. Crime is complex, multifaceted human behavior. Punishment is a reaction, not a solution.

In 1975 Faye Brown sat in the front seat of her boyfriend's car while he and two friends robbed a bank. Later, when the car was pulled over by law enforcement, a man in the back seat shot and killed the officer while Faye, exhausted from a night of partying, slept. All four occupants of the car were tried, convicted, and sentenced to death—but only one person pulled the trigger. At what point did Faye have a chance to think through her actions or predict what another person would do? How many of you have been in the car with friends when one of them did something unexpectedly stupid or illegal? The unfortunate fact is that the law punishes you harshly for your friends' decisions, whether you know about them or not.

Faye's death sentence was overturned on appeal when a court agreed being an accomplice to murder didn't qualify one for the gas chamber. Resentenced to life in prison, Faye became a role model to other women, educated herself, and maintained a job, but still spent forty-five years in prison before dying of COVID-19 in the spring of 2020 at sixty-seven.

Maybe you think deterrence should be a condition of confinement, borrowing from the origin of the penitentiary, where prisoners were put in solitary confinement with only a Bible. Roughly 90 percent of all prisoners will return to society. If the goal of their incarceration, after incapacitation and retributive punishment, is to make sure they don't come back, deterrence fails here too. Between 1994 and 2007, the US Bureau of Justice Statistics found that under half (45 percent) of all re-entering citizens return to prison within three years while some analyses put the average national recidivism rate at 65 percent.[1] All of the supermax prisons, repeat offender laws, decades-long sentences, harsh prison conditions, lack of incentives or prison education programs, and abolition of parole only increase the likelihood of reoffense. It sends the message that state officials don't care about people caught within the criminal legal system, and therefore, those people who exit prison have little reason or resources to care about staying out.

Criminologists can benefit from applying the theory of behavioral psychologist B. F. Skinner, whose work with pigeons progressed our understanding of how behaviors can be positively or negatively reinforced. Without going into a deep dive on operant conditioning, let me give you a simple example: Children are more likely to behave when you reward good behavior (positive stimulus) than when you punish bad behavior (negative stimulus). What's more, harsh punishments like spankings increase the likelihood of violent behavior in adulthood. The tough-on-crime era ignored this concept. Where incentive-based corrections gave prisoners opportunities to pursue college degrees and vocational skills for job placement and time off for good behavior, warehousing removed these incentives and extended the length of all sentences. Longer prison terms don't mean lower crime rates, they mean violent penal environments and people who lack the appropriate skills for successful reentry.

Incentives are about more than dangling a carrot in front of a mule. Where prisoners are concerned, it's important to provide hope for relief from the pain and deprivations of incarceration and to instill the belief one can earn one's way back to freedom. To make that belief realistic, corrections officers must invest in a rehabilitative philosophy. The rehabilitative philosophy is simple: All human beings have value; habilitation (equipping someone with basic tools for survival) and higher education are essential to successfully returning to society and reducing prison violence. Completing this process means maximizing one's potential as a contributing member of a community. A prison environment must promote improved mental health, education, and accountability. Spirituality is also a critical element in all of this. Suffice it to say, authentic maturation in prison requires acknowledging a power greater than oneself.

Mental health programming should include counseling, anger management, conflict resolution, access to Alcoholics Anonymous and Narcotics Anonymous programs, and psychotherapeutic groups focused on communication, team building, and critical thinking. Considering over 20 percent of prisoners suffer from mental illness, a number three times that currently in US mental hospitals,[2] increasing treatment options is important to lasting rehabilitation.

As an extension of the rehabilitative philosophy, there are three main arguments for access to higher education. If 90 percent of all prisoners return to the community, public safety demands a skillset that improves one's chances of being a productive member of society. Proactive efforts to prevent crime that begin in prison—on the first day of incarceration—address recidivism before it starts. Beyond qualifying for jobs that pay a living wage, higher education develops critical thought, organizational skills, time management, goal setting, and a broader understanding of the world that enables better decisions. Whether or not one has a release date, college-in-prison programs reduce prison violence throughout the population because both staff and prisoners invest in and respect the pursuit of higher education when it's part of the penal philosophy. Policies that promote human value support greater levels of compassion throughout a population.

It's cheaper to invest in the higher education of one person than in his or her incarceration for a single year, let alone long-term imprisonment, postrelease supervision, and additional costs for recidivism. How much cheaper? The average annual cost per federal prisoner is roughly $30,000. This same amount could pay for GEDs, vocational programming, and a two-year degree from a community college for three prisoners. That education reduces their likelihood of recidivism by 40 percent.

Maybe you're wondering why, if these things so obviously work, they're not implemented on a broad scale. The answer is that they were. Then the rehabilitative philosophy met the misinformation driving tough-on-crime politics. The data of what works could not compete with fearmongering from populist politicians, political pundits misrepresenting statistics, and the amplification of false narratives in the media. It has only been in the absence of incentive and second-look mechanisms, in the sprawling face of mass incarceration, human rights violations in public institutions, and crippling costs that the public is once again looking for solutions that have been there all along.

Chapter 13

Paroling Michael Pinch

The ceremony took place in a tall concrete room on death row.

Our blue plastic chairs sat in three semicircles before a scarred wooden podium. The front of the podium bore the great seal of North Carolina, with its motto in stark lettering: Esse Quam Videri. To be rather than to seem.

Two Franciscan priests sat in the front row with Michael's confirmation sponsor. The rest of us watched as Bishop Gossman conveyed a final blessing and anointed Michael with perfumed oil, proclaiming him to be a confirmed Catholic. The moment was a snapshot of his twenty-six years on death row, an era during which many of us learned from Michael Pinch.

We were relieved when Michael's death sentence and conviction were overturned in 2005. No one who met the humble, quiet man believed he should be executed. Michael had a stabilizing influence on the row, enough so that even prison officers sought his advice.

Ken Harris, former Central Prison associate warden, used Michael to counsel young troublemakers. "Mike always had something intelligent and beneficial to hear," Harris told the *Greensboro News and Record*. "He'd tell them, 'Look, if you don't change now, if you don't get yourself off of drugs and alcohol, if you don't change your attitudes, you can end up right where I am.'" Harris echoed the sentiment that many officers felt when dealing with Michael: "I'm old-school and hard to fool . . . But Mike's above-board. I think the world of him."[1]

Former deputy state attorney general Joan Byers Erwin publicly said in 1996 that Michael should not be put to death, even though it was her job to oppose his appeals and fight for his execution. Erwin had been hearing testimonials about Michael from lawyers and others for fifteen years. She said the case did not "have the feel of a death case . . . The person the jury saw is not the person he really is."[2]

Convicted and sentenced to death for the 1979 shotgun slayings of nineteen-year-old Freddie Pacheco and eighteen-year-old Tommie Ausley at a Greensboro bikers club, Michael spent a quarter century on death row before an appellate court found that the police and prosecutors withheld evidence. They hid the fact that Pacheco and Ausley were small-time drug dealers and that Pacheco had stabbed at least four people. The court acknowledged such information would have helped Michael's attorneys prove the murders were not premeditated. Rather than retry the case, district attorney Stuart Albright of Guilford County offered a plea deal: plead guilty to one count of second-degree murder and one count of first-degree murder and in exchange, receive a sentence of life with parole. While Michael was saved from execution, he was still far from freedom. His future depended on navigating North Carolina's arduous and uncertain parole system.

Parole in North Carolina is only an option for crimes committed before October 1, 1994, when a new state law, the Structured Sentencing Act (SSA), went into effect. The law abolished parole, instituted mandatory minimum sentences, eliminated judicial discretion in sentencing, and made life without parole—or death—a mandatory sentence for first-degree murder.

An earlier law had allowed for parole-eligible life sentences, time off for good behavior, and indeterminate sentencing, but the SSA replaced all of that with inflexible, punitive policies. Fortunately for Michael and others sentenced for crimes under the "old law," the SSA is not retroactive and cannot affect any crime committed before the date of its enactment.

This is especially important because many death sentences have been commuted to life as a result of successful appeals. After North Carolina reinstated the death penalty in 1977, but before one execution was carried out, fourteen death row prisoners had their sentence reduced to life with parole. Four of those prisoners were paroled by 2000. More recently, James McDowell was sentenced to death in 1988, resentenced to life with parole in 1991, and paroled in 2018.

No life sentence was ever guaranteed parole, merely the possibility. Even for those who are still parole-eligible, the path to freedom is anything but certain. Contrary to the popular myth that parole is an automatic exit for these lifers, the North Carolina Post-Release Supervision and Parole Commission has strict guidelines for attaining parole candidacy.

The parole process begins when a person has served their minimum sentence; for Michael Pinch this was twenty years. As soon as his death sentence was converted to life with parole, the parole commission assigned a case analyst to research Michael's file and prison record. During the initial review stage, the case analyst looks at psychological evaluations, custody-level history, visitation history, gang membership (if there is one, and whether the prisoner has renounced ties), and home plan. Special weight is also given to the brutality of the crime, whether a prisoner has been convicted of a sex offense, and whether he or she ever tried to escape.

Any one of these factors can prevent parole, and any combination may prevent consideration beyond the first stage of review. Too many infractions in prison is a common reason for rejection. "Write-ups" as we call them, are not always serious; they can include failing a drug test, disobeying a direct order, possession of contraband, and disrespecting staff. Some staff who have a vendetta against a prisoner will claim the prisoner broke a rule, process a write-up, and that infraction can prevent parole for another year.

After completing the first stage of review, the parole case analyst makes a written recommendation for or against parole, to be considered by the parole commission in secret. Each case analyst is responsible for over a thousand offenders. Considering that each parole commissioner reviews about ninety-one cases on a typical day, with as many as two thousand cases voted on each month, it is hard to believe every case receives a fair hearing.

Commissioners usually vote "no." On the rare occasions when they allow a review to proceed, commissioners recommend the case analyst "investigate" the prisoner. This is typically when an analyst would determine a prisoner's level of remorse, rehabilitation, social adjustment, goals, and support on the outside. If the investigation reveals a promising candidate for parole, the commission will normally greenlight them for the Mutual Agreement Parole Program (MAPP). The MAPP contract provides opportunities for community work release, participation in educational or vocational training programs outside of prison, and other programs that prepare incarcerated people for reentry to society. MAPP is mandatory for parole and lasts one to five years—and that's after the many years it takes a parole-eligible lifer to attain a MAPP contract in the first place.

North Carolina's parole commission does not hold parole hearings. When it comes time to make a final decision, each commissioner votes independently, in separate rooms, at differing times of the day. When a lifer is considered for parole, the commission notifies the prisoner, the district attorney where the offender was convicted, the head of the law enforcement agency that arrested the prisoner, any of the victim's immediate family who requested to be notified, and any media outlets in the county where the prisoner was charged and sentenced.

In January 2019, news of Michael's parole investigation flashed between two longer news segments on National Public Radio, so cursory it would have been easy to miss. "North Carolina's Parole Commission is considering whether to release a murderer who spent a quarter century on death row after the shotgun killings of two teenagers at a Greensboro motorcycle club. The parole commission said it could release a fifty-eight-year-old Michael Edward Pinch despite the 1979 double murder." The broadcaster then announced that Republican state representative Phil Berger would seek to prevent Michael's release. Berger has represented the district where Michael's case played out since 2000.

It is not uncommon for politicians to interfere with the parole process, as Democratic governor Beverly Perdue did with Bobby Bowden and a few other parole-eligible lifers who were on MAPP contracts in 2009. The governor forced the parole commission to halt their release, not because there was a legitimate public safety concern, but because parole-eligibility did not align with her purported belief that "life means life." At the same time, it came to light that, four years earlier, Perdue had supported the parole of a lifer who had worked in her office while on a MAPP contract. In that moment, constitutional protections were ignored for the sake of politics.

The stance that officials like Perdue and Berger have taken is the sort of punitive obstructionism and political grandstanding common to the politics of parole-eligible life sentences. Commissioners often fear losing their jobs for making politically unpopular decisions, especially if they are contrary to the tough-on-crime rhetoric of elected officials. This is partly because voters respond less to broad positive reforms in criminal justice—like the national effort to release low-level drug offenders in the "First Step Act," signed into law by then-president Donald Trump in 2018 and still in effect today—and far more to sensationalized crimes.

The result is a tendency to generalize the outcome of a single released prisoner who goes on to commit a violent crime as indicative of all prisoners if they are given the chance. In reality, such outcomes are rare, even more so among parole-eligible lifers who earn release.

Lifers who earn release from prison have the lowest recidivism rate of all parolees. One Stanford University study of 860 murderers paroled in California found only five returned to prison for new felonies, and none for murder.[3] In 2012 Maryland's appellate court ruled in *Unger v. State* that life sentences handed down before 1981 violated due process. As a result, more than one hundred lifers have been released, and none have been convicted of a new felony as of 2016.

Unfortunately, the politics of crime do not heed the evidence of sociological research, even as the nation searches for ways to end mass incarceration. Representative Berger's decision to interfere with Michael's release is not based on any evidence he might reoffend, or that the parole commission's process is too lenient; it is simply an extension of his draconian politics. Parole-eligible lifers approved for release by the parole commission should not have to worry whether some politician is going to sabotage their parole, either by leaning on parole commissioners or violating the state constitution.

On May 2, 2019, the parole commission announced that Michael was approved for a two-year MAPP contract. When Michael accepted his plea arrangement it was with the belief he would be paroled if he worked hard enough. On death row he committed himself to making his life count for something. He would ultimately spend forty-one years in prison, released in May 2020, as many short timers were during the COVID pandemic. The early release of people like Michael who had done their time was resisted by some in the North Carolina General Assembly, but that was to be expected. It is time for North Carolina lawmakers to be true representatives of all people in this state, not just those who fit a tough-on-crime agenda.

Esse quam videri indeed.

Chapter 14

Mob Mentality in Politics

A Viral Space Where Bad Laws Are Made

I watched from my cell as the January 6 Capitol insurrection unfolded on the TV bolted to the wall. Later, labels like "domestic terrorism" and "anti-government extremist protocols" were used by various journalists and lawmakers calling for justice. Incoming US Attorney General Merrick Garland promised to prosecute perpetrators of the attack and anyone responsible for undermining democracy. Although law-and-order rhetoric is intended to rally and reassure, it's reminiscent of an era in the 1990s that wrought the Violent Crime Control and Law Enforcement Act, the Antiterrorism and Effective Death Penalty Act, and the rise of mass incarceration.

The last time Garland prosecuted an infamous domestic terrorist, it was Timothy McVeigh, the man responsible for the 1995 Oklahoma City bombing that killed 168 people. Congress had just passed the omnibus crime bill. The prison industry boomed and law enforcement multiplied and militarized. The wars on drugs, crime, and immigration converged on Black and brown communities, rural communities, and marginalized citizens such as the homeless and mentally ill. The hype of the "tough on crime" era signaled a cannibalistic iteration of Manifest Destiny.

Right-wing conservatives exploited the tragedy in Oklahoma City by using the prominence of capital punishment and rage of a grieving nation to focus attention on reducing the time between a death sentence and execution, establishing extensive new limitations on federal judicial oversight in state courts. They called it the Antiterrorism and Effective Death Penalty Act (AEDPA).

On its face, the AEDPA imposed a one-year time limit for death row prisoners to file a federal habeas corpus petition. It also created an "unprecedented deferential standard of review" that made state court decisions virtually indisputable. The only way a federal court can overturn a state court decision is if it was so unreasonable and unconstitutional that no rational jurist would have reached the same conclusion.

The AEDPA contained numerous other procedural hurdles that so complicated filing a federal habeas corpus petition that it initially caused a spike in executions as capital defenders struggled to figure them out and missed the filing deadline. While this may have restricted federal litigation of capital cases and, only briefly, shortened the delay between death sentences and execution, attorneys found other ways around it in state courts. And this, in turn, bogged down the process until capital cases languished under state review for decades. Nationwide, the average amount of time a defendant spent on death row slowly increased while executions decreased. AEDPA went far beyond capital cases and destroyed the process of federal review for all criminal defendants, preventing them from using the courts to challenge the denials of their constitutional rights. AEDPA was the predictable result of politicizing criminal justice policy and was also part of the backlash to the Civil Rights era.

Noncapital defendants bore the worst of the AEDPA because, unlike capital defendants, they lack legal counsel to navigate the procedural kudzu on a habeas petition. Even the most fervent jailhouse lawyers struggled to meet the one-year deadline, let alone get past the procedural bar against issues not raised at the state level. Prisoners with legitimate claims of police, prosecutorial, or jury misconduct; ineffective counsel; disproportionate sentences; and clemency were ignored. Even if a defendant presented evidence of legal innocence and a state appellate court upheld his or her conviction, under AEDPA the federal court could acknowledge that person is probably innocent, but still defer to the state court.

In the time since I've fought to overturn my wrongful convictions and sentence, and I've learned a lot about criminal procedures, rules of evidence, expert testimony, ineffective assistance of counsel, false confessions, and a pattern of prosecutorial misconduct. The harsh reality is that the criminal legal system has nothing to do with truth or justice, and AEDPA is all the evidence one needs.

My trial lawyers got a lot of things wrong, not just their representation of my case. After the jury rendered its verdict, I asked how long I had until the state executed me. "Don't worry," said my lead attorney. "You've got appeals, maybe ten years, sometimes more." Two or three years for direct view of the trial record, four or five years for the state-level habeas, known as a motion for appropriate relief, one year for the federal habeas petition, maybe a few months for clemency. "You might even win," he said as they took me away. All of it was a gross oversimplification. None of it reassured me.

Thirty-one executions were carried out my first seven years on death row. Then, litigation over doctor participation and drugs used in lethal injection initiated a de facto moratorium. Many of the people were strangers, some were friends I still think about, but all of them were human beings fighting for their lives just like me. In the brutal moments after someone is put to death, understanding criminal justice policy and the law becomes a matter of survival. But it's like dying of thirst and sipping from a fire hose to quench it.

Prior to the passage of the AEDPA in 1996, the average span of time between trial and execution was ten years. By 2015, that timespan increased to nearly nineteen years.[1] In death penalty states like North Carolina, where no executions have been carried out since 2006, the span of time prisoners spend on death row has become the equivalent of life imprisonment with the remote possibility of death. AEDPA, in other words, had the opposite of its intended effect. Rather than shorten delays, it doubled them. By reducing federal judicial oversight, it forced state courts to step up their scrutiny of capital post-conviction appeals. For example, in North Carolina, by 2015, over seventy percent of all death sentences were reversed on appeal. Twelve people were exonerated between 1973 and 2020.[2]

The fact is, without judicial scrutiny and legal representation, the number of death sentence reversals would be dwarfed by executions. When a death sentence or conviction is vacated, it may be a glimpse of justice, but the process also exposes how difficult it is to achieve equal justice in a system not designed to help those it impacts. The criminal legal system isn't broken—it works exactly as intended. AEDPA and the omnibus crime bill are proof of that. If anything, our trust has been broken. Elected officials are supposed to rise above the mob mentality's desire to seek revenge upon us, to do the right thing for the poor and marginalized, not embrace the status quo or settle for half measures. True justice has no exceptions, yet embedded within the Thirteenth Amendment's prohibition against slavery, there is a loophole through which millions have gone and will continue to go as long as populist politics determine criminal legal procedure instead of equity. Rather than pick at the threads of the rope with minor reforms, as I have now witnessed five presidents do, it's time to dismantle the scaffold. Repeal the 1996 Antiterrorism and Effective Death Penalty Act.

Interview with
Kerwin Pittman

April 13, 2022

Kerwin Pittman is currently the director of policy and programming at Emancipate NC, a nonprofit organization in Durham, North Carolina, that strives to reduce sentences, improve prison conditions, and hold the criminal legal system accountable through litigation. Pittman was also a member of the North Carolina Task Force for Racial Equity in Criminal Justice (TREC), initiated by governor Roy Cooper and led by attorney general Josh Stein, and North Carolina Supreme Court associate justice Anita Earls. Members include American Civil Liberties Union attorney Henderson Hill and Kerwin Pittman, founder of Recidivism Reduction Educational Programs Services (RREPS), a reentry service for formerly incarcerated people. On the task force, Pittman tried to find mutual ground where community policing could be reformed, and from this work he became a vocal community advocate after incidents of police brutality and shootings of unarmed citizens and is often a go-to commentator for local ABC news affiliate WTVD, Raleigh. He is a 2022 Soros Justice Fellow.

Lyle May (LM): How did you get into activism after your release from prison? Who and what inspired you?

Kerwin Pittman (KP): Before I was released from prison [during an eleven-and-a-half-year sentence] a chaplain asked me what I'm going to do when I get out. "I want to be an activist," I said. I was so used to seeing prison officials make and break their own policies. I wanted to do something to change that, to make it a better environment, and keep people out of prison, among other things. I ended up going to a meeting called "Bring Back Our Community" when I got out. While there, I met Dawn Blagrove [the director of Emancipate NC], Dr. Kimberly Muktarian, Wanda Hunter, and Deidre McCullers, all of whom got me into activism around police brutality.

LM: What has activism in the community meant to you? What are some specific examples?

KP: Activism has meant being on the front line of fighting for the community and those who struggle to advocate for themselves. To speak up for those who suffer and die at the hands of law enforcement.

LM: Who and what represents the greatest threat to community organizers and what can be done to counter that threat?

KP: Racism and white supremacy are the greatest threats to our communities. Look at every institution where racism is embedded. We can't dismantle each one immediately, but it has to be done. So you do it slowly, a piece at a time through policy reforms.

LM: What kind of organizing have you done? I remember calling you once and you were in the middle of a protest. I could hear chanting in the background.

KP: I've organized group demonstrations in the wake of George Floyd's murder. I even had to become an organizer of organizers in the younger generation, letting them lead with fire and pizazz. It definitely has been a learning experience. But we stay connected through social media, organizing in increasingly larger groups. We basically say to people, "If you know someone interested in this issue, we're having a meeting. Tell them to tell people they know."

LM: As a member of Governor Cooper's Task Force for Racial Equity in Criminal Justice, what is some of the progress you have seen come from that work? What have been the biggest problems?

KP: A duty to intervene policy for law enforcement officers who see their coworkers engaging in brutality or other unlawful conduct, mental health assessments for law enforcement officers, a ban on chokeholds and hog-tying suspects. We helped redefine "use of force" for law enforcement in North Carolina, but recent legislation has chipped away at that by making records of what law enforcement officers do secret. We also helped design new policy for law enforcement handling protesters. And, of course, the Juvenile Sentence Review Board. [An executive action by Governor Roy Cooper created the JSRB to review certain cases involving juveniles who received long sentences, already served many years in prison as a result, and demonstrate substantial signs of rehabilitation. The board is necessary because there is no parole for crimes that were committed in North Carolina after October 1, 1994.]

LM: What do you see as the future of criminal justice reform? What will it take to prevent regression toward the status quo where Black people, Indigenous people, people of color, the poor, and mentally ill people are targeted by law enforcement and state budgets reinforce incarceration rather than community?

KP: It's going to take lawmakers in particular, and white people more generally, to experience police brutality and injustice before they really understand enough to change.

LM: Kind of like different responses to the crack epidemic—which largely devastated urban minority communities—versus the opioid epidemic, which has largely impacted rural and middle-class white communities. Where mostly BIPOC [Black, Indigenous, and people

of color] were incarcerated during the crack epidemic, the approach to opioids has been treatment-oriented despite the fact many, many more people have died and continue to suffer.

KP: Exactly.

LM: Who has influenced your activism? Who inspires you?

KP: I analyze and draw strength from people like Dawn Blagrove, Elizabeth Simpson [assistant director of Emancipate NC], Kristie Puckett-Williams of the ACLU, Whitley Carpenter of Forward Justice, and Charles Rodman, a neighbor of mine who, when I was younger, used to try talking some sense into me. I thought he was talking junk, but when I became older, I better understood that he spoke from a place of love, interest in my welfare, and experience as an activist from the Civil Rights era.

Interview with Marsha Owen

April 16, 2022

Marsha Owen, of Restorative Justice Durham and the Religious Coalition for a Nonviolent Durham, is a community leader pursuing an end to the adversarial criminal legal system. She is currently working with Durham County district attorney Satana Deberry to bring about true community justice.

Lyle May (LM): Do you think restorative justice is activism that can impact incarceration?

Marsha Owen (MO): I think it's the means to end mass incarceration. The only tool we currently have is retributive punishment. There needs to be an alternative. Restorative justice is that alternative. It says that crime happens to the community, not just individuals. I've sat in on many homicide trials. There's no feeling there. Restorative justice turns that on its head.

I led a restorative justice conference on a homicide recently. Over the period of a year, we asked each party—the person who committed the crime and the victims' family—five questions:

What happened?

What did you think about it?

What is your thinking now?

Who was impacted and how?

What needs to be done to reduce the harm now?

Every circle begins with the value brought to the discussion by each person. We focus on love and respect, the qualities of responsibility, integrity, honesty, compassion, and confidentiality. There are three specific guidelines for a circle:

Confidentiality is key—in other words, we have an agreement with the court not to divulge a discovery from the circle. Lessons can leave the circle, but stories cannot.

Listen to understand, not respond.

Take all the time you need.

LM: How is restorative justice different from group therapy?

MO: Restorative justice is better and more powerful than group therapy. It's not about diagnoses or costs of insurance tied to group therapy; it's about the people impacted by crime and people with the agency, power, wisdom, will, and ability to make things right. Restorative justice reduces the costs associated with incarceration by reducing the need for incarceration. Group therapy can't do that.

LM: How do you get lawmakers on board with restorative justice–centered approaches to crime and punishment? What about victims' rights groups that support more punitive responses?

MO: It's kind of like climbing Mt. Everest. Nobody knows it can be done until it's done. When I was executive director of the Religious Coalition for a Nonviolent Durham, we conducted vigils for victims from 1997 and on. We developed relationships with enough people in the criminal justice system in Durham to ask elected officials—judges, district attorneys, sheriffs—to support restorative justice. Crime is currently seen as a violation of the law and state, not people. No one goes to folks who have been harmed and asks: What do you need? How have you been harmed? No one is ever asked: What can be done to heal this pain and trauma? The focus is purely retributive. The more we can be in relationships with people the more we can shift the law to serve people. Violations create obligations. Punishment doesn't heal relationships. Relationship heals. There must be more relationship building for restorative justice. The duality of the victim-offender relationship is false. Crime affects the community and should be addressed as a community.

LM: How can ordinary citizens without any connection to the criminal legal system get involved with or help promote restorative justice?

MO: Restorative justice is voluntary and volunteer based. Regular people who want to find a better way can engage in restorative justice by reading up on the subject to tell others about it, or by training as facilitators for circles.

LM: The Durham County Commission is planning to build a $30 million youth jail when the United States is trending away from pre-trial confinement and is trying to reduce the number of youth in confinement. Where do you stand in this effort? How does a new brick-and-mortar facility fit with restorative justice principles?

MO: Right now, we need a place for kids who are committing harm. Currently, a lot of them are placed on house arrest with ankle monitors and they lack supervision. We have used some diversion programs, and they work beautifully, but we need more than one, two, or even three options. We also need to have a complete and thorough answer to handling children with mental illness. The current youth facility would allow for so many things, more programs and treatment-oriented care. Not just confinement like a traditional jail, but one with a rehabilitative focus in the design. Someone once said, "Love is the intensity of attention." We have to address the reality of crime with compassion and care.

PART III

CULTURE OF CONTROL

CHALLENGING THE NARRATIVE

Chapter 15

Draconian Ideals

In 2017 after Sergeant Meggan Callahan's death at a medium-custody prison in Windsor, North Carolina, we knew there would be hell to pay. Sensational murders tend to generate anxiety on death row because they usually renew the push for executions to resume. This time was different: a prison guard had been beaten to death with a fire extinguisher. It's generally understood that when one prisoner kills another they are likely to be sentenced to death; when a prisoner does the same to a guard, the entire prison system pays.

At Raleigh's Central Prison (CP), my residence since 1999, death row staff wore somber black ribbons in Callahan's honor. In the unit manager's office, a photocopied picture of the young woman hung from a wall, beneath it a single word: REMEMBER. When staff clustered in the hallways, scowls and hard accusatory looks twisted some of their faces.

On the block, a number of us worried whether executions would begin again; over forty death row prisoners were out of appeals. Most dismissed the Chicken Little thinking, since a moratorium on executions is maintained by lawsuits pending in the state courts. But outrage would reach us in other ways. Under the guise of safety and security, the state's wrath would impact every prison; a murdered guard was a license for punitive reprisals throughout the penal system.

Callahan's murder was not just a lapse in security or one bad actor who took someone's life; her death was a consequence of long-standing dysfunction in North Carolina's prisons. The vacuum left by the death of the rehabilitative idea, end of incentivized sentences, and absence of any form of empathy for the incarcerated was filled with retribution, violence, and hopelessness. The prison population metastasized, overburdening state budgets, and in North Carolina, undermining the Department of Public Safety's (NCDPS) ability to maintain secure prisons.

In the years leading up to Callahan's murder, plenty of signs indicated the decay in North Carolina's penal system. In 2012, at the same prison where Callahan died five years later, Willis Gravley hanged himself in his cell. While a prisoner committing suicide may not be extraordinary on its own, an investigation later found that staff had failed to check Gravley's unit that night and falsified records to show they made their rounds. Six guards were fired when investigators learned this was a common practice. Gravley's death marked the fifth in three years that occurred because of staff negligence.

CP has also had problems for many years. Unit One, the most notorious solitary confinement unit in the state, was rife with abuse. Brutal cell extractions, beatings out of camera view, and prisoners pushed down flights of steps while handcuffed behind their back were common. The conditions were akin to any dungeon: mentally ill prisoners lived in their own filth, swallowing batteries and mutilating their genitals just to receive medical attention and time out of the cell.

Not until a 2013 lawsuit, joined by eight prisoners, did conditions on Unit One begin to improve, but only after a federal judge demanded changes. Although a number of guards implicated in the more egregious abuses were transferred, at least two received promotions shortly thereafter: then-warden Kenneth Lassiter and shift sergeant Brent Soucier, a man as notorious as the unit itself.

Around this time, a North Carolina legislative mandate required mental health experts to implement therapeutic programs for large groups of prisoners taking psychotropic medications. The reform addressed a growing awareness of the need to treat the mentally ill in and out of solitary confinement. No case better exemplified that need than the 2014 dehydration death of Michael Anthony Kerr.

A schizophrenic man held in disciplinary segregation at a close-custody prison in Taylorsville, Kerr, fifty-three, was handcuffed in a cell without water, lying in his own waste for five days. When staff finally checked on him, Kerr was unresponsive and died in transport before reaching the hospital. Though the state ultimately paid his family $2.5 million in a settlement and fired or disciplined at least twenty-five employees, most of these staff gained work at other prisons.

It takes effort not to despise those responsible for Kerr's neglect, but the real fault lies in a defective system that criminalizes mental illness and punishes those incapable of helping themselves. Later that year, in 2014, the National Sheriffs' Association and Treatment Advocacy Center published a joint report on the treatment of people with mental illness in prisons and jails. The report found "there is probably no state where mental health services have deteriorated as much as they have in North Carolina in the past decade."[1] Seventeen percent of the state's inmate population had a mental health diagnosis, but many of those individuals went untreated as the state outsourced prison mental health services to private providers.

Because of the 2013 NC legislative mandate and the 2014 report, mental health at CP came into greater focus. Unit One (solitary confinement), Unit Three (death row), and Unit Six (mental health unit) were assigned a psychological programs manager, Dr. Peter Kuhns.

On Unit One, Dr. Kuhns created a process for a step-by-step resocialization and reintegration of prisoners who have been in solitary confinement for years. He also oversaw the installation of video-monitored suicide cells and de-escalation training for Unit One staff accustomed to using force on mentally ill inmates. Both on Unit Six and throughout CP, Dr. Kuhns retrained all of the mental health staff to act more like counselors than prison guards. On Unit Three, he provided a number of therapeutic programs: art therapy, mindfulness and meditation, drama, creative writing, speech and debate, and more. All of Dr. Kuhns's reforms at CP gained support from then-warden Carlton Joyner and Lassiter, who was by that point deputy director of prisons.

The advent of therapeutic programs on death row infused a sense of hope and excitement that things might change with constructive activities to break up the monotony that causes a prolonged decay in socialization and critical thinking.

Over half of the death row population consumes psychotropic medications of one sort or another. Before Dr. Kuhns instituted therapeutic programs, these medications were used as tranquilizers meant to stave off the worst hallucinations and mood swings of death row phenomenon.

Through the programs, our interaction and communication with unit staff increased and improved. Dr. Kuhns, his staff, and volunteers from Duke Divinity School and the nonprofit Hidden Voices treated us as equals. It was liberating. In a period of six months, morale on death row significantly improved.

Of all the programs Dr. Kuhns implemented, it was the death row drama group that altered the way CP staff perceived us. After a production of the play *12 Angry Men* earned support from Warden Joyner, word spread throughout the prison. The second performance was standing room only. No longer were we viewed as stereotypical death row prisoners; we became actors who cooperated on a project bigger than our circumstances.

As one of those *12 Angry Men* performers and a frequent participant in Dr. Kuhns's groups, I thought meeting and speaking with NCDPS officials was a turning point. After each performance, staff and prison officials asked how the programs improved our lives, and we related how important constructive activities had been to us. At one such discussion, superintendents from Maury and Bertie Correctional Institutions, two juvenile justice officials, and visiting representatives from the Vera Institute of Justice expressed an overwhelming need for more structured rehabilitative programming in North Carolina prisons.

In January 2017, CP's administration turned over, as it does every few years. Edward Thomas, the new warden, claimed three things are essential to a safe prison: "Security. Security. Security." Though Thomas remained supportive of Dr. Kuhns's programs, a faction of staff at CP resented the programs and attention paid to death row. They despised the idea that any inmate should be treated as an equal, or that use of force should be a second option rather than the first. John Juehrs, a member of this particular group of staff, became the unit manager of death row, mimicking the warden's security mantra and openly expressing his disdain for Dr. Kuhns's innovative programming.

After Callahan's death in April 2017, the *Charlotte Observer* published "Wrong Side of the Bars," a five-part series detailing staff corruption that allowed drugs and other contraband into NC prisons.[2] It also claimed that staff shortages and poor training contributed to Callahan's murder. The series went on to describe how some staff engaged in sexual liaisons with incarcerated people and one unit manager ordered gang hits on prisoners. The articles enraged a number of legislators, and Republican Representative Bob Steinburg, head of the Justice and Public Safety Oversight Committee, launched an inquiry into these security failures.

In prison, a legislator's wrath is felt in ways the public never experiences. We are at the mercy of every official whim no matter how contrary to safety or effective corrections. Because of this, prison is a punishment factory, where output is measured in suffering, and human potential is wasted.

An internal affairs (IA) investigation of Dr. Kuhns's volunteers was initiated after it was alleged they had "inappropriate" relationships with prisoners on death row. Volunteers were trained to keep prisoners at a physical and emotional distance, much as staff are. Prison officials claim this is to stop prisoners from taking advantage of volunteers who may not be streetwise enough to recognize they are being manipulated. While there are those in prison who do try to use people, the circumstances around Dr. Kuhns's volunteers was much different and related to their concern for our well-being. Investigators also scrutinized his use of the Mental Health Department budget to purchase books and supplies for his programs, connections to prisoners beyond therapy, and guest speakers he brought to death row (such as Bryan Stevenson, long-time *News & Observer* columnist Barry Saunders, and Michael Hardt). The problem seemed rooted in the fact Dr. Kuhns's programs filled a gap where the Programs Department should have been providing activities but was not. The IA investigation, focus on volunteers, and effort made to push Dr. Kuhns out of the prison were due to bureaucratic jealousy. Viewed another way, it was the rehabilitative ideal battling the poison of anti-intellectuals and losing.

As a part of the investigation, five death row prisoners were sent to Unit One, solitary confinement. I was one of them.

It took me a while to figure out what happened, and there are still some pieces missing. None of the prisoners under investigation were charged with violating policy, because all of Dr. Kuhns's volunteers quit so there was no way for IA to question them. This was just another case of prison officials using an investigation against prisoners who have done no wrong but are nonetheless punished. After I got off lock-up, in a conversation with unit management, I was told, "You guys are on death row. We can't have volunteers telling you they love and care about you. That's undue familiarity." The volunteers had been labeled sympathizers who undermined safety and security. They committed a cardinal offense with their compassion.

"We don't need some doctor roaming around the prison thinking he can do anything he wants," the unit manager said. "Now the problem has been solved."

The investigation ended mental health programs on death row, ousted eleven volunteers, and restricted Dr. Kuhns's practice to those being treated at CP's hospital. Lieutenant Soucier, who conducted the investigation, received a promotion to hospital unit manager. There, Soucier created such a hostile work environment for Dr. Kuhns that he ultimately left CP to work in the juvenile justice system. It did not seem to matter that Soucier was previously fired for abusing handcuffed prisoners in the Vermont Department of Corrections, or that he was a defendant in a 2013 lawsuit alleging similar abuses on Unit One.

Later that year, in October 2017, Pasquotank correctional officers Veronica Darden, Justin Smith, Wendy Shannon, and Geoff Howe were killed by four prisoners attempting to escape the high-security prison in Elizabeth City. It was the single deadliest attack in modern North Carolina penal history, and prompted investigative reports and calls for the National Guard to secure the state's prisons. Some reports concluded that these murders and other prison violence were primarily attributable to staffing vacancies, poor training and surveillance, and a lack of proper protective equipment for staff. Representative Steinburg believed the key problems were a lack of morale and respect for officers.

Just months later in June 2018—despite promises of improved safety and security from Lassiter, NCDPS Secretary Eric Hooks, and

Representative Steinburg—Lieutenant Soucier was cut, stabbed, and beaten by two regular population prisoners at CP. Though he was severely wounded, Soucier survived the attack and tensions between staff and prisoners at CP reached a boiling point. Lassiter significantly stiffened penalties for assaults on staff, threatening the use of an interstate compact to send them to solitary confinement in another state.

In 2018 a number of former and current corrections leaders were appointed to the North Carolina Prison Reform Advisory Board. They discussed everything from security upgrades and intelligence gathering methods, both within and outside of the prison system, to tougher sanctions needed to punish the incarcerated. Based on the board's recommendations, the Legislative Oversight Committee on Prisons pushed the North Carolina General Assembly to relinquish more funds to the prison system. The money would be invested in recruitment, training, and equipment to make the prisons more secure but did nothing to address the underlying cause of the tension between staff and the incarcerated.

Of the nearly thirty-seven thousand incarcerated citizens in North Carolina, most will get out, bringing their prison experiences back into the community. The prisoners responsible for the murders of officers Callahan, Howe, Smith, Darden, and Shannon will not. They lacked something the NCDPS push for safety and security does not provide: a positive connection to outside communities reinforced by education and accountability.

Many in the public believe murders like these are why the justice system should show no mercy. But not showing mercy is how we arrived at this point. If legislators, NCDPS administrators, and prison officials continue to disregard what prisoners think, remove meaningful incentives, undermine rehabilitative efforts with punitive reprisals, and fail to provide models of good behavior, the penal system will cease to exist. In its place will be a collection of savage human warehouses, where public safety is a hollow ideal and everyone is in danger.

Chapter 16

Freeing the Press in Prisons

The public has a right to know what happens in state prisons, but how can they when the information comes from a single, limited source?

In 2019 an intern for WUNC, the National Public Radio member station for a large swath of central and eastern North Carolina, wrote to ask if I would consent to a taped interview for a show on local politics and culture called *The State of Things*. The segment would cover my writing on North Carolina's abolished parole system, as described in an article I wrote for issue 16 of *Scalawag* titled "Paroling Michael Pinch." I agreed to a telephone interview, assuming nothing else was needed. The show's producer, however, felt obliged to contact the Department of Public Safety (NCDPS) Communications Office. I never heard from the radio station again.

As a prisoner of North Carolina since 1997, I have witnessed the deterioration of the penal system from the inside. The neglect of North Carolina prisons can be laid at the feet of lawmakers who implemented the Structured Sentencing Act (SSA), which effectively abolished parole in 1994, removing incentives for good conduct and lengthening the amount of time people spent incarcerated. By 2004 North Carolina's carceral population tripled. Facilities grew crowded, dysfunctional, and violent while state legislators ignored the consequences, and the public remained oblivious. The story of what has been going on in North Carolina's penal system has always been there, but not necessarily accessible.

Freedom of the press does not fully extend into prisons. Members of the media cannot interview prisoners at will or freely investigate troubling events as they do with the general public. In North Carolina, journalists must go through a convoluted bureaucratic process to enter a prison or talk with a prisoner. Access is never guaranteed. Most information comes from the North Carolina Department of Adult Corrections (NCDAC) Communications Office, designated prison officials, or the official NC-DAC website and social media accounts.

Violence in prisons is nothing new, so the lack of attention can be partly excused. Nevertheless, in 2017, after five North Carolina prison officers died in the line of duty, the violence could no longer be ignored. Reporting and legislative oversight focused on training and filling staffing vacancies. A report commissioned by the governor's crime commission and the creation of the Prison Reform Advisory Board seemed to quell calls by some lawmakers for the national guard to man the walls and protect the public.

Since then, three prisoners have been killed in North Carolina prisons: two at Columbus Correctional Institution in Whiteville and one at Maury Correctional Institution in Greene County. There was no uproar over these deaths. They were not even linked to the bevy of reporting on a penal system in crisis. That prison officers' lives are valued more than prisoners has never been in doubt, but any death linked by the same cause should be a matter of concern reflected in the reporting. Was this failure to connect prisoner and officer deaths attributable to shoddy media coverage? Or have NCDAC and US Supreme Court restrictions on press access in prison so discouraged journalists that they are satisfied with parroting the penal narrative?

In trying to understand why WUNC never followed up with me about the interview, I discovered an extensive NCDAC policy that governs public relations and media access to prison. While the general policy facilitates public access by "reasonable" means, "factors that compromise security, disrupt orderly administration, damage morale, and/or mitigate against the effectiveness of correctional treatment may limit that access."

Even prison officials are not completely free to speak with the media unless they coordinate what will be said with the communications office. Interviews with prisoners are subject to numerous restrictions. Access to death row prisoners, for example, requires written consent of the prisoner and his or her attorney, agreement from the warden, the director of prisons, and the communications office. Print reporting on the state's penal system is usually done by newspapers such as the *Charlotte Observer* and the Raleigh *News & Observer*. The reliance on newspaper reporting may be because video footage in prison is highly restricted.* Often, the public will only see outside shots of the fence, wall, and building, or old stock footage of blurred faces and closing doors, the cameras angled at prisoners' feet. Prisoners' faces cannot be shown without prior approval from prison officials and written consent from the prisoner. Unless it's a feature story about a criminal case, incarcerated citizens are a nameless, faceless, unrepresented mass.

This particular media restriction is ironic in light of the tour groups regularly walked through Central Prison and other facilities. Criminal justice student groups, prison officials from other states and countries, legislators, governors, and judges have all observed prisoners in the hallways and chow hall, on the recreation yards and cellblocks. Meanwhile, a ranked officer or the warden spin out the common penal narrative: descriptions of daily operations and security measures that keep "offenders" in check; specific criminal cases in the news and how that offender would be processed in the system; horror stories of "bad guys" intended to further isolate people in prison and justify anything done to them.

North Carolina prison tours give the appearance of transparency, but prisoners are forbidden from communicating with such groups and are punished if they try. After the 2017 prison officer deaths, Republican state representative Bob Steinburg, head of the Legislative Oversight Committee on Prisons, spoke out against carefully sculpted accounts of these prisons. He warned that withholding information from the public would create greater dangers in North Carolina's penal system: "If it's not going to be brought forward publicly then chances are pretty good that we are not going to ever know what happened and we're not going to be adequately able to prevent something like this from happening again."

---

* As of 2023, these policies have undergone some changes and, though less convoluted, continue to discourage interviews with incarcerated people.

Constitutional Limitations

While people on the outside have the full benefit of the First Amendment, the incarcerated do not. In several cases between 1974 and 1987 the US Supreme Court restricted press access in prison. The court held that as long as the restrictions are "content neutral," and other means of communication exist, the press has no special right to information in prisons beyond that of the public, which includes interviews with specific prisoners.

One case in particular addressed the extent to which prison officials could control the flow of information, and what "meaningful" press access means. In *Houchins v. KQED* (1978) the court held that nothing in the constitution "[compelled] the government to provide the media with information or access to it on demand."[1]

Some might argue these limitations are reasonable, that journalists are too intrusive anyway, or that specific media outlets are slanted. However, for marginalized groups at the mercy of negligent, careless state agencies, the press are arbiters of the truth who should be able to look under every rock and rotten log—wherever they lie.

Counternarrative

Considering the restrictions on media access and the stigma of having been convicted of a crime, it is difficult for people in prison to challenge the penal narrative. But it's not impossible. In the 1920s people confined here at Central Prison in Raleigh published the *Prison News*, a newspaper that "told of religious revivals, performances, baseball games, and boxing matches." On Saturday nights prisoners even hosted a radio program broadcast by Raleigh's news and talk station WPTF. While these opportunities were likely sanitized by the warden, they were presented as early efforts to humanize an incarcerated population, a trend that ended when penal ideology shifted to retributive punishment and incapacitation. A century later, no such programs exist in any of North Carolina's prisons.

Over the years prisoners have produced writing that has appeared in newspapers, journals, magazines, and books. This represents only a small percentage of millions, many of whom do not have the resources or ability to get published. Writing for public audiences also depends on which publication circulates the writing. A lot of mainstream publishers are reluctant to get involved with prison writers because they don't want to be viewed as coddling criminals. The advent of online publishing and social media, without the strict standards of traditional publications, made it somewhat easier for prisoners to be heard, but a number of states have prohibited the incarcerated from using social media, even through a third party. Regardless, the internet advances the conversation on mass incarceration in ways the traditional press cannot.

Online messaging is also a new strategy being promoted and used by the NCDAC. In an October 2019 report on improving NC prisons from the Prison Reform Advisory Board, there is a sense of urgency behind the "internal and external communication" of their efforts. Some of the initiatives appear to be normal for a large organization trying to attract new employees and increase cohesion within its workforce. For a state agency in crisis after a significant increase in prison violence, corruption among staff, and personnel shortages—other communication strategies smack of propaganda. According to the report, "Additional staff capacity will allow for opportunities to promote 'good news' stories of what's happening inside facilities and more timely posts on social media."

Like the advisory board's own report, "good news" stories propagated by the NCDAC on social media will not discuss issues like prison overcrowding or why, exactly, they would rather hire more people than incarcerate fewer. Those "good news" accounts will gloss over or ignore the continued use of long-term solitary confinement on mentally ill prisoners. If prison violence or the rate of assaults on staff and prisoners do not go down, the NCDAC is unlikely to tweet about it or post about it on Facebook. There will be nothing about the lives of prisoners in these "good news" stories. None of their messaging will warn that upon entering the prison's gates, constitutional protections are optional.

The NCDAC "good news" will be a carefully sculpted narrative given to the press, repeated, retweeted, posted, and regurgitated to the general public, who will then accept it as gospel, because anything contrary is fake news.

It is time to free the press in prison and give them unrestricted access to North Carolina prisoners and staff. Allow the substantial population to contribute to the conversation on its own reformation. Let the general public see and hear what really occurs in its institutions—not just the good news stories or the violent ones. In doing so, lawmakers can better address the needs of the penal system and the people contained within it, the public can evolve its understanding of prisons, and the press can regain its authority as a check and balance against government powers.

Chapter 17

Prison Journalism

Fighting the Narrative of Control

Gary Fields, in trying to gain access to a prison for a 2012 story for the *Wall Street Journal*, wrote that "each prison is a fiefdom." Wardens are feudal lords, guards their militia, and prisoners the serfs. While rules govern each prison, and the penal system at large loosely controls the collective of prisons in a state, there is still some autonomy among wardens. Their main cohesion, however, can be found where the flow of information is concerned. In this way, the penal narrative is as much a wall keeping out the public as it is keeping prisoners incarcerated.

Contrary to popular belief, state and federal prisons are public institutions. They are supposed to be governed by constitutional protections like freedom of the press and the prohibition against cruel and unusual punishment, but US Supreme Court rulings over the last thirty-five years have eroded these checks against state power.[1] As a result, what occurs on the inside is often hidden from the public, and, when stories of abuse leak out, riots occur, and prisoners or staff die, the public is left wondering why.

Prisons are controls for the marginalized, hidden behind the curtain of tough-on-crime rhetoric, manipulated by the stigma of a criminal act that suppresses one's humanity. Film, television, and the media help maintain that curtain. Viewers are unlikely to realize the exact forces at play behind the narrative of control in *The Green Mile* or *Oz*. Rather, they consume a singular philosophy: criminals deserve to be punished. Prison serves as that punishment. And what's wrong with retribution against the wicked? Prisons make neighborhoods safer, right?

No. That logic would imply that mass incarceration "works," thereby making America the safest country in the world. It is not.

The problem with the narrative of control is that it narrowly focuses on one aspect of behavior, crime, to the exclusion of all other environmental and social influences. This narrative carries all the way through the politics of crime, criminal legal policies, and public institutions like schools. The media echoes and amplifies it. Hollywood glorifies it. In turn, the public consumes, internalizes, and bases its understanding of incarcerated people on it. Any attempt to dissolve the carceral state must challenge and change the crime control narrative to one of crime prevention, equal justice, and accountability.

Prison life does not neatly fit into movie and TV archetypes. Television shows about prison often depict scenes of the rec yard, where everyone is cliqued up by race or gang. This may be a semiaccurate illustration of a California prison like Folsom or a New York prison like Sing Sing, but it's in no way a representative sample of all prisons. Yes, gangs are a growing problem in prison, but not for staff as much as for the ordinary prisoners trying to do the right thing to get home. But even this is subject to variation. While some gangs do raise the threat of violence, sometimes they impose order, acting as subcontrols beneath those of the prison.

This, too, is part of the crime control narrative. But if the information provided is tailored to make prison officials look good and prisoners bad, in leaving out prisoner perspectives it fails to answer a very basic question: Why have gangs proliferated in prisons? The crime control/penal narrative response is that criminals are opportunists who resist sanction and violate laws in any environment. The reality is closer to the way that gangs proliferate in poor neighborhoods and schools where economic and educational advancement are limited, and law enforcement uses brute force to maintain control. The same is true in prison: officials allow idle time and a lack of education to be filled with suborganizations, which swiftly fill gaps in leadership.

You will not glean these factors from the movies and TV shows that glorify and venerate law enforcement. Authors of these screenplays are typically limited in their access to information: they are shown the stories prison officials want them to tell. The same is true of journalists. The counternarrative would expose the overwhelming failure of crime control and its disconnect from reality. It attributes responsibility to prison officials for the problems in their facilities. On a more basic level, the counternarrative expects prison officials to correct behavior and guide rehabilitation through positive reinforcement and education. Even dog trainers will tell you coercive control isn't as effective as positive reinforcement.

There's a lot of nuance between prisons. Prior to the reinstatement of Pell Grants for prisoners in the 2020 FAFSA Simplification Act, New York prisoners had greater access to higher education than most other state prisons. Others, like Angola in Louisiana, are modern plantations, primarily full of Black and brown people. Some are minimum security, like the women's prisons in *Orange Is the New Black*. Others are maximum security, like the one depicted in *Shawshank Redemption*. This variation matters because of both the experience it provides to the incarcerated and the legislation derived from people leaving and returning to prison. Violent prisons breed violent recidivists. Gang-infested prisons breed more gangs in and out of prisons. Similarly, greater learning opportunities, mental health services, and job training on the inside create more productive reentering citizens and fewer recidivists.

Unfortunately, television shows and movies depict violent crime as a crusade of good against evil, where law enforcement officers (LEOs) are usually the "good guys" and judges, defense attorneys, and other elected officials as the personifications of truth, justice, and American ideals. Suggesting that militarized police are responsible for innocent civilian deaths or that too many people are in prison as a result of overpoliced BIPOC communities is a counternarrative. Arguing that judges who were once prosecutors are incapable of giving defendants a fair hearing because they have an implicit bias challenges the established narrative of judicial impartiality. Suggesting that sheriff's deputies contribute to in-custody jail deaths as a regular part of their criminal negligence is, in many circles, worth creating laws to hide. Holding criminal justice system actors accountable in the light of public scrutiny also means explaining how those actions are part of the mainstream narrative and common responses to crime and punishment. Without a counterbalance to that narrative, those public officials are rarely held accountable even to the standard ordinary citizens must follow. Because there is not a strong enough counternarrative exposing bad actors in the criminal legal system, the crime control narrative creates a double standard: accountability is for the underclass, but not the ruling one.

In 2018 and 2019, twenty of the top fifty highest-rated prime-time television programs were law enforcement oriented. None of them focused on the fruits of their labor: overcrowded prisons. All of them glorified some element of crime control while denigrating and devaluing those on the receiving end of "justice." Law and order are upheld, the bad guy gets killed, and the audience is sated on disinformation.

Is it any wonder, considering this steady diet of crime dramas, that when George Floyd and countless other Black and brown people are publicly murdered by law enforcement, many Americans are skeptical about the roots of racial injustice? Or that, in response, they would in fact double down on law-and-order rhetoric or pursue confirmation of their biases in online echo chambers? Prisons themselves are a long-standing, physical extension of that willful ignorance.

The widely circulated video footage of Floyd and others murdered at the hands of police raises a new question for abolitionists: Would televising prisoner executions lead to similar outrage and action? Let's say executions were broadcast on the nightly news. First, the condemned would appear strapped to a gurney, IV in arm (crotch or leg if he or she had collapsed veins from drug use). The warden reads off the crimes and names the victims and, after asking if he or she had any last words, the warden signals to begin the lethal injection. It probably wouldn't make for prime-time coverage though, because a botched execution can take up to or over an hour to kill, exposing the fact the condemned do in fact visibly suffer. I'm sure there would be commentators to dramatize the event, with cut-away interviews and suspense over potential last-minute reprieves. It still probably wouldn't impact abolitionist efforts though, because, let's face it, how many innocent men, women, and children have been killed by law enforcement, captured on video, and widely circulated online before large swaths of America expressed moral outrage?

Executions were originally removed from public view because they incite greater violence, which isn't a good look for civilized capitalism. The spectacle itself reveals the heavy hand of control over the marginalized. Prison came in to tame the more barbarous practices of corporal punishment and fill the void left by abolition of slavery. But the root of this flawed logic still pervades this country—found now in the prison itself, disappeared from public sight, behind the veneer of law and order.

But between the indoctrination of the crime control narrative, mass shootings, and vitriolic disinformation tweeted from Donald Trump's White House, the stage is set, and public executions could very well make a comeback in the modern era. As George Orwell would say:

War is peace.
Freedom is slavery.
Ignorance is strength.[2]

I don't think executions should occur at all, let alone on TV. But I do believe that the press should have unrestricted access to prisons and the people therein. The only way to counter the narrative of control is by injecting perspective into the conversation. Show the public what really occurs in prisons. It is the purpose of the fourth estate to act as a check and balance against judicial, executive, and legislative branches of government. These powers converge in the policies of mass incarceration. Without the media to examine their impact at every level, and without a check against some of the more egregious abuses against people in confinement, prisons will remain black holes where information and people disappear.

When people do reappear, crippled by their experiences on the inside, many in the public seem not to understand. Why? Because their information about prison isn't based in reality, but a one-sided dramatized version of it. Here are some basics you should know about prison, ones you won't find in fictionalized and sanitized state-sponsored narratives:

- Ninety percent of those who go in come out, many of them worse off than when they entered. Many prisons lack robust educational programs, and the time spent away from the job market compounds an incarcerated person's lack of skills, while collateral consequences of a felony record make it incredibly hard to earn a livable wage or even find a place to live. Prison reentry programs are not only insufficient, but inaccessible to many.
- Most people who go to prison are ordinary citizens who made mistakes rooted in economic instability. These factors are exacerbated by systemic racism, classism, and the criminalization of mental illness. Most television viewers are likely a paycheck or two away from having more in common with those they see demonized on TV than they realize.
- Over half of all prisoners have experienced some form of mental illness like depressive episodes or addiction, while at least 20 percent suffer from a serious psychological disorder and lack access to adequate mental health care in prison.
- Sociopaths and psychopaths, used to drive draconian sentencing policies and illustrate a majority of the "bad guys" in crime shows, make up less than 1 percent of the prison population.
- Gangs and drugs occur in prison as much as recidivism does outside of it. Most people in prison want to do better, but prison officials lack the personnel, training, resources, and motivation to prevent violence on the inside. A lack of access to adequate education, resources, and second chances solidify a similar fate upon release.

Much of the above relates to prison officials never being held accountable, reliance upon misinformation/disinformation to establish criminal justice policy, and an often-indifferent public that fails to recognize prisons are their responsibility, too. Neglecting that responsibility has contributed to mass incarceration and the highest recidivism rate in the world.

Prison journalism is one concrete step I'm taking to counter the narrative of control. My experiences and those of others within the criminal punishment system generate a deeper understanding of which policies do or don't work. My skill as a writer and opportunities to speak with the public are what enable me to convey that understanding, and to challenge the narrative presented on TV and in film. Critical thinkers must question what they're accustomed to hearing about crime control and public safety, dig deeper than the rhetoric, and seek out the facts wherever they can be found.

Chapter 18

Developing a Career from Prison

It Takes a Team

Higher education gave me an edge when submitting my first article for publication to *Scalawag*. Where someone less knowledgeable in essay writing might have struggled with structuring their argument, organizing information, and using sound logic, I found it normal. This gave me confidence. Drawing from lessons learned in writing and rhetoric, and from literary masters like George Orwell, I recognized my advantage. Accordingly, my first *Scalawag* article advocated for greater access to higher education in prison. Being a trained writer, however, is only part of the publication process.

Publishing while incarcerated is hard. Lack of access to computers or the internet or even a typewriter means handwriting (and carbon copying) submissions, then waiting on snail mail. Most publishers don't accept handwritten manuscripts, so you have to send out the work to be typed and mailed in again. Research and revisions are similarly difficult. After putting forth so much effort, receiving a form letter rejection is discouraging.

My first rejection came with a note explaining how seldom the organization published, that many submissions by great writers are turned down, and that I should keep trying. No signature, feedback, or guidance. I was left to wonder if I had an awkward tone, the wrong politics, the wrong topic, or just bad writing. Maybe my lack of resumé and imprisonment were the only causes for rejection they needed.

Whatever the reason, rejection is part of the writing process. Stephen King impaled his many rejections on a nail in the attic where he wrote *Carrie*. Success in a writing career demands practice, determination, creativity, and resilience. Though the author gets the credit, publishing only happens with help from other people.

I knew early on that publishing a few essays about my experiences on death row and in prison would not be enough. I felt an overwhelming need to counter the one-sided sensationalism of mainstream journalism that typically excludes incarcerated voices and experiences. I wanted to challenge the "official" reporting on North Carolina's penal dysfunction, which too often fails to hold state officials accountable.

"Career" had not made it into my lexicon when at a visit with my first *Scalawag* editor, Danielle, we discussed where I saw my writing going.

"I want to be the one you rely on for an insider's perspective," I told her. "Most newspapers don't describe us or only as a living extension of a crime. We have no representation in the media, and I want to change that."

My familiarity with prison journalism came from Wilbert Rideau's and Kerry Myers's work on the *Angolite*, Earlonne Woods's and Nigel Poor's work with *Ear Hustle*, and several independent writers whose work frequented PEN America collections and the Marshall Project. But the writing largely focused on infamous prisons and lacked coverage of thousands of facilities throughout the United States. Also, labels like "inmate" and "offender" were attached to writers, their criminal conviction listed at the end of an essay like an asterisk.

It frustrated me to think that there are journalists in every town of America, their names in print without a qualifier, but not in its prisons. Several US Supreme Court decisions over the last forty years have restricted press access to prisons, making it unlikely that they can accurately cover what happens in a given facility or penal system. Without incarcerated writers and their firsthand experience, reporting about the criminal legal system and mass incarceration carries the odor of propaganda. It takes editors willing to be inclusive, and not accept state officials' word as gospel or parrot state-reported statistics, to correct this fatal journalistic flaw.

There is no shortage of material to write about in prison, because it is an authoritarian society sponsored by an apathetic democracy. It's more about choosing the most important and timely topics. Danielle made pitching topics easy by trusting my experience and judgment.

When it came to revisions, she was not heavy-handed and explained why a paragraph needed to be moved or cut or restructured. Though I knew a lot about the politics of mass incarceration, policies of the criminal legal system, and life in prison, she reminded me that good journalism is story driven. It was the kind of instruction I needed to become a better writer.

Citing sources of information is an ordinary part of any article, but fact-checking takes on added importance for prison journalists. It's good to be meticulously grounded in facts, because an incarcerated writer's integrity will always be in question. Citing facts and their sources makes editorial support easier, and harder for prisons to assail or censor the writing. Challenging the penal narrative from the inside carries an inherent risk few other journalists in America experience, which is why strong editorial support is critical, far beyond just the writing process.

In 2018 *Scalawag* published my article, "Measures Meant to Make North Carolina Prisons Safer Do the Opposite" (see chapter 15, "Draconion Ideals"). After five guards were killed in 2017, prison officials "cracked down" on the incarcerated population. Draconian policies and vindictive officials cut much-needed rehabilitative programs, harassing an already frustrated group of people. From minimum-custody facilities to death row, an increase in tension caused more assaults. These did not make the news. Instead, corrections officers were characterized as law enforcement heroes who did no wrong. Prisons were understaffed, not overcrowded. The responsibility for prison violence belonged to violent inmates, not a complete lack of incentives, antagonistic guards, or penal mismanagement. After publication of my article, I received a not-so-subtle threat from unit management: "You need to get your story straight. What you wrote is wrong. It wasn't in the news, so it didn't happen like that. You think you have it hard? It can get a lot worse."

I told Danielle about the interaction, and she was ready to provide whatever help she could. It reassured me to know the support went beyond an awareness of the risk from prison journalism, something parachute journalists on the outside do not face. *Scalawag* has a genuine interest in representing marginalized people. Danielle's concern was not curiosity, charity, tokenism, or mutual benefit—she cared about what happened to me as a human being, friend, and member of the *Scalawag* team.

What more can a writer ask for than to be represented and taken seriously by an editor? Professional treatment produces professional outcomes. The same cannot be said if the writer is treated as less than, a distraction, or someone whose ideas are good enough to appropriate but not credit.

A recent experience showed me the difference between the good editorial communication and support I receive from *Scalawag*, and the poor communication I received from a national newspaper. Some friends arranged a meeting with a journalist and two editors. I was asked to prepare several pitches in advance of the meeting to be forwarded to the editors through the journalist. The phone meeting went well, and the editors assigned an article with a two-week deadline for an initial draft. Within ten days, I submitted a draft, followed by revisions three days later. That was it. I never heard back from the editors, and they ignored emails from my friends. I had been dismissed with silence.

What happened to me is likely common, especially for incarcerated writers. It was infuriating and depressing, but not the end of the world. After all, rejection and opposition make up the air we breathe in prison, and one develops a certain amount of resilience that cannot be overcome by a professional snub. Danielle commiserated with me even as she celebrated the potential of publishing with the newspaper. It's the kind of professional support and communication that has helped me flourish as a writer.

Stability enables innovation. The accessibility of *Scalawag*'s online format made it easy to share my articles with criminal justice students. In 2018 I began speaking events with undergrad classes at University of North Carolina at Chapel Hill, Ohio University, and the University of

Minnesota at Minneapolis. Students were assigned some of my *Scalawag* articles, and over the course of two fifteen-minute phone calls, my voice amplified by a speaker in the classroom, I answered questions about capital punishment, executions, life imprisonment, higher education, penal reform, and criminal justice policies. By spring 2021, with the aid of Zoom, I connected with a number of private high schools, church groups, podcasts, and over a dozen professors at eight different universities for a total of fifty speaking events. My writing for *Scalawag* and other publications became a platform from which I could teach the public about the myths and misperceptions surrounding crime and punishment.

It takes a special level of determination to keep learning and striving as a writer in prison. If success is defined as publication, this is unlikely without the help of friends or family at some point. Similarly, developing a successful writing career takes a special level of interest from editors who recognize and cultivate a writer's potential. All of it requires mutual respect and hard work. None of it happens without support on the outside. Writing in prison was never meant to be an isolated practice; it is a community-building event that takes a team.

Chapter 19

On Retaliation against Incarcerated Writers

Scalawag published a piece I wrote, titled "Prison Officials Cut Off Higher Education for People on North Carolina's Death Row," in the fall of 2019. The article shined a light of accountability on petty bureaucrats who decided to obstruct my access to privately sponsored college correspondence courses. It was the kind of arbitrary, mean-spirited, and punitive decision that causes much of the dysfunction in North Carolina's prisons. A North Carolina Department of Public Safety (NCDPS) official responded to the article on *Scalawag*'s Facebook page, simply stating that my access to the correspondence courses had been restored. The internal response by prison administrators was not so polite.

A few days after the official responded publicly to *Scalawag*, an Internal Affairs (IA) lieutenant and one of her staff locked me in a holding cell. Neither said a word and I was left to wonder if they were placing me under "investigation." Due process disciplinary rights suddenly become flexible or nonexistent when you are being investigated by IA, and many lose months in solitary confinement.

After an hour, the IA lieutenant and her staff left the unit without ever talking to me or the unit manager. I was released from the holding cell and told to return to my cellblock. No one had answers for me, but when I saw that my typically neat cell had been trashed—papers, books, clothes, and pictures littered the floor, sheets stripped from the bunk, chair turned over—I got the message: writing about prison officials has consequences.

In 1989, a federal appeals court ruled that the First Amendment prohibits retaliation against prisoners for exercising free speech.[1] In a later decision in which a man incarcerated in a Washington, DC, prison claimed a violation of his First Amendment rights, the US Supreme Court stated, "Retaliation offends the Constitution because it threatens to inhibit exercise of the protected right."[2] However, despite clear constitutional protections, covert retaliation still occurs because most prisoners lack the knowledge and resources to file a lawsuit. Some prison officials know this and use it to their advantage.

Prison accountability is what makes prison journalism critical to representing interests of the marginalized and oppressed, and why incarcerated writers put themselves at risk. The writing is less about individuals and more about examining the policies and laws that fail to protect everyone in the system, with the goal of pursuing change. Prison officials often view this unwanted attention as a challenge to their control.

Retaliatory punishment is a common response to such challenges. Threats, harassment, revoked privileges, interference with the mail and access to the courts, destruction of property, hindered communication, solitary confinement, physical abuse, and transfer to more dangerous prisons in other states are just some of the retaliatory measures that have been taken against prisoners for exercising their right to free speech.

Incarcerated writers have to expect officials will ignore prohibitions against retaliation. The people who manage state penal systems are not held accountable often enough for anyone on the inside to believe the courts or public will assert any rights for the incarcerated. There are exceptions, like the COVID-19 lawsuit filed in Wake County, North Carolina,[3] or a lawsuit to secure hepatitis C treatment for incarcerated people filed in one of the state's federal district courts in 2018.[4] Both lawsuits mandated access to adequate medical care in prison and requisite safety protocols because prison officials had refused to provide them. But these issues impacted prisoners as a class and were also tangible threats to public safety, which made them relatively easy wins for civil rights groups filing class action lawsuits. Had these health issues just impacted people in prison, COVID-19 and hepatitis C would be running rampant. The problem with this standard of accountability is that one cannot expect help from the outside unless a civil rights group with their own interests is willing to take up the cause. Otherwise, North Carolina prisoners have to depend on an ineffective grievance remedy procedure officials use to rubber stamp complaints, and underfunded, understaffed Prisoner Legal Services that rarely pursue cases. As a result, the incarcerated suffer.

The risks associated with incarcerated reporting are worth taking because the public is ultimately responsible for what occurs within its prisons. Mainstream media narratives that regurgitate what state officials feed them cannot be allowed to dictate public perceptions of their incarcerated class. Editors stand as information gatekeepers who must be aware of their responsibility for fully informing the public, and the value of incarcerated writers in that process.

Media organizations protect and invest in the things they value. Any good editor will stand by their writers after a story has been published. Most editors, however, do not typically need to get involved with their writers' work when there is negative criticism. Most critics cannot punish writers with solitary confinement, billy clubs, degrading searches, destruction of their property, or longer prison terms through negative parole reviews because they exercised a right that too many take for granted.

Standing by incarcerated writers does not mean an editor must file a lawsuit if public officials inhibit, retaliate against, or otherwise silence free expression; but some public officials are hardheaded and power hungry. "Please stop" will not be enough. The point is to call them out publicly every time, not just when it is convenient. Address them on social media, call them up directly, and write follow-up articles that address the image they have of their position of authority. However it is done, a demonstration of support in the face of opposition can be enough. Support can take many forms, and it's a good feeling to know someone has your back, that you are not alone in the fight. Accountability is a community in action, serving the interests of its members, and providing strength in numbers. It's the only way to bring about lasting change.

Chapter 20

Keeping the People Ignorant

When Censorship Contributes to Misinformation
around Mass Incarceration

In June 2022 the Durham County Commission voted to include a $30 million youth jail in its annual budget. Once built, the facility would primarily confine Black and brown children under the age of eighteen. Prior to the final vote on the budget, my friend Danielle asked me to write a letter to the commission describing my experiences in the juvenile justice system. She believed that, in addition to public protest, if the commissioners read an honest account of growing up in the criminal legal system, they might reconsider building another jail.

The letter described some of my encounters with abusive staff in a youth detention center, how it undermined my ability to trust or adjust as an adolescent. I argued that the national staffing crisis made building another jail a bad idea that would lead to many of the problems caused by understaffing in adult prisons: neglect, suicide, and violence. I urged the commission to instead invest in community-based alternatives to incarceration that paired youths with mentors and rigorous after-school programs. Then I had nine of my death-sentenced peers, who also suffered in the juvenile justice system, sign on to the letter. I had the letter notarized and sent certified mail to the commission.

Charlotte West, a friend and journalist with Open Campus Media, helped get a version of the letter published online at YouthToday.org.[1]

Danielle knew journalists at three different media outlets: two who wanted to interview me over the phone about my letter to the commission and one who would submit our coauthored op-ed to her editor. The journalist for NPR affiliate WUNC asked about my experiences in the juvenile justice system. She wanted to know how I got involved in activism from death row, my thoughts on what the commission should do instead of building a new jail, and how incarceration as a youth impacted my life. The network TV reporter for ABC affiliate WTVD News also asked about my experience with solitary confinement as a sixteen-year-old, wanting to know why a newer facility would have the same problems as the old one. She said the interview might air as part of a larger story on the rise of youth confinement in North Carolina. For the op-ed, Danielle and I wrote about our opposition to funding the jail, and how it was an investment in incarceration instead of youths who had yet to even commit any crimes. The jail would grow the prison-industrial complex and undermine the community, not make it safer. We submitted the op-ed through her contact at the *News & Observer*.

We thought at least one of these efforts would make it to the public, but none of them did. Danielle followed up with her contacts to find out what happened. WUNC claimed they previously interviewed family members of teens confined at the old youth jail in Durham. The journalist's editor claimed not to want to appear biased by airing another interview on the same subject. WTVD did not give a reason. Their story about the rise in youth confinement lasted about three minutes in the afternoon and included brief statements from academics with no personal stake in the jailing of America's youth. The new $30 million youth jail in Durham County was never mentioned. The *News & Observer* journalist was at a loss to explain why they did not publish the op-ed.

The lack of coverage about a $30 million youth jail in a county where schools are underfunded and test scores are below the state average was aggravating and all too customary. Especially when the *News & Observer* published an article about the Durham County commission passing the nearly billion-dollar budget and referencing investments in law enforcement and raises for commissioners, but nothing about the jail.[2]

I wanted to call out the local media for continuously failing to report on the advance of mass incarceration and the prison-industrial complex in its most obvious form. The public had a right and need to know where it begins and who is responsible. I began looking into setting up a third-party social media platform. It would be a way to fill coverage gaps and immediately respond to the misinformation that often corrodes mainstream reporting on the criminal legal system. Social media would also be a way to hold public officials directly accountable. What I discovered, though, was yet another obstacle that made getting information to the public as difficult as before.

In 2021 the North Carolina Department of Public Safety, Division of Prisons, enacted a policy that prohibits incarcerated people from maintaining third-party social media accounts.[3] Facebook, Twitter, TikTok, and similar platforms were off limits. The new social media ban holds that violators would be reported to the platform's security system management for immediate termination of the account. For attempting to exercise their First Amendment rights, the incarcerated are punished with solitary confinement, losing access to the phone, tablet, and visits.

❧

The seed of my desire to be a journalist was planted by the one-sided narrative of my arrest as a nineteen-year-old in 1997, and my trial, wrongful conviction, and death sentence in 1999. That desire blossomed in the years following North Carolina's 2006 moratorium on executions. Then came the back-to-back release and exoneration of Jonathan Hoffman, Levon Jones, and Glen Chapman. During this period two media outlets—the *News & Observer* and WTVD—sought interviews with random death-sentenced prisoners. Then–Central Prison Warden Gerald Branker was a staunch death penalty advocate. The warden had death row's unit manager "specially select" people for interview and they chose two severely mentally ill prisoners. On camera one man claimed the state treated him better than he deserved. In a newspaper article, the other man spoke about wanting to die and how he hoped executions would resume to end his suffering. No one else was interviewed. Maybe the journalists asked for others and were refused. Warden Branker certainly had the power to control who is interviewed and what information is disseminated to the public from a prison. All prison wardens, sheriffs, and state officials do.

Despite belonging to taxpayers, prisons, jails, and other confinement facilities are closed to the press and public. The control of information that goes into or comes out of these institutions belongs to the facility head or the state. The US Supreme Court enshrined this authority over free press, speech, expression, and other constitutional rights in *Turner v. Safety* (1987).[4]

The state can withhold information, restrict access to prisoners, detainees, and their records, even limit a confined person's ability to communicate with the public as long as it is "reasonably related to a legitimate penological interest." This phrase has granted state officials broad latitude in the suppression of information and communication and helps keep the public ignorant about what really occurs behind the fences of prisons, jails, and detention centers.

For the press to access information state officials don't want to provide, first a Freedom of Information Act (FOIA) request must be filed naming the information; then if they are still not forthcoming, a lawsuit.

In February 2021 Forsyth County prosecutors asked a judge to prevent journalists from accessing John Neville's death records, which were in possession of the Department of Health and Human Services (HHS).[5] Considering the records belonged to the HHS, not prosecutors, the request seemed suspicious because these same prosecutors would have to pursue charges against the sheriff's deputies responsible for Neville's death in the county jail. A litigatory battle over the records ensued; the lawsuit filed by the *News & Observer* was joined by eleven other news organizations. Also drawing national attention to the case was the NC General Assembly's passage of SB 168, a law that would conceal in-custody death records and investigations of the sort that prosecutors now sought to stall in the court.[6] Fortunately, the governor vetoed SB 168 in large part because of the attention generated by activists and the joint lawsuit filed by a dozen media outlets.

It bears mentioning that the level of attention paid to John Neville's death and passage of SB 168 would likely not have happened without the international uproar over the death of George Floyd. Bystander cameras caught the merciless act by law enforcement just as jail cameras caught deputies asphyxiating John Neville. Footage of Floyd's death spread online and generated momentum that forced a more thorough examination of the way BIPOC communities are disproportionately targeted by law enforcement and oppressed in the criminal legal system. Mainstream media did not cover the story until after it circulated online. More than ever before, this cultural moment demonstrated the power of social media to hold public officials accountable, which the fourth estate is supposed to do, but instead frequently parrots accounts given by state officials without engaging in due diligence. This cultural moment is also why the NC Division of Prisons now prohibits the incarcerated from accessing social media.

The irony of the social media prohibition by prison officials is that the incarcerated are allowed to submit writing for ordinary publication. I can, for example, write an op-ed and get it published in a newspaper. My only concern then is whether prison officials decide to retaliate for its content. That is the assumed risk of incarcerated journalism though. But that same op-ed cannot be posted on a Facebook page set up in my name. The policy is about controlling the flow of information. Most incarcerated people are not going to be able to get their writing published. It's why there are thousands of jails and prisons, but only a few dozen people who might claim to be incarcerated journalists. Social media removes the hurdles of editors who vet stories, check for grammar, or refuse to publish content because it is "unsuitable." Through social media, even the most senseless and deranged Twitter feeds attract followers and voters. We see this increasing with every new election cycle.

It could be argued the social media prohibition is intended to prevent scams and attempts at harassing members of the public or engagement in other nefarious activities. Someone unfamiliar with institutional policies can be forgiven for thinking that makes sense. The reality is such things are equally possible through snail mail. Also, technological advances have made it easier for prison officials to monitor, scan, disrupt, or block any incoming and outgoing communication, whether by phone, tablet, or mail. No, the prohibition against social media use is about the speed with which information travels online and the inability for state officials to control the narrative once it gets away from them.

In 2019 the *New York Times* resisted publishing graphic images depicting three years of extreme violence in the Alabama penal system. An anonymous prison officer at St. Clair Correctional Facility downloaded over two thousand images from the prison's computers and onto a thumb drive, then mailed them with a cover letter to the Southern Poverty Law Center, with fifty ending up at *Splinter News*, and just five going to the *New York Times*.[7] The images depicted prisoners who had committed suicide, been beaten and stabbed to death, pools of blood, and unfathomable amounts of gore and brutality. The *New York Times* refused to publish all but a few of the images, more concerned with "audience sensibilities," the inability to "provide more context for specific incidents depicted," and the "suitability of the images for publication."[8]

Shaila Dewan, the *New York Times* journalist who wrote the article accompanying the few images that were published, claimed, "The photos are incredibly dehumanizing and gory, so from the point of view of people in the photos we have no way of knowing how they would feel about having those published."[9]

A more disingenuous excuse for censorship and failing to fully investigate a story, or act as a check and balance against a state government has never been uttered. The dead expect their stories to be told. Especially those who have been discarded by society while they were alive. The images were not dehumanizing; the cruel and inhumane conditions of confinement were. Hamilton Nolan, senior writer for *Splinter News*, authored the article that accompanied the St. Clair images the publication posted online. Nolan insists "there's a public value to people being able to see behind those walls. One of the biggest problems with mass incarceration in America is that it's completely hidden from public view."[10]

Penal violence occurs because the people locked away in these brutal cesspits are shown they are not even worth basic human dignity. Their suffering is dismissed as deserved and unsuitable for public consumption. Then the causes of the systemic dysfunction—policy and politics—are obscured or omitted in the coverage of crime and punishment. Into the mix goes all the stereotypes and "tough-on-crime" rhetoric that fills the minds of the public with misinformation that undermines their ability to comprehend why youth jails and prisons fail.

Salman Rushdie said in a May 2022 speech to the PEN America Emergency World Voices Congress of Writers:

> Above all we must understand that stories are at the heart of what's happening, and the dishonest narratives of oppressors have attracted many. So we must work to overturn the false narratives of tyrants, populists, and fools by telling better stories than they do, stories in which people want to live. The battle is not only on the battlefield. The stories we live in are also contested territories.[11]

Despite the prohibition against North Carolina prisoners using social media, I will nevertheless work hard to publish articles that explore and explain the politics and policies of mass incarceration. Difficult as it may be, this is both the story I and millions of others live and a contested territory that demands public attention.

Chapter 21

"A Modernized, Streamlined Incarceration Experience"

New Prison Technology Surveils Life on Both Sides of the Wall

---

Before my incarceration at age nineteen in 1997, my formal experience with technology ended with Windows 2.0 as a high school freshman. I played Sega Genesis and Super Nintendo video games or paid quarters for tokens at an arcade. I saw dial-up internet exactly once when my girlfriend logged into a chat room to find out when to purchase some concert tickets.

Technological learning curves were even steeper for those who entered prison in the 1980s, anchored as they were in *Star Wars*, laser tag, and *Knight Rider*. Whatever decade we got there, our memories of digital things collectively faded over time against the distant buzz of the dot-com era, URLs, and cell phones.

All of us who entered prison before the tech evolution of the early 2000s watched it play out on a television inside a prison dayroom, struggling to grasp new developments in our isolation outside of time. We were reminded of our isolation whenever someone new came to death row and spoke about "the internet." After a while though, they, too, became encapsulated in the concrete of yesterday, witnesses of the free world's technological glamor from a disconnected distance.

North Carolina prisons resisted technological advances until the mid-2000s, when canteens went cashless and a number of minimum- and medium-custody facilities provided limited access to pay phones. Weekly rec department movies were still 8 mm films displayed on pull-down silver screens. Televisions were analog behemoths bolted to the dayroom wall. Nobody had hot plates, tape players, microwaves, or any tech other than a cheap digital watch and a hand-held AM/FM radio that used two triple-A batteries.

On death row, we shared a single wall-mounted, steel-wired phone—identical to a pay phone, but without the coin slots—between twenty-four people. This system obviously came with its own limitations under normal circumstances. Those problems were exacerbated during the COVID-19 lockdowns when frustration and anxiety drove everyone to the phone, and tempers flared.

For a time, violence seemed inevitable—until a memo appeared on the block bulletin board in June 2020. In bold capital letters, it announced: NEW PRISONS TECHNOLOGY PROJECT. "The Division of Prisons will introduce a new technology project that provides tablets to every offender, at no cost to you or the state of North Carolina, at all prison facilities."

Those reading the memo on death row at the time averaged twenty-five years in prison, each near the age of fifty. The concept of a "tablet," while simple to understand in a TV commercial, lacked any context in the carceral world.

Nationally, at the same time as the rise of social media and flip phones, an overburdened carceral system faced a growing crisis for mass incarceration. In 2005, as public officials searched for ways to cut budgets, Corrections Corporation of America (CCA) warned its investors that the demand for private prisons' goods and services would be negatively impacted by relaxed conviction and sentencing measures.

It was a perverse admission of the industrialization of prisons. More people in prison meant more money for private companies building correctional facilities—or supplying telephone services, tasers, electronic ankle monitors, and GPS tracking.

The 2008 recession supercharged the private prison industry when state governments struggled to maintain overcrowded facilities and bloated penal budgets without releasing more people from prison. By 2010 in the South and Southwest, 7 to 9 percent of all prisoners were in private facilities, compared to just 2 to 3 percent in the Northeast and Midwest, according to the US Department of Justice.[1]

Privatized prison services impact nearly everyone in the system. One such company to rise out of the 2008 recession is the online prison profiteer JPAY, a Florida-based money transfer service. JPAY streamlined the collection of money from friends and family members of incarcerated people, charging a fee for every transaction and depositing money in the prisoners' trust fund account.

It was not until 2012 that JPAY eventually came to serve North Carolina prisons, leading the way for other profiteers to follow. Soon after, prison telecom giant Global Tel Link (GTL) contracted with the North Carolina Division of Adult Corrections (NCDAC) to provide phone services to every cellblock of every facility. By 2016 they reached Central Prison's death row. Before the phones' arrival, if one didn't write letters or get visits, a single collect call around Christmas was the only other way to connect to the outside world.

GTL—which was, and is, the defendant in numerous individual and class action lawsuits for its aggressively opportunistic and predatory business practices, including improperly retaining money that was deposited in accounts after they went inactive for a short period of time—was the first to meaningfully connect incarcerated people with their friends and family.

For a fee.

By 2019 GTL—which rebranded itself ViaPath Technologies in 2022—reported revenues of $318 million for services provided to nearly two thousand prisons and jails in all fifty states.

As beneficial as access to a phone is to the incarcerated population in spite of the fees, it also meant something else for prison officials: a new, amplified way to gather information from prisoners, and anyone communicating with them. No longer did penal servitude stop at the gates of a prison. Now, it invaded the home, car, workplace, town, state, and country of anyone daring to accept a call from the inside. Through GTL, the carceral state received limitless access to the private lives of law-abiding citizens.

For us, reacclimating to a telephone seemed a silly thing at first. Who forgets how to use a phone? But after going without one for years, the rules of conversation, delay between lines, and fifteen-minute time limit for each call made communication discouraging for some. A number of older guys refused to use the phone. I stumbled and tripped over words while speaking to my parents. Even though an automated warning announced every call would be monitored and recorded, the prerecorded message soon became background noise when it came to talking with my family.

Considering the frustration and despair caused by the pandemic and understaffing, the June 2020 memo announcing the New Prisons Technology Project was a welcome distraction. "From the tablets," it read, "you will be able to make phone calls and enjoy a variety of programs and activities, such as health-focused offerings, self-help programs, and re-entry related programming, to name a few."

These programs were especially tantalizing given that in 1994, the national Violent Crime Control and Law Enforcement Act stripped most prisons of educational programming and incentives for good behavior. What was referred to as the "no frills" prison experience was really the human warehousing of many bored, frustrated, and dehumanized people with nothing but time.

The new memo about the tablets boasted video visits, a comprehensive education package that met "state standards," and a law library that had been absent from North Carolina prisons since the 1970s. Still, despite knowing the state has never been a benevolent caretaker, everyone immediately spun elaborate fantasies about movies, TV shows, music, and games. Conspiracy theories spawned rumors and misinformation, twisting talk of the tablets with dystopian cynicism.

The New Prisons Technology Project hung like a giant carrot dangling from the perpetual stick that is life in prison. Most understood the tablets as incentives for good behavior in a system devoid of them—and, of course, as a money-making scheme for prison profiteers. But many who read the memo overlooked the primary purpose of the new technology: an extension of the state's surveillance.

Screens that watch you back

As helpful as increased communication with the outside world seemed, it also allowed prison officials to monitor, record, and gather more data on incarcerated people, and their families and friends. While the impact of that access was not always apparent, there were obvious cautionary tales. In early 2020, a prison administrator testified at the bond hearing of a man whose conviction and sentence were vacated and who awaited retrial. Using the transcript of a phone conversation between the defendant and a codefendant who turned state's witness, the Central Prison administrator helped to get the bond denied without her testimony being considered "hearsay evidence." When clips of the administrator's testimony aired on WNCN Channel 17 news at noon, it was a chilling reminder that the only private conversation in prison is the one you don't have.

Prison is fundamentally about incapacitation, punishment, control, and surveillance. Penal philosopher Michel Foucault held that in addition to surveillance, prisons should be considered places for the formation of "clinical knowledge" about the incarcerated, both in behavior and the "deeper state of mind."[2]

Advances in technology increase the body of knowledge prison officials build by seamlessly integrating surveillance with the ordinary course of life—and making prisoners dependent on technology in the process. This in turn allows law enforcement to collect information on ordinary people who unknowingly surrender their right to privacy by communicating with a prisoner—be it by mail or by tablet.

North Carolina prisons saw a marked increase in the use of technology after five prison guards were killed in 2017 (see chapter 15). The increased violence, national coverage, and assumed causes revealed systemic dysfunction that embarrassed lawmakers. The Governor's Crime Control Commission hired Duke University's Sanford School of Public Policy to study the penal system's problems. From this study came a staffing and security report containing recommendations for nine urgent improvements in personnel, organizational culture, and facility safety.

All of their suggestions advanced the use of technology in North Carolina prisons; from social media "good news stories" that drew attention away from the violence to infomercials about career opportunities to infrared scanners on perimeter fences and cell phone interdiction tech. The seventh recommendation, in particular, would more closely identify the penal system as a law enforcement entity by sharing information with the State Bureau of Investigation, the Federal Bureau of Investigation, Immigration and Customs Enforcement, and local police through an "intelligence management system," citing similar models in Pennsylvania and Tennessee, which they say have "allowed for more comprehensive investigations that expand beyond the prison walls to reduce crime both in prison and the surrounding area."[3]

After the publication of the staffing and security report, the Legislative Oversight Committee on Prisons with the Department of Public Safety (NCDPS) created the Prison Reform Advisory Board to advise the NCDPS on policies, programs, and services that would improve prison safety and security. Chaired by retired Major General of the US Army Beth Austin, and composed of current and former high-level prison officials, one discussion from a June 19, 2018, board meeting is especially telling.

One board member asked what the current "largest" drug problem is in North Carolina prisons. Another member replied that "synthetic cannabinoids" like K2 and spice—which are legally sold online and in tobacco shops—are especially problematic, because they are cheap and do not show up on traditional urine screens.

The meeting's minutes continue: "Mr. Mohr asked what intelligence gathering strategies are used inside the prison system. Ms. Sutton replied that phone calls, informants, and letters sent to offenders are used. Ms. Sutton stated that facilities use local law enforcement officials to assist with criminal investigations and they work with the department's Special Operations Intelligence Section."[4]

After the Prison Reform Advisory Board submitted its findings and Todd Ishee, a former warden from Ohio's penal system, was hired as commissioner of North Carolina prisons, the next phase of the intelligence-gathering operation began. It would quickly exacerbate the dysfunction in North Carolina prisons.

Digitized and sanitized

Piloted in women's prisons in February 2020, TextBehind is another predatory profiteer like JPAY that receives, scans, and sends digital files of personal mail to North Carolina, Wyoming, Colorado, Arkansas, Pennsylvania, and West Virginia penal systems. More states could follow.

Physical mail sent to TextBehind's Phoenix, Maryland, P.O. Box is digitized and sanitized. No more scented letters or tear-stained notes from girlfriends or wives. No more four-by-six photos of siblings that remind us of a time when the whole family was together.

I had a small pop-up card collection that became my Christmas decorations. Each year, I received a new one and exchanged it with one of the old ones. When I told my mom about the switch to scanned mail, she said, "They've taken everything from us." What remained was a grainy copy of whatever was sent, several weeks after the fact, if it ever arrived at all. Physical mail became more uncertain and undependable, requiring certified or tracked letters just to be sure TextBehind could not claim they never received it.

Some states, like Florida, make prisoners pay for a paper copy of their own mail. While this does not include letters from attorneys and court documents or books and periodicals mailed from a vendor like Amazon, fewer people receive scanned mail, because either it is lost in this convoluted transit or people on the outside have no desire to relinquish their privacy to the carceral state.

Commissioner of Prisons Todd Ishee claims TextBehind is needed in North Carolina prisons to screen out contraband, especially liquid cannabinoids sprayed on paper.

However, according to the US Department of Justice, prison staff are the primary source of drugs, cell phones, and other contraband entering prison. The Federal Bureau of Prisons and the state of Pennsylvania, the latter of which uses TextBehind, found that once they began scanning mail through an intermediary, drug positivity rates in prisons actually increased.[5]

Ironically enough, the North Carolina Prison Reform Advisory Board admitted at its meetings that prison staff are the primary source of contraband in North Carolina prisons too. If prison staff are the cause of the drug problem, then the switch to TextBehind was always about creating an easily accessible digital file for the Special Operations Intelligence Section and law enforcement.

Virtually identical to TextBehind, competitor MailGuard, of Florida-based Smart Communications, has "a smart tracker" surveillance system that gives officials a cache of intelligence into the public sender: home addresses, IP addresses, email, GPS tracking names, and location of devices in use, as well as any accounts connected to them.

These programs, as Stephanie Krent of the Knight First Amendment Institute at Columbia University told the *Intercept*, "force writers to leave a lasting digital footprint of their words, even if they opted to send physical mail because they preferred greater privacy."[6]

The final phase

In 2020 when the tablets were first given to every incarcerated person at Central Prison (except those in disciplinary segregation or designated mental health segregation), a GTL sales rep/technician gave each cellblock a twenty-minute lecture on how to use them. The Android device, with its touchscreen, facial-recognition software, and security code entry system, felt alien. The digital image of my face above the glowing keyboard appeared much older than what was reflected in the steel mirror on the wall of my cell. Others gave similarly bemused or perplexed looks. Some listened to the fast-talking sales rep, struggling to absorb an entire technological world in that fast-moving moment.

No internet access. A select number of apps to be downloaded through the GTL GettingOut platform. Some of the apps, like Edovo and CypherWorx (renamed "Hope University"), were free. Most of the apps, including messaging, access to digital photos, and music, cost $0.03 a minute—a fortune for anyone without money or an income.

One older mentally ill man in a wheelchair grew frustrated and wheeled off, leaving his tablet on the table. Another watched *Jerry Springer* on the TV, the tablet forgotten in his lap. It would take most of us days to puzzle through a device that had evolved during the decades of our confinement. Eventually though, the day room stayed empty for the length of the tablet's battery life.

That was another part of the tablet's purpose: control through fascination. Distracted people are less likely to think critically about the prison system's designs or reasons for their sudden willingness to provide access to technology. The advantage of greater communication aside, self-isolating people reduced both likelihood of violent confrontation and questions about the information gathered by prison officials.

Within a few weeks of the tablets being passed out, a prisoner was violently assaulted at Central Prison. The attack was bad enough that a crime scene photographer was brought in. As a result, the facility went into a series of lockdowns made worse by familiar structural problems like power outages and understaffing. Now, there was even more frustration when the Wi-Fi signal grew weak or inconsistent.

Sometimes the new technology worked. Sometimes it didn't.

When the GTL sales rep tried to convince leery incarcerated people that we needed the tablets, it was the same pitch used by every prison profiteer to date: a modernized, streamlined incarceration experience. Technology is touted as a privilege in prison, but it's a superficial fix— one that's both monetized and monitored at every turn—replete with the same dysfunction, violence, and other subterfuge that always hides what really happens in prison.

Interview with Kathy Williams

March 17, 2022

Kathy Williams is an instructor of the dramatic arts at the University of North Carolina at Chapel Hill, associate director of North Carolina PlayMakers Repertory Company, and associate director of the nonprofit organization Hidden Voices, which amplifies marginalized voices through artistic mediums. As a function of Hidden Voices, Kathy directed *Serving Life*, a play cowritten by director Lynden Harris and six men on North Carolina's death row, and helped the incarcerated writers bring their work to life. *Serving Life* was performed on death row for hundreds of staff and prisoners, changing the way an entire prison population perceived people sentenced to death. *Serving Life* would go on to be rewritten and renamed *Count*, which was performed by the NC PlayMakers Repertory Company for the general public.

Lyle May (LM): Do you believe your work is activism?

Kathy Williams (KW): I've always looked at my work in theater as activism. Mainly, through my work with kids and y'all. Just me being in a play is an act of activism.

LM: How did you get involved in activism?

KW: I'm a child of the sixties. My parents were both journalists, so we grew up informed. We went to protests. Politics were always discussed around the table because Dad covered DC politics. They told us, "You have a responsibility to be part of this world. You do that by getting involved in it." My activism became theater pretty early on.

LM: How can the average citizen, without any experience, get involved in their community and maybe even disrupt the school-to-prison pipeline?

KW: Get involved with public schools. Pre-K and early childhood development are so important. Something as simple as reading to children. We need more programs for postbirth through sixth-grade children. Also, stay involved with school policy. You should know things like testing score averages in reading and math, and find out why kids are falling behind. The best approach is to treat every child as if they were your child, your brother, your sister, and want the best for them.

LM: How do you think technology has improved today's activism and organizing?

KW: It's definitely made it easier, but it's also gotten easier to create echo chambers on social media. It's critical to get people to understand they have the power to change things, but [it's] also necessary they realize that goal by communicating and working together.

LM: Are strikes and demonstrations still effective?

KW: Yes, absolutely, but in today's world we must harness the power of social media in a way that drives strikes and protests. If we do that, then people come out like they did in the middle of a pandemic to protest the murder of George Floyd. This is how we make more lasting and impactful changes.

LM: What is the greatest threat to activism around social justice issues?

KW: Misinformation is our greatest challenge. People have to decide if they want to be together or divided. As the old spiritual goes, "Which side are you on, my brother?" You must live and speak your truth, but have the courage to listen to, and love, those who insult or hate you.

LM: In recent years more companies—big brand providers of goods and services in the US and around the world—have engaged in activism when state and federal officials fail in their moral and social obligations to the citizenry. Do you think this strategy has longevity, and can it be turned against the prison-industrial complex?

KW: Companies that speak out or withdraw their services do it from an executive level, and this doesn't require any individual sacrifice. From the top-down it's more of an investment analysis of costs versus benefits. From the bottom up it's harder to give up creature comforts. If people who buy a given company's products are willing to boycott that company as a result of its policies or because they think the company should be more socially engaged—this can work. Really, if people just got their shit together, we could vote out more problematic officials and not need to rely on any of these companies. People are too often conditioned to believe it's hopeless, that voting doesn't matter, when it really, really does.

Interview with
Tessie Castillo

March 12, 2022

Tessie Castillo is a former lobbyist for the North Carolina Harm Reduction Coalition (NCHRC), a nonprofit organization that pursues legislative change helpful to marginalized people, including sex workers, formerly incarcerated people, and the homeless. While transitioning out of NCHRC, Tessie began volunteering at Central Prison's death row, teaching journaling to a number of the men there. Surprised by the humanity she discovered, Tessie submitted an op-ed about her experience to the Raleigh *News & Observer*. When the op-ed was published, Tessie was fired from her volunteer job. She would go on to collect essays from four men in her journaling classes and create *Crimson Letters: Voices from Death Row*, published by Black Rose Writing in 2020, later renamed and released with new material under the title *Inside: Voices from Death Row*, by Scuppernong Books in the fall of 2022.

Lyle May (LM): How did you get involved in activism?

Tessie Castillo (TC): I came from a conservative background, one that taught that people who became involved in the criminal justice system "deserve it," and the justice system is always right and fair. I would

164

eventually discover, both through my work with the Harm Reduction Coalition [HRC] and volunteering at Central, that is not true. The criminal justice system is wrong all the time and some people can't help becoming part of the system because they are unfairly targeted and treated because of their race, mental health, and class.

LM: How did you become a lobbyist?

TC: When I worked for the HRC it was part of the job. I didn't have any training in lobbying. I just had to go and knock on doors and explain to lawmakers why they should support a particular bill.

LM: Were you successful at doing that without the money of a political action committee behind you?

TC: Yes. It takes a lot of hard work and persistence. A lot of patience. But we managed to get the 911 Good Samaritan Law passed, which allows citizens to call emergency services for people who overdosed without fearing arrest or criminal prosecution. I also helped pass a needle exchange bill, which enables addicts to acquire clean needles in exchange for used ones to reduce the risk of infectious disease and hazardous waste.

LM: Were there any losses that made your work more difficult?

TC: Yes. We fought and lost against the death by distribution law, which allows prosecutors to charge someone with murder if they provide another [person] with drugs that result in overdose and death. We fought to pass a Ban-the-Box bill, to make it easier for people with felony convictions to at least make it past the job application stage when searching for employment, but we lost this too. These losses seemed to negate the ground we made with the previous bills. It was discouraging, but I know there are people who are alive because of the work we did.

LM: How can the average citizen become an activist?

TC: Get involved with local elections: [district attorneys], sheriffs, judges, state representatives, county commissioners, and school boards. Everyone has the ability to be an activist through the simple act of voting, both in the primaries and main elections.

LM: Is there anything you would do differently from your initial foray into community activism?

TC: Yes. I would make sure the people I was advocating for actually wanted the help. It's really important [for] people who advocate for others do so in coordination with those in need, not from some paternal relationship or because they think their social status gives them special authority. This is especially important for white people to remember. Those in need of help or representation need to signal as much or lead the process. There are a lot of well-meaning activists who don't bother to ask what a person or group actually needs or wants. They come into a situation and proffer help where sometimes it is overbearing or misguided. Activism is a collaborative effort.

PART IV

WITNESS

ADVOCACY AND ABOLITION

Chapter 22

Science vs. Anti-Intellectualism and the Death Penalty

The federal execution of Brandon Bernard on December 10, 2020, was yet another manifestation of anti-intellectual populism masquerading as law and order. Brandon's execution after twenty-one years of incarceration exemplifies all that is wrong with the criminal legal system and those who contribute to its misguided, often unjust, application. The crux of the conundrum that is mass incarceration, the overwhelming problem, is that criminal justice policy is governed by political posturing and hate-mongering, rather than experts who rely on data-driven research and evidence-based facts. Capital punishment is a microcosm of the problem.

Brandon was eighteen years old in 1999 when he participated in a robbery that resulted in the deaths of Todd and Stacie Bagley. Though he was not the shooter, Bernard was convicted of murder and sentenced to death a year after the murder. The nineteen-year-old shooter, Christopher Vialva, was put to death in September 2020. The three remaining codefendants were under eighteen years of age at the time of the crime and received reduced sentences. All five teenagers were Black.

In Bernard's case, the federal prosecutor could just as easily have charged him with second-degree murder and robbery. No public backlash would have come of it. In proceedings like this, the desires of the victims' family members only matter when it is convenient. Even if someone protested the mercy, federal prosecutors are appointed, not elected. They are also *never* held accountable for abuses of power and overcharging, let alone consideration of a teenager's capacity for rehabilitation in prison. While the lack of independent oversight of a prosecutor's charging decisions is nothing new—they are the gatekeepers of the carceral state—this aspect of the law also serves as a distraction from other important facts.

At the time Bernard and Vialva were tried, not enough neuroscientific research had been done around adolescent brain development to help them, or the other tens of thousands like them. But that changed over the next five years. The US Supreme court, informed by a groundswell of scientific evidence and an evolving standard of decency, ruled that the death penalty is unconstitutional for defendants under eighteen years of age at the time of an offense. In *Roper v. Simmons* (2005), the court found that juveniles:

1. Lack maturity, impulse control, and adequate risk-benefit assessment skills
2. Are susceptible to peer pressure and emotional influence, which exacerbates immaturity when in groups or under stressful conditions
3. Lack fully developed character due to the neuroplasticity of the adolescent brain, meaning they have a better chance at rehabilitation than do adults because they are still growing

Using the same science from *Roper*, the court prohibited mandatory life without parole sentences for juveniles in *Miller v. Alabama* (2012), and then retroactively banned them in *Montgomery v. Louisiana* (2016).

In the years since the rulings, research in the cognitive development of adolescents between the ages of eighteen and twenty-one consistently demonstrates impulsivity, immaturity, poor decision-making, and neuroplasticity of the brain similar to the functionality of sixteen- and seventeen-year-olds.[1]

In other words, neuroscientists—not partisan elected officials or other laypersons—have shown, through peer-reviewed studies and

FMRI scans, that the adolescent brain continues to develop beyond the arbitrary age of eighteen and well into one's early twenties, thereby reducing criminal culpability. Signaling its support of this finding, in 2018 the American Bar Association (ABA) resolved that jurisdictions imposing capital punishment should "prohibit the imposition of a death sentence on or execution of any individual who was 21 years old or younger at the time of the offense."[2]

But the conservative US Supreme Court ignored the ABA resolution and other mounting scientific evidence supporting it. Much like the conservative justices who *dissented* in *Roper v. Simmons* (2005), *Miller v. Alabama* (2012), and *Montgomery v. Louisiana* (2016), the court declined to intervene and stop Bernard and Vialva's executions. Science is progress and the conservative court opposes it.

As with most sensationalized crimes that trigger the revenge-punishment reflex, there was no concern over the influence of race, socioeconomic status, geographic location, ineffective trial and appellate attorneys, or politics of the moment on Vialva and Bernard's sentences. These factors have everything to do with their deaths and the disproportionate number of African Americans on death row, which is partly why capital punishment was declared unconstitutional in *Furman v. Georgia* (1972), and why it should be abolished by Congress today.

The main argument maintaining the use of the death penalty is a myth. The deterrence effect of execution has long been discredited by southern states with active execution chambers and high murder rates. Meanwhile, states that abolished the death penalty, like New York, have seen declines in murder rates, and states without a death penalty maintain lower murder rates. Rarely is murder as premeditated and deliberate as prosecutors mislead juries to believe—most murders are the result of impulsive overreactions to an emotional state, or a product of mental illness. Such circumstances warrant treatment, not death.

The crimes committed by Bernard, Vialva, and the other codefendants should have been punished. But the long-term capacity of Bernard and Vialva to live with the harm caused to the victims, their families, and the community was squandered for the sake of anti-intellectualist votes. Bernard and Vialva's families have now been victimized. Lost is any healing and accountability that could have come through restorative justice. Gone is their potential to learn from this tragedy and one day become contributing members of society. Millions more languish in prison because society stubbornly resists what it knows to be right, but it doesn't have to be this way. We need only follow the science.

Chapter 23

Protesting Death[*]

 The Digital Abolitionist
@TDAbolitionist

The insurrection at our Nation's Capital & the president's responsibility makes pursuing the execution of #LisaMontgomery on 1/12 a vulgar display of power. Our nation needs reconciliation & restoration. Let it begin with a commutation of Lisa's sentence. -Lyle May, NC death row

5:37 PM · Jan 7, 2021 · Twitter Web App

ılı View Tweet activity

24 Retweets **6** Quote Tweets **39** Likes

---

* My friends at the Digital Abolitionist offered to amplify my comments on the criminal legal system after discovering one of my articles on Inside Higher Ed. At the height of the 2020/2021 election madness, when then-president Donald Trump and attorney general Bill Barr carried out twelve federal executions, I wanted to speak out. The TDA provided their Twitter platform and what follows is that feed.

THREAD: Lyle May, incarcerated on North Carolina's death row, offers his perspective on incarceration, mental illness, and the impending execution of #LisaMontgomery (all content from Lyle is relayed via authorized phone calls)

   💬 2   🔁 40   ♡ 41   ⬆   ᔕ

The Digital Abolitionist @TDAbolitionist · Jan 8   ···
"Over 1/2 of all federal & state death row prisoners suffer from mental illness. At least 20% from severe debilitating psychotic or anxiety disorders. #LisaMontgomery is such a person, and her execution would violate the 8th Amendment's prohibition of cruel & unusual punishment"

   💬 1   🔁 6   ♡ 10   ⬆   ᔕ

The Digital Abolitionist @TDAbolitionist · Jan 8   ···
"For people who commit crimes in the grips of mental illness, treatment is needed, not death. Commute Lisa Montgomery's death sentence." #SaveLisa

   💬 2   🔁 3   ♡ 7   ⬆   ᔕ

The Digital Abolitionist @TDAbolitionist · Jan 8   ···
"If we as a nation are pivoting the criminal legal system away from the prosecution of drug offenses and instead promoting greater use of treatment programs, that focus should extend to the mentally ill, who account for the greatest number of death and life sentences." #SaveLisa

   💬 1   🔁 6   ♡ 10   ⬆   ᔕ

The Digital Abolitionist @TDAbolitionist · Jan 8   ···
"Punishing mental illness is cruel & all too usual. It's a major link in the chains of mass incarceration. Diagnosis of the Carceral Crisis begins with a recognition mentally ill people who commit crimes have less culpability. Treatment means rehabilitation" #AbolitionNow

   💬 1   🔁 1   ♡ 6   ⬆   ᔕ

The Digital Abolitionist @TDAbolitionist · Jan 8   ···
Read Lyle's writing for @scalawagmag here:

The Digital Abolitionist
@TDAbolitionist   ...

"Lisa Montgomery's pending execution is an extension of anti-intellectualist populism. The type of might makes right rage-based extremism that ignores science & morality, attempts coups at the Capitol, & completely disregards public safety" -Lyle May, NC death row #SaveLisa

9:26 AM · Jan 11, 2021 · Twitter Web App

ılı View Tweet activity

6 Retweets   **12** Likes

Chapter 24

Inside the Tinder Box

COVID-19 in Prison

In the beginning, we joked about zombies and the Apocalypse when cruise ships contaminated with the coronavirus first found reluctant harbors. But as the virus spread through Washington and New York, daily White House briefings displaced talk of Democratic primaries, and news broadcasts grew ominous, a corrections officer made an announcement on every cellblock: "Gentlemen, listen up. Effective immediately, all personal visits and volunteer-based programs are suspended for the next thirty days. Legal and clergy visits will continue. These restrictions will be assessed after that thirty-day period."

He left a thick stack of stapled papers on the table, a surprising amount of information for a bulletin board usually littered with one-paragraph memos. There were memos to prisoners, wardens, and staff, screening procedures for entering the prison, and a COVID-19 daily briefing with a list of active coronavirus investigations within the state prison. But these safety measures, which also included mandatory cloth masks for prisoners, increased access to cleaning supplies, social-distancing requirements, and disinfectant fans, reassured no one. Before the pandemic, prisons were already overcrowded—staff undermanned, overworked, underpaid, and undertrained—and prison health care was spotty. COVID-19 exploited each of these weaknesses, and North Carolina then faced an additional hurdle of its own making: the abolition of parole, implemented in the Structured Sentencing Act of 1994. Without parole, prisons have few means to reduce prison populations, thereby increasing the risk of infection and transmission of COVID-19.

To be clear, even if North Carolina had a robust parole system, there was never any assurance of safety in the pandemic. Vivid CDC hand-washing signs appeared on random walls throughout CP, right beside older posters warning against the spread of staph infection, hepatitis, and influenza. New handwashing signs instructing us to "wet, soap, scrub, rinse, dry: repeat" were undermined by actual practices. Though the commissioner of prisons assured the public we would be issued two bars of soap each week, claiming this as a safety measure was laugh-able—most state prisoners have received two bars of soap every week for decades, and it hasn't prevented the spread of anything.

Unsanitary conditions in prison are common. Every area is a "high-traffic area" due to overcrowding, and chow halls and kitchens—where flies circle during the day and rats feed at night—are the worst. COVID-19 could find welcome on every filthy surface and be tracked throughout the prison, even if it was locked down. Sanitation and virus prevention have never been security concerns any more than the health and well-being of people in prison.

The NCDAC and CDC guidelines for preventing the spread of COVID-19 also said to "avoid contact with people" and to "stay home if you are sick," but minimum- and medium-custody facilities account for most of North Carolina's prisons. Living spaces are open dormitories of fifty or more people sharing toilets, sinks, and showers. Each bunk is three to four feet to the left, right, above, and below another bunk.

Even on death row, where a block contains only twenty-four sin-gle cells, viruses spread quickly. A month before COVID-19 struck the United States, a vicious strain of influenza swept through CP. Despite annual flu shots, and masks issued to any prisoner who asked, many peo-ple became sick. Prisoners who reported symptoms were tested for the flu and, if positive, quarantined via solitary confinement—no TV, radio, phone, personal property, or showers. During the flu outbreak, seven death row prisoners were quarantined on the mental health unit because the hospital had no room for them. Nurses routinely ignored calls for help and questions about medication, inconsistently checked on patients, and generally acted indifferent toward their welfare.

According to several staff, CP's hospital had no ventilators and only a handful of respirators. At the height of the pandemic, ventilators were already in short supply in the free world. The additional layer of apathetic prison hospital staff and their power to decide whether or not a patient went to an outside hospital, meant that prisoners with COVID-19 died in confinement. Given the choice between degrading and inadequate medical care in the hole or suffering in silence, many prisoners will choose the latter. As such, the coronavirus spread.

Elderly prisoners represent one of the fastest-growing segments of people in prison, largely due to the excessive long-term life sentences enforced in the 1990s. According to research of the Department of Public Safety's Research and Planning Automated System Query, among the approximately thirty-five thousand people incarcerated in North Carolina, more than eight thousand are over the age of fifty.[1] Prisoners are classified as "elderly" by the age of fifty because of both preexisting health problems and those that develop while incarcerated.[2] COVID- 19 is especially dangerous for people with asthma, autoimmune disorders, diabetes, heart disease, and hypertension. Such men and women compose a substantial portion of the prison population.

In late March 2020 at Neuse Correctional in Goldsboro, North Carolina, two prisoners reported symptoms of a virus, were quarantined and tested for COVID-19. When the results came back positive, prison officials ordered a facility lockdown—restricting movement and confining prisoners to the dorms. Fearing contagion, over two hundred prisoners staged a protest. It took local law enforcement to help restore "order." Three weeks later, over 460 of Neuse Correctional's 770 prisoners tested positive for coronavirus, one of the largest prison outbreaks in the nation, and the only state prison to have all of its inhabitants tested. Most were asymptomatic, but still contagious.[3]

Despite promises to halt all county jail and interprison transfers, state prison officials shipped the thirty-six "ringleaders" of the Neuse protest nearly 150 miles east to Pasquotank Correctional, a maximum-security prison near Elizabeth City. The wife of one correctional officer at Pasquotank, which reported several positive COVID-19 cases among the newly arrived Neuse prisoners, asked, "Why bring inmates that were exposed to [coronavirus] to a prison that didn't have any?"[4]

Similarly, six people at Johnston Correctional near Smithfield tested positive for COVID-19 in mid-April. Though three prisoners were quarantined, and three staff sent home, no one else was tested. State prison officials claimed they did not have the budget to test every prisoner, but while staff received testing upon request, only symptomatic prisoners were tested. A week after the positive COVID-19 cases at Johnston Correctional, prison officials closed the facility, sent its employees to help out at Neuse, and transferred six hundred prisoners to two western North Carolina prisons.

By late April, nine of North Carolina's fifty-five prisons had confirmed coronavirus cases, including CP, the Correctional Institute for Women in Raleigh, and Butner Federal Correctional Institution (FCI).

Around the same time as the Neuse outbreak, FCI had already reported seventy-six cases of COVID-19. Fearing for his life, Richard Cephas escaped from a minimum-security building. The fifty-four-year-old, who was incarcerated for a nonviolent drug offense, had about eighteen months left on a five-and-a-half-year sentence, but has neutropenia, an autoimmune disease. Cephas applied for the Federal Bureau of Prisons home confinement program, which has released a little over 1,000 of the 175,000 federal prisoners at the time, but was denied.[5] After turning himself in, Cephas received an additional eighteen months added to his sentence for his escape, and returned to Butner FCI, where eighteen prisoners have now died from COVID-19, in addition to twenty others across other federal facilities. The majority had underlying health conditions.

There are too many people in prison, evidenced by insufficient space, correctional staff, medical resources, and funding for programs. In acknowledgment of prison overcrowding and the danger it represents, especially during the coronavirus pandemic, public health experts at Duke University and the University of North Carolina at Chapel Hill pushed for an immediate reduction in North Carolina's incarcerated population. In early April, Dr. Gavin Yamey, director of the Center for Policy Impact in Global Health at Duke, wrote and asked Governor Roy Cooper to commute sentences for elderly medically vulnerable prisoners, or those who have less than a year remaining on their sentences. "We have an on-going campaign with statewide administrations through multiple channels to try to make the case that jails, prisons, ICE detention centers, [and] juvenile correctional facilities are all tinderboxes when it comes to COVID-19."

Likewise, in a letter to Durham County District Attorney Satana Deberry, Durham Congregations, Associations, and Neighborhoods (Durham CAN) asked Deberry to consider sentencing relief for some eight hundred prisoners whose cases originated in Durham County. "Criteria could include, but not be limited to, individuals who are 65 or older, individuals who have served three-quarters of their sentence, or individuals serving sentences for low level felonies or probation/post-release supervision violations."

In mid-April, a coalition of civil rights groups filed a lawsuit asking the State Supreme Court to immediately release vulnerable prisoners. They argued that Governor Cooper and the Department of Public Safety (NCDPS) had "a legal duty to take action before large-scale outbreak results and deaths inside the prisons in and surrounding communities."

Responding to the demand for release of more prisoners, the NCDAC allowed only five hundred men and women with 2020 release dates to serve the remainder of their sentences at home under community supervision. The effort to minimize public and legislative backlash by releasing only pregnant women and select elderly prisoners was a disingenuous and potentially deadly game: between January and April of 2020, 6,900 incarcerated people earned release by completing their sentences.

The NCDAC could do more to reduce overcrowding in state prisons, thereby reducing the risk of coronavirus spread and strain on penal resources. However, resistance to such common-sense safety measures remains strong. It comes from the same quarters that created and supported the Structured Sentencing Act without any long-range vision for how it would overburden state prisons. It abolished parole without any data showing that early release is contrary to public safety or that longer prison terms improve it. The threat to public safety has always been indifference towards the incarcerated.

People in prison do not lose all their rights and are constitutionally entitled to a certain level of dignified care. When the penal system is no longer capable of maintaining its responsibilities because there are too many people in prison, it is time to reinstate parole for all the incarcerated, and close some prisons.

Chapter 25

When the Thermometer Breaks

In 2020 reporting from the Raleigh *News & Observer* on COVID-19 in North Carolina prisons seemed to keep apace with the growing number of positive cases and in-custody deaths. From the initial cases at Butner Federal Correctional Institution, newspaper coverage relied on North Carolina Department of Public Safety (NCDPS) data. Over-the-phone interviews with prisoners and their advocates described unsanitary conditions, overcrowding that mocked social-distancing orders, confused responses by medical and custody staff, and a lot of sick people living among the others already in poor health. These experiences refute the NCDPS narrative of control, as did the constantly rising number of COVID cases and deaths around the country. This dissonance between the numbers and the facts also casts suspicion on the state's reported in-custody deaths and medical care in prison.

Prior to the coronavirus pandemic, North Carolina's penal system was in a fragile rebuild. Investigative reporting by the *News & Observer* uncovered rampant corruption, severe understaffing, incompetent leadership, and underreported in-custody deaths. While Republican legislators had finally been prompted to action following the death of five correctional officers in 2017 (one at Bertie and four at Pasquotank correctional facilitites), their primary motivator was the perception of increased danger to prison staff. The North Carolina Prison Reform Advisory Board recommended numerous new safety and security protocols, which the commissioner of prisons began implementing in 2019, but none of these changes addressed conditions of confinement.

Then, COVID-19 struck.

A pandemic raises the standard of acceptable decisions by governments and their agencies. Effective leaders are troubleshooters who provide as much safety and security as is reasonable under the circumstances. Those unable to meet that standard of leadership fail in their duty of care. Such failures cost lives.

Interprison transfers increase the risk of spreading COVID from prisons that are experiencing outbreaks to those that are not. Between April 12 and May 25, 2020, over 1,100 NC prisoners were transported both from jails to prisons and between prisons. State officials claimed these transfers were necessary, but had been reduced. Prior to the pandemic the same number of prisoners were transported every week. Despite rising numbers of positive cases and COVID deaths around the state, between May 26 and June 12, 2020, prison officials transported an additional 2,600 prisoners.

Shortly after that, the American Civil Liberties Union (ACLU) and other NC civil rights groups filed a lawsuit to halt jail and prison transfers. Shifting untested, potentially COVID-positive populations endangered prisoners, staff, and the community. Wake County Superior Court Judge Vinston Rozier Jr. agreed, saying that the state "failed in its duty to care" and that NC prison conditions are "likely unconstitutional."

Despite the multiple outbreaks in NC prisons some officials refused to acknowledge the seriousness of the pandemic. Shortly after prison spokesman John Bull said NCDPS officials were not "aware of any confirmed, active cases of COVID-19" at the North Carolina Correctional Institution for Women, the facility was confirmed to have over one hundred positive cases of COVID, and at least one death, sixty-seven-year-old Faye Brown. The women in the minimum-security "Canary Unit" where Faye died continued to leave the prison during the pandemic to clean NCDPS offices—like those of John Bull, Commissioner of Prisons Todd Ishee, and NCDPS Secretary Erik Hooks.

To underscore the state's casual disregard for incarcerated people, in an email to one prisoner's lawyer an NCDPS representative said the agency "is not in a position to permit COVID-19 concerns to prevent it from fully utilizing available space at operational facilities." The prisoner involved tried to stop his transfer to Neuse Correctional, which had 460 positive cases and two deaths as of July 2020. Afterward, Judge Rozier stopped interprison transfers and ordered the state to test its 32,000 prisoners.

On the surface, journalists tracked the progression of the pandemic in North Carolina prisons and kept officials under constant scrutiny. However, that oversight is only as accurate as the COVID statistics provided by the NCDPS. Accurate numbers helped health experts fight the pandemic. Underreporting positivity and death rates helps no one. If state officials wanted to appear more competent and in control than they are, tailoring statistics is one way. Claiming the virus will just "go away" or "disappear" is another. Considering recent efforts by the Republican-controlled NC General Assembly to pass a bill that blocks public access to medical examiners' reports on in-custody deaths, suspicion is warranted.

According to NCDPS.gov in July 2020, testing showed a 2.1 percent positivity rate—one of the lowest in the country. Over 29,000 prisoners were tested, with 619 positive results, who were then placed in isolation. Seventeen prisoners had died of COVID while in custody, though there had been no running tally and this number had to be parsed from the headlines.

Overall, the NCDPS website paints a rosy, competent, "we're rounding the corner" picture. It helpfully compares positivity rates from New Jersey, Tennessee, Michigan, and Texas prison systems—all of which are many times higher than North Carolina. Maybe this was accurate and not an example of extreme comparisons meant to make state officials look good. Maybe, after years of constant mismanagement, NC prisons are now carefully controlled and disease resistant. Maybe my perspective is cynical, and it doesn't take two weeks for a nurse to respond to a sick call request. Perhaps prisoners are generally healthy, and we receive stellar medical care.

Contrary to NCDPS reports, COVID-19 was spreading unchecked in NC prisons. The pandemic did not solve understaffing, poor training, or violence—it just made all these things easier to hide with too many people suffering in the free world to question prison officials. Ignoring reality with false optimism and disinformation does not change the facts.

NC prisoners are suffering, but not just from COVID-19. Punitive measures masquerade as "safety protocols." Where most medical appointments occurred at prison hospitals and infirmaries, now only emergency care is provided. Among an aging population that requires attention to underlying illnesses, this has meant more emergency trips to outside hospitals. Each trip requires two to three guards per prisoner escort. According to one guard I spoke with in the last week of October 2020, twenty-five prisoners—a tenfold increase—needed emergency care. Only one was for COVID-19. In an understaffed facility on COVID lockdown, new protocols meant no programs or visits, poorer quality and smaller quantity of food, and reduced outside recreation. And as frustrations mounted, so did assaults on staff and prisoners. CP is just one of fifty-five NC prisons. But these things no longer make the news, nor are they mentioned on NCDPS.gov. Instead, just a 2.1 percent positivity rate. Somebody better check the thermometer because it needs to be replaced.

As of March 15, 2020, the ACLU and plaintiffs of the civil suit before Superior Court Judge Vincent Rozier Jr., settled for the early release of 3,500 prisoners from North Carolina facilities over a period of six months. More than 9,800 prisoners had tested positive since the beginning of the coronavirus pandemic; fifty died.

Chapter 26

Thank You for Your Service

Punishment and Disposability

The fallen and military veterans deserve honor and respect in our society, especially those who do not escape the horrors of war unscathed. Over the last thirty years there has been an increased awareness and treatment of mental health issues among soldiers returning from combat. Post-traumatic stress disorder (PTSD), initially a buzzword thought of as a weakness by military commanders, is now a recognized but treatable problem. Yet many veterans do not receive the necessary help or even recognition for their service despite these unseen injuries.

The dysfunction created by the deinstitutionalization of the mental health system is apparent in Veterans Affairs (VA) hospitals. Notoriously mismanaged, underfunded, and backlogged, the VA has always struggled to treat troops and veterans for PTSD and other mental illnesses through outpatient treatment centers. This is especially true of soldiers, sailors, and airmen from the Vietnam era forced to "tough it out" on their own, despite the prevalence of PTSD.

Over 830,000 Vietnam vets experienced behavioral impairment related to PTSD symptoms. Four out of five struggled with chronic symptoms twenty to twenty-five years after the war.[1] Suicide, homelessness, and violent crime are common among vets who suffer severe PTSD symptoms, such as flashbacks, insomnia, angry outbursts, disassociation, and other symptoms that make the adjustment to life post-trauma extremely difficult. Unable to resocialize within civilian life, some vets ultimately succumb to their mental illness.

But when violent crimes are committed as a direct result of the trauma experienced by combat veterans, the criminal justice system is unsympathetic. Retribution replaces mercy, and "Thank you for your service" becomes a meaningless platitude cast among the spent shells of a silent war . . .

Vietnam was a war without room for diagnoses in a deadly, wet environment where rats climbed the pants legs of sleeping soldiers, mosquitos fed upon exposed flesh, and the indigenous population bristled with antipathy for American troops. The distant whir of helicopters cut thick jungle air with the promise of deliverance. In Vietnam, a place where explosions of molten lead ripped through flora and fauna alike, one either lived or died on a coin flip, and young minds decayed beneath the onslaught of horrors.

James Davis joined the army to escape an abusive home. The man who claimed to be his father spoke with a leather strap and broken mop handle, cursing his children in a drunkard's slur and threatening to cut their throats while they slept. James's father went so far as to lock the freezer while at work so his children only ate by his offering. They went hungry a lot. When James turned eighteen and graduated high school, he knew joining the military would provide sustenance, housing, and escape.

James learned a lot in the army. His time at Fort Jackson, South Carolina, trained him to march, run, fight, and shoot. "If you couldn't shoot a rifle, you were out," he told me when I asked about basic training. Stories of vets who went in-country always fascinated me. "They taught us to be killers. [Vietnam] was about living and dying. Both were possible." Train to live. Live to kill. Kill to win.

James took pride in voluntarily joining the army when so many others had to be drafted. "It was a patriotic choice. The draft had already begun. It was for people who wouldn't volunteer. Mostly the poor. Later, college kids once the government suspended draft deferments. There was a lot of people angry about this. Protests on campuses happened because people were against the war, but not when the poor were drafted."

Upon his arrival in Vietnam, James was assigned to an artillery unit, where Death greeted him with a welcome grin. "When your number comes up, you die. When it doesn't, you live. Some guys got there and were shot dead on the first day. What was scary to some guys was being 'short'—getting ready to go home—and being sent out into the bush. One guy was short and went out. Raised his hand up and a sniper got him . . . We didn't think about living and dying. We couldn't. They trained you to do a job and put the rest out of your mind. Otherwise, you make mistakes that get you killed. Or you go crazy."

On his first tour James's artillery unit (six 105 mm TOWs, big crew-served howitzers) moved around frequently. When they weren't changing position to avoid enemy detection, they dug foxholes and trenches, filled tens of thousands of sandbags, and stole what little rest they could. At times, digging holes, filling sandbags, and breaking open ammo crates seemed to be all they did. That is, until they received orders to fire their weapons or took incoming enemy fire—then the smell of cordite, explosive concussions from their howitzers, and screams of the dying reminded them they were at war.

That first tour marked the best year of James's life. "Even though it was hard—the constant rain, mosquitos, heat, lack of sleep, and death—it was the best. I can't explain it any better." On second consideration, he told me, "This is one reason: it was better over there than anywhere else." James was becoming psychotic. He and others would engage in combat with the Viet Cong (VC) and North Vietnamese Army (NVA) and laugh. Their training to block it out could only go so far. After a while, the trauma of war corrupted his already damaged psyche, though James did not understand how.

At the end of his tour, James returned to North Carolina for a thirty-day leave. For a time, he haunted Shoney's Drive-In, where girls on roller skates took orders and the crooning of Elvis and Patsy Cline played from the radio of James's '61 Galaxie Starliner. As he listened, the oppressive heat and death of Vietnam a world away, James remembered how intensely alive he felt and knew he wanted to go back.

By the time James shipped to Fort Hood, Texas, he knew something was wrong with him. Loud noises startled him. He grew angry over simple things. His thoughts, disjointed and plagued with a sense of an impending attack, were fragmented. Much of his leave in the States felt alien, as if the Vietnam War was the only reality that mattered.

James's second tour nearly killed him. A chemical spill set his pants on fire, hospitalizing him for a week with second- and third-degree burns. Then came the Tet Offensive. The NVA and VC pushed ground attacks at major cities and American outposts in Vietnam, firing rockets and mortars in an attempt to soften targets. A lot of people died.

James's unit had dug in at Chu Ci firebase. "We were firing back and forth when a mortar landed behind me. It blew out several truck tires and hit me. I reached down and felt my leg was wet with blood. There were five of us [manning the 105 mm TOW] and we hurried up and took cover in a bunker. The injury burned. Hell, there was hot shrapnel in my leg!"

Ultimately, James's time in Vietnam ended with an incident as serendipitous as any in the war. Standing guard one night, he "threw a grenade down the hill out of boredom and got lucky. It was so dark you couldn't see your hand in front of your face. The next morning, they found a VC who had tried to sneak into camp, dead from a grenade. The supply sergeant said, 'Good job!' and gave me some more grenades."

Returning to Asheville, North Carolina, proved a welcome relief this time. The war had physically and mentally exhausted James. Yet his training did not prepare him for the transition back to civilian life. Now that thinking about his experiences would not get him killed, voices of soldiers and former commanders tormented his every waking moment. The thunder of artillery and chatter of machine guns echoed in his mind again and again. James tried to move on, briefly marrying a woman, but the war would not let go. He attempted suicide. While hospitalized, a VA physician diagnosed James as suffering from paranoid schizophrenia, depression, and severe PTSD.

Neighbors and coworkers who met James knew he had mental health problems, but no one seemed inclined or able to help a military veteran. Besides, soldiers returning from Vietnam were not treated with respect or lauded as heroes. This sentiment was magnified by both James's paranoia and the fact that people whispered about how he shot at imaginary groundhogs in his front yard or talked to himself. The community that should have embraced a soldier who needed help after protecting their freedoms further ostracized him.

Maybe this led to the fight at work. Another whispered conversation. A snide comment said within earshot. Whatever it was, in 1995, twenty-five years after the end of his second tour of duty in Vietnam, James got into a fight at the Asheville tool company where he worked. Fired as the instigator, James snapped. Two days later he returned to work with a semiautomatic rifle and pistol, fired about fifty shots, and killed three people.

The state of North Carolina tried and sentenced James to death for the triple murder. At trial, his public defenders failed to develop a mental health defense. James's military service came up during sentencing, but the prosecution used it to convince jurors this made the Vietnam vet *more* responsible and cognizant of what he did. In an era where yellow ribbons adorned light posts, cars, and front doors in honor of those fighting in Desert Storm, this sentiment turned to hypocrisy in the criminal justice system.

James is not alone. Approximately 15 percent of prisoners incarcerated for homicide are military veterans. Though the number varies by state, 22 of the 139 prisoners on North Carolina's death row are vets.[2] By 2004, about 16,400 veterans nationwide were serving either a life or a death sentence. The percentage of incarcerated vets who served in combat is unclear, but for those who did, PTSD, depression, anxiety, substance abuse, and other serious mental disorders are common.

Violent crimes impact everyone in a community, not just those immediately involved. Accountability is always necessary when addressing such crimes. However, often an individual's level of culpability should be balanced against restorative efforts to, where possible, repair the harm done and root out the causes of the crime. In this way, the person responsible can better understand those harms, and those harmed can begin to heal. Not everyone who experiences PTSD and schizophrenia commits violent crimes, but combat vets who decline into mental illness, experience psychotic breaks, and lack social supports are most likely to do so. When the symptoms of any mental disorder go untreated, the root cause does not disappear, but often worsens and finds a violent outlet.

Not until 2013 did PTSD become a serious mental disorder recognized by the American Psychiatric Association's DSM-5, a diagnostic manual that lists mental disorders, their severity of impairment to functioning, and symptoms.[3] A PTSD diagnosis for combat vets who are experiencing symptoms at the time they commit a crime should then, in theory, limit culpability and preclude capital punishment.

Except ineffective trial and postconviction counsel, a history of mental illness, and military service are common factors in hundreds of death penalty cases. In these ways, James is not unique. Like so many others, he has been abandoned and failed by people incapable of doing their duty even as he volunteered to do his.

After thirteen years on death row, James's appellate attorney hired therapist and retired army chaplain Jim Johnson to talk with his client. Even on his good days, James could be combative and difficult, so it was hoped that Johnson, himself a Vietnam vet who struggled with PTSD, would be able to connect with James and get him to talk. In one of those conversations, Johnson learned that James never received a Purple Heart for being wounded in combat.

Johnson made some calls and got the paperwork moving. James's appellate attorneys were surprised that it worked, and that their mentally ill client would be awarded two medals for his military service. Johnson wanted a ceremony for James at Central Prison to award both the Purple Heart and Good Conduct medals. He believed, even though the man lived on death row, James was entitled to recognition for his service. Initially, the warden refused, but after some intervention from the regional director of prisons, James French, who also served in Vietnam, the ceremony happened.

When asked what the medals meant to him all these years later, James thought a moment, adjusted his thick state-issued glasses, and said, "You have to go back to 1968. It took over forty years to get those medals. A lot has happened." He looked at his yellowed nails, then at me. "I don't know why it took so long, but the point is I lived to see those medals. Here, more than anything, it was recognition from other guys and officers who were surprised I was getting a medal. It meant a lot more to them, and that means a lot to me."

After a while, James went back to his daily routine on death row. A few television programs, maybe an old movie with John Wayne, then an afternoon nap. Later, he would work in his coloring books sent by attorneys unable to help the seventy-two-year-old veteran in any other way. Eventually, he would roam the dayroom talking to himself. Maybe he thought of thundering salvos of 105 mm TOWS or the scream of fighter jets before they dropped napalm. Maybe he remembered the burning sensation of shrapnel in his leg while sleep took cover in its own foxhole. Maybe regret for the victims invaded his mind in more lucid moments. Whatever his thoughts, James lives with the pride of having served his country even though it ultimately failed him.

Chapter 27

Jesus as a Man on Death Row

Unlike most other death rows in the United States, the cell doors on North Carolina's death row stay open from 7:00 a.m. until 10:45 p.m. There are about twenty-four people who live on each of the six cellblocks, divided between two floors. On a typical day, much of our time is spent on the block, except for one hour of outside recreation, meals at the chow hall, visits, medical appointments, or religious services. In terms of size, I have spent the majority of my life in a seven-by-nine-foot cell, walking the same two-hundred-foot length of hallway, playing and exercising in a dirt-and-grass lot roughly half a square acre. I suppose it could be worse: at least we don't have cellmates.

Throughout the day we are left to our own devices. Most of my time is spent writing and reading. A lot of guys watch TV or play tabletop games like cards or chess. There is also a small library of mostly donated books on our unit. We even have counseling services. After so many years, guys develop their own routine, doing what they can do to occupy their time with meaningful activities. It's important we do so because of how readily the mind decays without something to stimulate and stretch it. Even then, some lose touch with reality.

It is not an exaggeration to say we're lost in time and cut off from the real world. Without computers or internet access, this is even more true now than it was in the '90s. Our information still comes from dated newspapers and magazines, or mainstream television news affiliates like ABC, NBC, CBS, and Fox. It wasn't until 2016 that we received regular access to a phone. Before then we were given one ten-minute collect call per year around Christmas. Coupled with the stigma of a death sentence and the information desert that is prison, this technological deficit ended a lot of relationships. Already tenuous connections dissolved because—who has time to write a letter in the fast-paced free world?

Fortunately, over the years we've been able to rely on one another. Our interaction has eased the sense of isolation and abandonment. What for an outsider would be seemingly scary situation—living among people convicted of murder—is mundane for us. We share the same fate, for the same crime, have gone through the same legal process, and experience many of the same problems. It makes it easier to identify with one another, and while there is still a pecking order and various cliques, we are more equal than not.

The main thing to remember is that we are all flawed human beings who experience the same needs, hopes, fears, and persecution. When one of us has a bad day, for example, someone is usually there to hold him up. Like individual bricks, we don't amount to much on our own, but together we support and fortify each other. Death row may be the unlikeliest of communities, but for many of us it's the only family we have.

My mom raised my siblings and me in a Catholic household. She taught Sunday school, and we were all altar servers at some point. Though I left my faith behind in adolescence, I rediscovered it upon coming to death row in 1999. I've been confirmed since 2000, and have attended Catholic mass every week during my time on death row.

It wasn't easy at first. Father Dan, one of the priests who delivered mass on the row, tried to convince me to return using the parable of the prodigal son. He reminded me that we all stray from God, and the important part is to repent in humility and reconcile that relationship. I was angry and defiant, questioning him incessantly as I saw people I came to know put to death. When his original approach didn't work, Fr. Dan used Pascal's Wager. If you believe in God and it turns out to be a story, you've lost nothing; but if you choose not to believe in God, in all that the Bible instructs, and it turns out to be true, then you, my friend, have lost everything in this life and the next. Fr. Dan's belief in the eternal mercy of Jesus Christ and his infinite love and patience saved my life.

For me, it was the manifestation of Jesus as a man on death row. Endless patience. Unconditional love. Mercy. I paid attention.

In Luke, chapter 23, verses 39–43, there is a scene not repeated in any of the other gospels. As Jesus hung on the cross between two criminals, one reviled him, saying:

> "Are you not the Messiah? Save yourself and us." The other rebuked him and said, "Have you no fear of God, for you are subject to the same condemnation? And indeed, we have been condemned justly, for the sentence we received corresponds to our crimes, but this man has done nothing criminal." Then he said, "Jesus, remember me when you come into your kingdom." Jesus replied to him, "Amen, I say to you, today you will be with me in paradise."[1]

The first time a friend of mine was executed, I had been on death row for less than a year. Harvey and I exercised together and grew close. Like Fr. Dan, he urged me to pursue God. Ask my questions. Be angry but confess my sins and be constant in my relationship with Him. Harvey was one of my early mentors. He was vocal both in the Sunday Protestant service and on the block. He admitted his crimes and repented and urged others to do the same. In him I witnessed the rebuke of the second criminal crucified with Jesus; the plea for mercy and redemption. Before they took him away, Harvey urged me not to let death row define me like the State intended it. He told me, "You. Are. Valuable."

My friend's death hurt me as so many after his would. The second manifestation of Jesus as a man on death row was recognizing my faults and being unafraid to change and grow from them. But Harvey also taught me to live.

How do you reckon with being in the shadow of the valley of death? The enemy uses helplessness, despair, fatalism, hatred, and self-loathing to break us down. These things erode one's ability to resist violence and animal urges governed by prison norms. A loss of identity, failure, betrayal, and constant disappointment drains the ability to resist. It makes prison a miserable experience and daily battle.

I often draw inspiration from Viktor Frankl, Holocaust survivor and author of *Man's Search for Meaning*. Frankl's experience in captivity provides a blueprint for finding purpose amid unimaginable pain and suffering. He lived in a place where innocent people were stripped of their humanity, starved, beaten, tortured, and executed in the millions. He made it through multiple concentration camps, his mind intact, and discovered a radical resilience that made sense of the misery when it would have been so easy to succumb. What right do I have to do anything less?

Frankl provided a map to thrive in any environment, but there had to be more. What would thriving look like for me?

A third manifestation of Jesus as a man on death row came in the form of an offer to enroll in some college correspondence courses. Before prison, I had dropped out of high school and earned a GED in a reformatory because it was required of delinquent youth. College had never been a thought. But needing something to do, and genuinely curious what it would be like, I accepted.

It turned out to be the best decision of my life. I discovered I'm a capable student and avid reader; that my ability to write was an untapped talent. Within a few years I knew that as long as my sponsor was willing to fund the courses, I would complete them. Higher education transformed my life on death row in ways I could never have imagined. It became the key God handed me to unlock any door I chose. The more I learned, the greater my sense of responsibility grew to use this wonderful gift to help my brothers.

One John, chapter 3, verse 14 says, "We know that we have passed from death to life because we love our brothers. Whoever does not love remains in death."

Lutheran theologian Dietrich Bonhoeffer posited that the ongoing incarnation of Christ happens in the community. The Church is the Son of God working among us. "Not only does this contain the notion that social interaction is the point of departure for understanding Christian faithfulness, it means when I encounter another, I encounter Christ, and that [person] places an ethical demand on me."[2] Bonhoeffer said that to be disciples of Christ, to follow after Him, we are called to act vicariously on behalf of others. Bonhoeffer was executed for speaking out against

Hitler and the Nazis.

This is how love for our brethren is carried out.

My access to higher education on death row is unique, but it gives me a more objective and informed understanding of the criminal injustice system. I realized that America is not the land of the free, but that it has become a place where prisons proliferate and fill with the poor, the uneducated, and the marginalized; where human potential is sent to die.

I write not merely to advocate for those who lack a voice or an ability to articulate their needs, but out of a sense of Christian duty to use my gifts effectively and broadly and as an act of faith. All of us are more than our mistakes; we are human beings. I take every opportunity that comes along to pull back the curtain of judgment and reveal how the incarcerated continue to live, think, feel, and learn.

Mass incarceration is a colossal, seemingly insurmountable problem. When broken down by state and community it can become more manageable. Prisons are a testament to what society thinks about the least of its citizens. If there is no investment in the people you believe are problematic enough to confine, those problems don't disappear—90 percent of them return to your communities.

I shouldn't need to convince people of faith of the value of human potential or dignity of life wherever it exists. Rather, I implore you to consider the following question, and once you do, answer it with action: how can your faith community impact the carceral state?

Don't sit idly by and think the answer will occur on its own or that someone else will do it for you. Community involvement, spiritual accountability, and personal action are essential to building up the world we want to exist.

Interview with
Jonathan Wilson-Hartgrove

March 16 and 17, 2022

Jonathan Wilson-Hartgrove is a noted author, Christian minister, Duke University Divinity School faculty member, and a member of the National Steering Committee of the Poor Peoples' Campaign. Jonathan protested and stood vigil during executions in North Carolina between 2003 and 2006. He also created the Rutba House, a way station for the wayward and formerly incarcerated who need a place to call home for a while. Between 2014 and 2017, with the aid of several Duke Divinity students and Mennonite minister Isaac Villegas, Jonathan led a creative writing group on death row at Central Prison where numerous personalities and activists were introduced to the group. While the purpose of the group was instruction in creative narratives, Jonathan directly linked activism around death penalty and prison abolition on the outside with the people it served on the inside, helping us to understand and invest in that activism by writing.

Lyle May (LM): How do you combat misinformation campaigns intended to discredit your efforts as "too liberal" or as being "soft" on people convicted of crimes?

Jonathan Wilson-Hartgrove (JWH): First, by communicating the humanity of incarcerated people. On an organizational level, campaigns have to communicate through direct mail, phone, and social media to keep a consistent message. Without communication the campaign will be ineffective. Second, disinformation is meant to disparage, discourage, and distract movements. To combat this, you have to expose the lies, but return to the main issue at hand. Disinformation is successful when it uses wedge issues that distract and undermine consensus, such as allowing others to focus on a particular type of crime to justify use of the death penalty and drive focus away from the facts. [When it] is applied in a racist manner, innocent people are incarcerated on death row, and no human being should have the authority to take the life of another.

LM: Who or what represents the greatest threat to community organizers? What can be done to counter that threat?

JWH: The media and cultural climate in which injustice occurs are threats to community organizing. But the biggest obstacle or threat is whether people believe change is possible.

LM: In what ways do you think George Floyd's murder, and the subsequent prosecution and conviction of the law enforcement officers responsible, has reinvigorated calls to change the criminal legal system?

JWH: The murder of George Floyd and subsequent prosecution and conviction of those involved did a lot to galvanize consensus, to create broad public support for Black lives. This can shift political power on a national scale to pass major legislation. In reality, we've only seen minor, local changes. No major legislation. Defunding the police, for example, was disinformation used as a wedge issue to undermine any consensus and distract from the goal of deeper systemic change.

LM: You and the Reverend William Barber III organized, mobilized, participated in, and got arrested for Moral Monday Protests

at the state building in Raleigh from 2012 to 2015. How did that get started?

JWH: I had gotten involved in protests to make life easier on poor people. [There is] no way to change policies without changing the politics. The protests were helpful by grabbing public attention to what [Republican] governor [Pat] McCrory was doing. He won office as a middle-of-the-road politician, but in reality, he supported really radical policies that targeted marginalized people. The protests forced people to remember that. It's why I believe he was a one-term governor. Moral Monday protests were a form of a "moral fusion movement," a term created by Reverend Barber. They demonstrate nonviolent campaigns are as effective as they were in the 1960s when people joined for a singular cause. We're also seeing this with the Fight for 15 to raise the minimum wage, Black Lives Matter, March for Our Lives gun control campaign, and the movement for climate change. The Poor People's Campaign is working to fuse with these movements, networking, helping to organize and otherwise find common cause. The thing about mass movements is nobody ever knows what's the one thing that tips public opinion. It took nearly twenty-five years for the Civil Rights Movement of the sixties to manifest change. We might be halfway to the next major civil rights change. There's still a lot of work to do, but we're making progress.

PART V

THE FURY OF RESISTANCE

Chapter 28

The Hole

To Live Means to Resist

My first experience with solitary confinement occurred in 1994 at the age of sixteen. I ran from an officer who was trying to arrest me for violating curfew while on juvenile probation. Once caught and returned to the Maine Youth Center (MYC), as punishment for running from law enforcement, MYC staff stripped me to my underwear and put me in ICU—the intensive control unit.

A long hallway of cells extending from the infirmary and intake building, the ICU was a difficult place for a kid struggling with drug addiction and a history of self-mutilation. Silence smothered dimly lit cells. Talking was forbidden, so we communicated in hoarse whispers through a crack beneath the cell doors. No books, magazines, TV, or music. We lay on the cold concrete, flicking ants and centipedes out of the way as we traded stories about our brief lives in the free world. The ICU staff kept an erratic schedule, withholding food, showers, and our allotted hour of rec in a bigger cage. Without a clock, and wire mesh covering a painted window, it was hard to know day from night. The light always stayed on.

The hardest part about time in ICU, other than the boredom and loneliness, was listening to staff beat a fifteen-year-old kid who gave them lip. They threatened him, but the kid kept talking. After opening the door, they rushed in, meaty thuds of fists on flesh echoed alongside curses, cries, and pleading. We yelled. "Hey! Cut it out! STOP!" But the beating continued for merciless minutes. When they quit, a few chuckles and heavy breathing, then the cell door slamming shut followed by two sets of footsteps. A pause, the ICU door buzzed open and slammed shut.

Though the Maine Youth Center in South Portland shut down in the late 1990s after reports of systemic abuse, it reopened with a few structural changes and a new name: Long Creek Youth Detention Center. They likely rehired the same staff.

A little over two years after my first experience in ICU, in North Carolina, I found myself charged with two capital murders I did not commit. Facing the death penalty, the county sent me to the Western Youth Institution for "safekeeping." It was August 1997. Safekeeping is a practice where county jails outsource pretrial detainees until they can be tried. Rather than keep me in the jail as a "security risk," or send me to an adult prison as a nineteen-year-old, I was shipped to the Morganton High Rise.

The sixteen-story high rise kept safekeepers in solitary cells without running water or toilets. Locked in these "dry" cells behind wooden doors for twenty-three hours a day, the confinement was the most difficult of my life. A single communal restroom with three toilets—to be used upon request—served twenty-four youth between the ages of fifteen and twenty-one. A request to use the toilet did not guarantee access. Some guards tormented people who needed to go, ignoring or delaying requests. Empty milk cartons, Styrofoam cups, and bottles were a must.

When I arrived on the thirteenth floor of the High Rise it had the same quiet oppression of the Maine Youth Center. Three guards, after taking the handcuffs off, took me to the nearest open cell and pushed me in. A short, fat guard rushed me, grabbed two fistfuls of my mustard-colored jumpsuit, slammed me hard enough against the wall to bounce my head forward, and backhanded me. Letting go, he whipped out a baton, jammed it against my throat, and pressed hard as I flailed my arms at him.

"I hate punks like you," he said. Panic squeezed my chest. I couldn't breathe. He jammed the baton harder. I choked and gagged, weakly pushing at his arms. A tall, lanky guard saw this and jabbed his baton into my ribs. Once. Twice. Three times. The biggest of the three blocked the open doorway and watched. Each impact of the baton buckled my knees. A fourth blow from the lanky guard and I lost control of my bladder then passed out.

Moments later the fat guard kicked me, laughing as I sobbed in air. Tears, snot, and blood from my busted lips came with each broken gasp. The air was not sweet like some claim it is after being without for a while. It tasted of terror and dominance and degradation. I knew in that air I was utterly alone.

The fat guard spat brown tobacco juice on the floor by my face. "If we hear a peep out of you, we'll come back and string you up. Ain't nobody gonna question it or care about you dyin' boy." In a falsetto he croaked, "I swear detective, we offered to get the boy help and he refused. I thought he might be suicidal, but when we let him out for showers, there he hanged." Blue-gray eyes bored into me. "You understand me, boy? We straight?" I nodded because it was all I could do beyond breathe and calm my hammering heart.

After they left, I sat on the floor hugging my knees for a long time. My only possessions—several letters, a toothbrush and toothpaste, paper and pencil—lay scattered and marred by boot prints. The people who wrote those letters could not help me. Staring up at a bare light bulb sprouting from the ceiling I considered breaking the glass and using a piece to cut my throat. What if they came back? I sat petrified, wishing I had something to defend myself against the next person to come through that door. Later, I found one of the long metal slats on the bunk was loose. It was thick, heavy, and cold. I pulled it up a bit and knew it could be broken. Listening for footsteps and hearing none, after a time I crawled into bed, pulled the covers up to my chin despite the sticky August heat, and stared at the light until it went out.

The light bulb or the metal slat. Me or them. I could hit the first one through the door. The others might get me, but the first one—probably the fat one—would not. Despite my growing hatred for them, I was drawn toward the escape of suicide. It was easier than fighting.

For the rest of the night and into the days, weeks, and months that followed, my thoughts jumped between the light bulb and the metal slat as the only two objects in my seven-by-nine-foot world that gave me power. Power over the fear, helplessness, isolation, and despair. The difference between submitting to their oppression or resisting was a choice between life and death, and I wanted to live.

Discipline, Punish, Torture

As one of the most extreme punishments in the American penal system, solitary confinement has many pseudonyms—A-seg, D-seg, restrictive housing, segregation, intense control, max control, the "bing," "box," or "hole." All of them are prisons inside of prisons designed to inflict pain and suffering despite prison officials' claims they need something to control the unruly, dangerous, and mentally ill among the incarcerated. In general, prisons maintain segregation units for "security threats," people who pose a risk to themselves or others, or who have violated institutional rules. The pretense of institutional order does not prevent systemic abuse of people in isolation or the violation of their due process rights. This is especially true of prisoners put in the hole because they angered prison officials after demanding and advocating for those rights.

In most penal facilities the hole is a cell the size of a parking space, often filthy, dark, and cold. Isolation occurs for twenty-two to twenty-four hours each day, usually with movement out of the cell restricted by handcuffs and shackles. Some county jails isolate people as a matter of policy, to reduce altercations and tightly control the population. Supermax prisons are similarly arranged, but isolate prisoners because they have been deemed a threat to the penal *system*, not just a facility. A number of death penalty states like Alabama, Florida, Texas, and Oklahoma maintain solitary confinement death rows solely because of the person's sentence, not from any additional threat they pose to institutional safety and security.

As of 2021, nearly sixty thousand people experienced solitary confinement in US prisons. In the *Solitary Confinement Sourcebook*, Sharon Shalev writes how acute social isolation, reduced physical and mental activity, limited or no environmental input, and the loss of control over virtually every aspect of daily life has a lasting psychological impact on prisoners.

Indeed, Dr. Craig Haney spent three decades researching the psychological effects of solitary confinement and found few that forms of imprisonment produce as much psychological trauma and as many pathologies. These psychopathologies can include:

- Anxiety—panic attacks, obsessive-compulsive disorder, and fear of impending death.
- Clinical depression—apathy, lethargy, withdrawal, severe mood swings, suicidal ideation, and catastrophic thinking.
- Aggression—rage and violence toward others.
- Cognitive disorder—a decreased ability to concentrate on mental tasks, notable memory lapses, disorientation, paranoia, psychosis, and schizophrenia.
- Sensory dysfunction—hypersensitivity to noise and smell, auditory and visual hallucinations, and derealization/depersonalization (doubting one's reality and existence).

These psychological and physical effects described by Shalev and Haney are not experienced by every prisoner in isolation, but they are recorded in historical accounts as far back as the birth of the penitentiary.

Nineteenth-century Quaker-inspired penitentiaries were the original "supermax," built on the belief that solitary confinement develops the moral character of prisoners through deprivation, penitence, and intense reflection. At the time, prisoners arrived at Eastern Prison wearing hoods, unable to see anyone around them. Though kept clean, shaven, and fed, prisoners were completely isolated and under a strict ban on communication.[1] The "Pennsylvania Model" of confinement sought to rehabilitate people by dividing them from "corrupting influences," different from other forms of incarceration that relied on the brutality of the whip and forced labor.[2]

The penitentiary may have appeared to instill perfect order in the carceral state, but Charles Dickens, noted author and social commentator, discovered an ugly truth. While on a tour of Eastern Prison he witnessed what every American who claims to support use of solitary confinement should: the "cruel and wrong effects" that drove one man to be addicted to peeling the skin from his fingers.[3] Shaken, Dickens went on to describe the penitentiary as a place of "torture and agony," and "which no man has the right to inflict upon his fellow creature."[4]

Some version of the hole has existed since the birth of the prison, but Eastern Prison institutionalized the practice. The "reformers" who believed they could reshape the carceral landscape in a way that "civilized" confinement, instead contributed to its brutality. As every type of prison—panopticon, penitentiary, penal farm, and labor camp—proliferated across the country, so too did "special housing unit," "segregation wings," and "intensive control units." In these places human beings were systematically broken, and the worst inclinations of those in authority were manifested beneath the banner of institutional control.

By 1971 solitary confinement was a fixed and common feature in prison, the "ultimate weapon" to "bring prisoners to heal," writes Professor Terry A. Kupers of the Wright Institute. This is especially true of officials who dread the "prisoner's capacity to think for themselves, to think critically, and to demand their rights."[5]

The Angola Three

In 1971 Robert King, Herman Wallace, and Albert Woodfox formed the first official chapter of the Black Panther Party (BPP) at the Louisiana prison farm known as Angola.[6] Aligning with Black radical organizing around food production, consumption, and distribution for collective political action, and drawing from previous incarcerated experiences, the Angola Three built solidarity among prisoners from every racial and ethnic group to achieve their goals.[7] King, Wallace, and Woodfox advocated for better food, health care, education, and an end to segregationist policies by first asking prison officials to change their policies, and then, once they were ignored, engaging in work slowdowns and stoppages, petitions, and labor strikes.[8] Their activism disrupted Angola's agricultural output to the point where it created modest changes, and landed them in the hole. This did not stop the Angola Three, who continued to encourage others and even initiated a forty-five-day hunger strike to get food slots cut into their cell doors (the food was previously slid across the floor as if the prisoners were animals).[9]

In 1972 Angola prison guard Brent Miller was killed the same day as kitchen workers went on strike. Then-warden C. Murray Henderson blamed the strike and murder on the Angola Three, claiming they organized the strike to carry out the murder. Each of the men denied the charges and had solid alibis, but they were ultimately put in long-term solitary confinement.[10]

Wilbert Rideau, incarcerated editor of the prison newspaper the *Angolite*, recalled how Miller's death prompted guards to "indiscriminate terror and violence against black [prisoners] especially those suspected of being militant."[11] Because the Angola Three, and their affiliation with the BPP, inspired others to organize and defy penal controls, prison officials went to great lengths to suppress that ideology.[12] It failed, in large part because the Angola Three fought for legitimate rights to humane treatment, equality, access to education, better health care, and due process. In their fight for better conditions of confinement, King, Wallace, and Woodfox advanced the prisoner litigation movement in Louisiana, though it cost them decades of torture.

Generally, most people in solitary confinement do whatever it takes to get out quickly. Some, like the mentally ill, are incapable of doing so. Others, like the Angola Three and gang-affiliated prisoners, are equally unable to leave the hole but for very different reasons. Gang affiliation is a permanent mark in prison that has lasting consequences. Woodfox, Wallace, and King were founding members of the BPP, and although they did not identify as a gang, prison officials believed otherwise. The Angola Three had opportunities to get out of solitary, but the price was too high. "Prison officials wanted me to renounce my affiliation with the Black Panther Party," wrote Woodfox in his book *Solitary*, "and they wanted me to give up my social and political philosophy, and just be a good little boy."[13] Woodfox refused and spent forty-four years and ten months in the hole, longer than any prisoner in US history. Prison officials who identify prisoners as gang leaders or "shot callers" hold them responsible for any recruiting and criminal activity attributed to the gang. This was the general purpose of the supermax in California known as the Pelican Bay SHU. The only way to get out, as the Angola Three discovered in Louisiana, is to renounce the gang. To turn on them. Most prisoners refuse to do this not only out of loyalty and pride, but also because it is a certain death sentence carried out by one's former gang.

To Live Is to Resist

Youth detention or adult prison, nineteenth century or twenty-first, isolation in a cell for more than a few weeks is torture. Prison officials know
it and use the hole to break people. History has recorded it. Most of the
general public either is vaguely aware and disinterested or buy into a
"just deserts" philosophy of punishment without a clue what that experience is like. While in the hole, suffering is a fact of life that hinges upon
whether basic needs are met or ignored. Resistance becomes a matter of
survival. But how does one resist being beaten, starved, and forgotten? In
that tiny crushing space, where despair blackens the air, sometimes resistance and insanity are confused. Imagine, for a moment, being trapped
and desperate enough to feel human contact that you swallow objects so
a surgeon has to cut them out of your stomach. Imagine so thoroughly
rejecting humanity the way it rejected you that language erodes into
senseless noise and fecal war paint. Imagine setting fire to your cell.

"CODE FIVE! CODE FIVE! CODE FIVE! ALL AVAILABLE
STAFF 1-A EAST!"

It was the height of absolute frustration. Tired of begging for toilet
paper, soap to clean a shower stall or cell, and their allotted time in a
slightly bigger cage, six people on Unit One, Central Prison's solitary
confinement wing, set their mattresses and some clothing on fire. The
fires were visible to the guard in the control booth, who immediately
radioed in the emergency.

When the "all available" call went out, Unit Three's sergeant locked
down death row, forcing everyone into their cells, and ran to help. It
was he who later explained what happened. Under normal circumstances
only extra staff responds to emergency radio codes, but throughout the
coronavirus pandemic, dysfunctional management and a staffing crisis
left a skeleton crew of a few hundred staff members running a prison
with a population of a thousand. Twenty percent of that population was
housed on Unit One. Under normal circumstances people in the hole
suffer, but understaffing and apathy made it worse.

Ray went to Unit One several times over the years, most recently in
2021. "Bro, you have to get their attention somehow. Staff won't give you

grievance forms, and even when they do it gets thrown in the trash. They ignore you down there, skipping rounds, showers, rec—everything—then excuse it by saying they 'short.' You kick the door to get their attention, maybe they come to the block long enough to hear what you got to say, but they leave and forget. Sometimes on purpose."

Nearly half of the people in isolation on Unit One are mentally ill or on the mental health case load. According to staff who worked there in recent years, these prisoners belong in Unit Six, the $155 million medical complex and mental health facility opened in 2011 for exactly that purpose.[14] One of the key needs Unit Six was supposed to address was the segregation of prisoners with a great need for mental health treatment while in long-term solitary confinement.[15] Despite the new facility and significant increase in staff, the same problems continued and Unit One filled with mentally ill people who received inadequate treatment or attention.

This left many long-term isolation prisoners to self-destruct and further decline in their ability to control their behaviors. They cut themselves open, swallowed batteries, flooded cells by flushing sheets or clothing, flung feces and urine, and assaulted staff. The last time Ray went to Unit One in 2021, an inch of sewage water covered the floor and staff pushed a food cart through it. The guards refused to let the designated block janitor clean it up or provide any supplies for the prisoners to do so. The attitude of staff was openly disrespectful and apathetic toward the prisoners' needs, health, or safety.

Unconstitutional conditions of confinement on Unit One is not a new thing. In 2012 a group of prisoners began a hunger strike protesting their treatment and conditions of confinement in isolation.[16] About one hundred people participated in the strike, calling for an end to the physical and mental abuse inflicted by staff and locking prisoners in their cells for weeks on end without access to recreation or showers.[17] Ultimately a class action lawsuit was necessary. Of the claims in that lawsuit, physical abuse by staff was substantiated in "'medical records which documented 'blunt force injuries including broken bones and concussions sustained while [the litigants] were isolated from other prisoners.'"[18] Prison officials denied all claims and even retaliated by informing the media those involved in the suit "racked up nearly six hundred violations."[19] As if the beatings were justified.

The lawsuit resulted in the installation of cameras on every Unit One cellblock. The North Carolina General Assembly also approved $12 million in additional funding to address mental illness in the prison system. The funding was part of the Task Force on Mental Health and Substance Abuse, created by Republican Governor Pat McCrory, in conjunction with the Vera Institute of Justice. The Vera Institute selected North Carolina to participate in a two-year study "designed to reduce the use of solitary confinement." The partnership with the nonprofit organization and additional funding did significantly reduce the number of NC prisoners in isolation, but it was a temporary fix. The abusive staff named in the original lawsuit found work in chronically understaffed prisons or gained rank. The general attitude toward people in the hole remained the same and the number of people serving extended terms in isolation crept back up.

People in the hole did not notice the change. Those with a firm grip on reality understood solitary confinement is like a baton across the throat—there because staff who abuse that authority can, and even if someone stops them, it only would be a temporary thing. Quiet on Unit One comes in fits and spurts. After the fires were extinguished, prisoners moved, and basic needs met, things returned to normal. It would begin with a mule kick to a steel door to draw the attention of staff. The sound booms throughout the unit—angry, frustrated, and nerve-shatteringly *loud*. Hunger strikes in the hole are a civilized form of activism for more organized prisoners. Some forms of resistance seem more like mental illness. Either way, the essence of activism in the hole is a fight to be heard, recognized as a human being, and treated as such.

Chapter 29

The Fury of Our Resistance

> "It was our hope that they would see the futility of resistance and would submit without compelling us to use force to bring them under control."
> —Commissioner of North Carolina Prisons,
> V. L. Bounds, April 1968[1]

We all vowed to go out fighting. To scream, bite, scratch, or punch whomever they sent. To defy the death squad when they came to execute us. To struggle against being strapped down as they inserted the needles. To curse them with our dying breath. Movies and televisions shows have an insidious way of obscuring reality with hyperbole and fantasy, even when you know better. When the prison brass came to the cellblock with an empty cart for the condemned's personal effects, the fury of resistance had been extinguished by the inevitability of execution. It left one numb, boneless, and defeated. The block would go silent, waiting for a signal that never came. Among the living, as our friends were escorted to their death, our fury burned brightly.

Activism, the kind that confronts oppressive policies, institutions, and public officials, takes many forms. Whether incarcerated or free, the pursuit of social change is rooted in service with and for others who suffer injustice and lack equal representation. It is a collective effort to fix society so that it works for everyone. Organizing and demonstrations such as petitions, boycotts, labor strikes, and protests are constitutional rights guaranteed under the First Amendment. In prison though, where injustice is the stale air we breathe, organizing and activism are punished severely.

According to current North Carolina Department of Public Safety Policy and Procedure for Adult Correctional Institutions, participating in a work stoppage, group demonstration, riot, or insurrection, encouraging others to do so, organizing such activities, or even appearing to make the attempt will result in six months to several years in solitary confinement.[2] An accusation of organizing from a confidential informant (also called a snitch) is enough for prison officials to launch an investigation and put the accused in solitary for the duration of said investigation, where one's due process rights grow murky and difficult to assert. Literature about prison activism and organizing on the inside is placed on the Publication Review Committee's "Disapproved Publications" list and banned from all state facilities. Recent examples include *Solitary: Unbroken by Four Decades in Solitary Confinement* by Albert Woodfox (2019), *Starve and Immolate: The Politics of Human Weapons* by Bargu Banu (2014), and *Blood in the Water: A History of the Attica Uprising* by Heather Ann Thompson (2017).[3]

Even writing about activism and organizing in prison carries a certain level of risk. This has a chilling effect on collective action on the inside, making it difficult to bring public attention to systemic physical and psychological torture, excessive use of solitary confinement, inadequate health care, poor quality food, a lack of access to educational programs, rampant disease, understaffing, a delegitimized grievance remedy procedure, and dysfunctional management practices that endanger staff and prisoner alike. Prisons are opaque institutions for the same reason authoritarian regimes maintain totalitarian states—officials want to sustain absolute control, and anyone who is perceived to disrupt or challenge that suffocating grip is a threat to be eliminated. Sometimes they are disappeared. Sometimes they are gunned down.

The Prison Rebellion Years: 1965–1972

The year 1965 was a significant turning point in prison activism because the judiciary finally determined that there is a minimum standard of care owed by the state, and it was not being met. The door opened for prison litigation when a federal court ruled in 1965 that an Arkansas state prison had to "change its practices and conditions" because they violated the Eighth Amendment's prohibition against cruel and unusual punishment.[4] Up to this point courts had never ordered prisons to improve their conditions of confinement.[5] That same year, the US Supreme Court sided with incarcerated Black Muslims in upholding their constitutional right to the freedom of religion. It was the first acknowledgment that incarcerated people have constitutional rights and ended the "hands off" approach to prisons practiced by the federal courts.[6] The stage for a revolution was set.

Incarcerated people filed numerous lawsuits against state and federal prison officials. They had been pushed beyond their ability to tolerate cruel and inhumane conditions of confinement and now had a legitimate way to challenge them. Yet rulings were slow to impact the penal environment. Cries from the public that prisons are too "soft" on criminals evolved into the normalcy of exceptional brutality and diminished value of human beings in confinement.[7] The desire to be treated as human beings instead of civilly dead slaves made prisons boil with the fury of resistance.

It shouldn't be underestimated how influential the civil rights movement and other external sociopolitical forces were on incarcerated people. Some prisoners developed radical political identities, aligning themselves with groups like the Black Panther Party, which established chapters in prisons across the United States to organize around more humane treatment and equal rights.[8]

When prison officials ignored or mocked reasonable requests, and were dismissive of the lawsuits filed against them, the incarcerated rebelled.

In April 1968 at Central Prison, North Carolina's oldest prison, 529 incarcerated people refused to return to work after a lunch break. Their complaints to prison administrators had been ignored. Now the protesting prisoners demanded the release of everyone in solitary confinement, an end to humiliating shakedowns, establishment of a prisoner-led grievance committee, payment of a "legally mandated" daily wage of one dollar per incarcerated worker, hot meals for lunch, additional TVs, and an increase in visitation hours.[9] Until Commissioner V. L. Bounds met with prisoner representatives, and agreed to the demands in front of reporters, the protesters refused to work, eat, or move.[10]

In response, prison officials isolated all 529 protesters in the prison yard, locked down the facility, and called local law enforcement. After several hours over one hundred prisoners surrendered as the number of armed law enforcement increased.[11] The remaining protesters likewise armed themselves, but with crudely made weapons and torches.[12] Prison administrators decided against negotiating with the incarcerated because even though their demands were reasonable, giving in to them would empower the organizers.[13] When a final order to surrender was ignored (incarcerated survivors claimed no such order came), guards advanced with attack dogs and law enforcement fired on the crowd of people.[14] Six of the incarcerated protesters were killed and seventy-six required medical attention; two guards and two state troopers received minor injuries from ricocheting bullets.[15]

The counterculture of resistance in prison is both an individual choice and collective response defying that control. Most protests are nonviolent, but sometimes they escalate to open warfare. This was especially true in California prisons such as San Quentin, where the saga of George Jackson, *Soledad Brother*, and the infamous "one-for-one" doctrine resulted in the deaths of nine guards and twenty-four prisoners from 1970 to 1971.[16]

The assassination of Jackson by California prison guards sparked violent protests in prisons throughout the country. Prisoners in Attica responded with a silent fast then three weeks later engaged in the most notorious prison uprising in US history. During the Attica rebellion, from September 9 to September 13, 1971, nearly 1,300 men protested horrendous conditions of confinement, and presented thirty-three demands that included better food, health care, education, the right to be protected from racist, abusive guards, and the right to be free from cruel and unusual punishment.[17]

On the fifth morning of the Attica uprising, it appeared that Commissioner of Prisons Russell Oswald and the protesters came to an agreement on twenty-eight of the thirty-three demands after days of nationally televised negotiations.[18] Except Republican Governor Nelson Rockefeller (of the infamous Rockefeller drug laws) had other plans. Against the advice of neutral parties observing the process and the state employees being held hostage, the governor ordered the violent retaking of Attica.[19] "Within 15 minutes," writes Thompson, "128 men were shot and 39 lay dead or dying—prisoners and hostages alike."[20]

The incarcerated revolt is a desperate measure. Most understand the risk, but take it anyway when basic needs are neglected by prison officials, and there are no legitimate means to end that suffering. The prison rebellion years marked a significant period of change for people on the inside, one that brought limited progress. However, the attention garnered was soon obscured by misinformation around the unrest. The deaths at Attica, San Quentin, Central Prison, and other facilities were blamed on the incarcerated. Conservative public officials such as Governor Rockefeller called for tougher punishments in prison and longer sentences without any evidence such policies or rhetoric improve public safety.

Carceral Experience, Social Impact

People who did not succumb to the tough-on-crime "law and order" rhetoric and disinformation around prison rebellions were often connected to those on the inside. Part of what made Angela Y. Davis's activism on the outside so important was her experience on the inside. This allowed her to be a bridge for outsiders seeking a way to end injustice for many who suffered under the heel of the criminal legal system. People like Joan Little.

In 1971 a young Black woman named Joan Little was confined in North Carolina's Beaufort County jail, pending an appeal of her breaking, entering, and larceny convictions.[21] While there, a sixty-two-year-old white jailer named Clarence Allgood sexually assaulted the nineteen-year-old Little at knife point. When he finished, Little gained possession of the knife and killed her rapist before fleeing the jail. Later, with help from her attorney, Little turned herself in.[22] The district attorney initially charged her with first degree-murder, wanting to seek the death penalty, but when he couldn't support a finding of premeditation, the charge was reduced to second-degree murder. (It should be noted that, in 2023, Joan Little would be tried for death without a finding of premeditation, simply because the victim was a law enforcement officer.) Little nonetheless faced a potential sentence of life in prison.[23] Believing she would not receive a fair trial in Beaufort County, Little's attorney sought and received a change of venue to Raleigh.[24]

Little's circumstances were not unusual—white men in positions of authority have historically abused and sexually assaulted women in general and Black women in particular. It is one dynamic that has made the criminal legal system especially unjust and torturous for women of color. Little's attorney recognized this and developed the defense around it, claiming his client acted in self-defense against a predatory white jailer accustomed to abusing his authority. Little's defense also got several other women who were victimized by Allgood while in confinement to testify on her behalf.[25] Joan Little became symbolic of "every victim of racism and sexual oppression" in a way that resonated with women both in and out of prison.[26]

Davis identified with Little and the odds she faced as a Black woman accused of murder. In 1970 Davis's advocacy on behalf of prisoners led to three capital murder charges and sixteen months of pre-trial confinement before a highly publicized campaign helped her win an acquittal in 1972.[27] The trauma of being tried for your life evokes a special kind of solidarity. Ten days before Little's 1975 trial, Davis representing the National Alliance against Racist and Political Repression, joined with Southern Christian Leadership Conference president Ralph Abernathy, and led a four-thousand-strong march through Raleigh, North Carolina.[28] Marching past Central Prison, which housed one-third (45 of 123) of the nation's death-sentenced prisoners, the protesters demanded an end to the death penalty and oppression of minorities. As they marched, members of the American Nazi Party, Klu Klux Klan in full regalia, and Rights of White People Party (an early progenitor of the alt-right) watched.[29]

At trial Little defended herself on the stand, saying Allgood told her if she resisted "no one would believe her claims of rape."[30] Prosecutors attacked Little's character and said she seduced her jailer to escape, but the defense countered that the strength of the young woman's resistance and willingness to turn herself in "demonstrated her character and dismantled the prosecution's claim."[31] Davis and others were not surprised prosecutors used racist stereotypes of Black licentiousness and criminality to make their case against Little. There was historical precedent. Davis would later write that slavery relied on sexual abuse as much as the whip. "Together with flogging, rape was a terribly efficient method of keeping Black women and men alike in check. It was a routine arm of repression."[32]

The case of Joan Little drew national attention and support, channeling the fury of those who long resisted oppression and injustice under the dominion of white male authority. Bernice Johnson Reagon wrote a song entitled "Joan Little." Rosa Parks formed a defense committee in Detroit. Davis spoke in Little's support.[33] Southern Poverty Law Center, with the Joan Little Defense Fund, raised over $350,000 for her defense. Also, the jury was evenly divided by race, with seven women and five men.[34] The racial makeup of the jury was critical to determining fairness at trial (as would come to be acknowledged years later in *Batson v. Kentucky* [1989]). Had Little contended with an all-white jury, she would likely have died in prison decades later, like so many do in her position.

The jury took seventy-eight minutes to acquit Joan Little, "making her the first American woman to ever be acquitted of murdering her rapist."[35] This was possible because of the essential legal help and advocacy provided by Davis, Parks, and Southern Poverty Law Center. Public knowledge of and support for Little allowed a nineteen-year-old Black woman to become the symbol of resistance to the carceral oppression experienced by the marginalized.

By the Light of a Candle

From 1984 until June 2002, North Carolina's death row was housed on Unit Two, of Central Prison. The cell windows of Unit Two face an access road that wraps around the back of the facility and its perimeter fence. Just beyond the fence is a set of railroad tracks. Before dusk on the eve of an execution, anti–death penalty activists straddled the tracks with signs and banners that read:

STAY STRONG! YOU ARE LOVED!
THE STATE DOESN'T KILL IN *MY* NAME!
WE STAND IN SOLIDARITY!

The guard posted on each cellblock to maintain order warned that anyone caught signaling the protesters would get sixty days in the hole. The threat didn't deter everyone, nor did every guard care enough to act on their threat. We recognized which guards didn't want to be there. Candles carved from a bar of soap, or made from an empty inhaler canister filled with mineral oil that soaked a piece of string for the wick, flickered small flames of acknowledgment. In that moment our resistance became a tangible thing that burned in the dark.

At night the protesters moved to the front of Central Prison for a candlelight vigil. People of Faith against the Death Penalty, ordinary citizens, friends of people on death row, and other activists sang hymns, prayed for a stay of execution or clemency, and discussed the need to abolish capital punishment. Some protesters tried forcing their way onto prison grounds but were stopped by the guards and law enforcement on duty. Sometimes there were counterprotesters yelling vicious things about the condemned and anyone who supported them.

After returning to North Carolina in 2003, Christian minister and author Jonathan Wilson-Hartgrove attended every vigil at Central Prison until the last execution in 2006. Wilson-Hartgrove had not always fought for the poor and marginalized. That came from an awakening of faith he related in a March 2022 interview: "When I was young I got involved in reactionary conservative politics. I began to realize, though, a tension existed between what I was taught and what my Christian faith told me. So I looked for another way to put that faith into action." Wilson-Hartgrove came to understand that "executions are an anti-Christian ritual sacrificing to the gods of the security state." Capital punishment, he explains, is "the tip of the spear that is mass incarceration."[36] Wilson-Hartgrove protested because he believed it his Christian duty, but also his obligation as a white man of privilege confronting a criminal legal system that disproportionately impacts the poor people of color.[37] Whereas Davis fought from experience, Wilson-Hartgrove was a convert much like the biblical Paul, who stood up against the Romans after God removed the scales from his eyes.

In addition to the protests, Wilson-Hartgrove and fellow activists sought help from NAACP attorney Al McSurley, who advised them on how to file a brief in court to block executions at Central Prison. It worked for a brief period in 2005, but the state found a way around it and still managed to execute five people that year. When asked if he thought the court is a useful way to pursue anti–death penalty activism, Wilson-Hartgrove said, "The court is one public venue. But to make the case for justice, there has to be a comprehensive effort for change."[38]

How do ordinary citizens fight for justice when entrenched criminal legal policies and tough-on-crime, law-and-order misinformation make the task seem daunting and endless? Progress from the prison rebellion years was short-lived and soon buried beneath a trio of laws that are the cornerstones of mass incarceration: the 1994 Omnibus Crime Bill, 1996 Prison Litigation Reform Act, and 1996 Antiterrorism and Effective Death Penalty Act. Human warehousing was unimaginable after Attica, yet it happened. Decades later, in the age of COVID-19, even releasing elderly prisoners to reduce overcrowding and the risk of death from disease is met with stubborn adherence to draconian sentences.

The abdication of responsibility for what occurs in prisons has left a void that can be filled by citizens willing to step in and force systemic change, but it requires dedicated collective resistance to the status quo. Social change comes from self-sacrifice and means "showing up for an issue you care about," said Wilson-Hartgrove. "Remember it takes work and be willing to be in it for the long haul."[39]

The long haul can be a lifetime in prison or in the free world. It means faith and devotion under the toughest circumstances. This is why the fury of resistance is the fire of the soul yearning to be free. Sometimes though, even the brightest flames flicker or feel tiny and too insufficient to shed any light. It is then that one understands resisting the carceral state is not a job for any individual leader or organization. Where one candle shrinks, others gather, and together they burn brightly, shedding light wherever darkness encroaches.

Chapter 30

Attention, Activists, and Election Cynics

Crowdfunding Local Political Campaigns Can Combat Mass Incarceration

Voting is the most effective way to protest bad decisions and policies made by elected officials. For example, "tough-on-crime" politics are detached from statistics and the reality of crime. Policies spawned from this rhetoric created mass incarceration and reflect some of the worst decisions elected officials can make. But mass incarceration devastates communities because of the decisions by local elected officials as much as if not more than Congress and state representatives. A district attorney, judge, sheriff, county commissioner, and school board member have a direct impact on the community with their decisions. Those who support militaristic, draconian, cruel policies that oppress the poor and marginalized are the gatekeepers of the carceral state. They ultimately control the flow of men, women, and children who enter, leave, return, and suffer in prison. The best way to hold these gatekeepers of mass incarceration accountable is by voting in down-ballot races, but that is no longer enough by itself.

Considering the turmoil around, and attempts to suppress, voter turnout of the people most impacted by "tough-on-crime" policies, it is more important than ever to get involved in elections. Directly helping or funding local campaigns is necessary. The idea may be cringe-worthy for citizens living paycheck-to-paycheck or busy raising children and working multiple jobs. However, name recognition of a political candidate and the associated agenda hinges on the dissemination of that information, which in turn requires money. In smaller campaigns for down-ballot races, fundraising can be difficult, but this is why crowdfunding is a useful organizing tool that allows activists to directly help oust the gatekeepers of the carceral state.

As an example of how effective small donations are at influencing local elections and shifting the politics of crime across an entire state, consider the rise of mass incarceration in California. In 1981 the California penal system accounted for 2 percent of the state budget.[1] Then came the unionization of the state's prison officers. In its first decade (1982–92), the California Corrections Peace Officers Association (CCPOA), which represents prison officers and other corrections workers, tripled in membership, then doubled again to thirty thousand dues-paying members by 2002.[2] The CCPOA became one of the largest political donors in California by using union dues (about eighty dollars per month per member) to raise wages first, then membership, and finally to win elections statewide.[3] By 2007 California's largest government agency, with roughly sixty-two thousand workers, was the Department of Corrections and Rehabilitation, which took up 7 percent of the state budget or $9.7 billion.[4] By 2009 union dues provided by the CCPOA reached an annual $29.7 million.[5] Once union dues were invested in political candidates with tough-on-crime platforms, these individuals went on to win and implement tough-on-crime policies at the county, district, and city level. More prison guards meant more dues, greater political influence across the state, more people in prison, and more prisons.

The CCPOA became a political action committee (PAC) that sold their scheme as public safety, but it was in fact BIPOC community oppression, responsible for the creation of the largest penal system in the country. Referring to the unethical nature of the CCPOA financing politics and laws that put more people in prison, former US Supreme Court Justice Anthony Kennedy publicly stated that the influence of the correctional officers' union passing the three-strikes law is "sick."[6]

Though not every state has a prison officers union like the CCPOA, police unions, district attorney conferences, and other law enforcement associations similarly influence public officials' carceral and criminal legal policies. The CCPOA is a case study on how organizing political funding influences local elections and criminal legal policies. This same system of organized, small donations by ordinary citizens can be invested in candidates willing to create stronger oversight bodies of law enforcement, prosecutors, and judges, close jails and prisons, redirect public funds to invest in more after-school mentorship programs rather than school resource officers (SROs), and shrink the carceral state one town, district, and county at a time.

The primary gatekeepers of the carceral state at the community level are members of the school board, county commissioners, sheriffs, district attorneys, and judges. The policy positions, professional acts, and coordination between these elected officials directly determine who is processed through the criminal legal system. Though not the only elected officials responsible for the school-to-prison pipeline, prison expansionism, overpoliced minority communities, life imprisonment, and capital punishment—these are the ones within reach of crowdfunded campaigns by activists interested in doing more than voting and protesting in the street.

School Boards

Citizens who run for and win seats on local school boards have agendas like every other elected official. This is evinced in the current moral panic over race and gender identity studies in the K–12 curriculum, and indicates a deeper corrupting influence of white nationalism and Christian nationalists in the public school system. The Texas State Board of Education, for example, proposed, when teaching K–12 US history, that slavery be described as "involuntary relocation" instead of brutal, inhumane, degrading treatment of other human beings because of their race and status as "property."[7] School boards also determine the presence of law enforcement on campus, SROs, and exclusionary discipline policies. In many public schools metal detectors, random locker searches, drug sniffing dogs, and uniformed guards prisonize schools. Students considered "troublesome" in these environments because of behavioral issues are labeled "suspects" in need of "interrogation" and "detainment" by SROs and vigilante teachers.[8] Minority students are disproportionally targeted by such policies and receive more exclusionary discipline as a result.[9] The school-to-prison pipeline construct begins with exclusionary curriculums, extends through exclusionary discipline and stigmatization, and ends up with former students pushed into the streets because it's difficult to get a job without an education. Without a job, the likelihood a youth commits petty crimes and becomes involved in the criminal legal system increases substantially.[10]

School board members who pursue racist, homophobic, history-revisionist curriculums, exclusionary policies, or those that criminalize mental illness, must be replaced with candidates who are learning-oriented, support diverse and inclusive classrooms, and advance public education that has students ready for college upon graduation. School board candidates do not typically require a lot of money, but this also depends on the district and population. One candidate in a suburban Michigan school district created a crowdpac.com account. The fundraising goal was $10,000. On the candidate's account page was her bio, goals as a potential school board member, and values as a "representative for everyone." Below the stated values of the candidate, a picture of a same-sex white couple with a biracial child. The message effectively demonstrated diversity, love, and inclusivity. The account drew nearly two dozen small donations to help lift the candidate's profile among the district's families.

County Commissions

County commissioners determine the county budget and how taxpayer money is spent. Generally, the commission votes on which items are put in the budget, allow time for public comment, then vote on the budget itself. On the surface, funding a county's needs like schools, law enforcement, and emergency services should be a straightforward process, with the public having a say in how additional money is spent. The reality is that commissioners ignore public comments contrary to their agendas. For example, in the fiscal year 2021–2022, Durham County commissioners approved a $794 million budget that included a $75 million increase in spending for law enforcement and $30 million set aside for a youth jail, but only an additional $11 million for Durham County public schools, which have some of the lowest reading and math proficiency scores in the state.[11]

Durham County commissioners ignored public protest over the proposed youth jail, instead investing heavily in law enforcement and the incarceration of children who had not even committed a crime. The jail would take years to finish building, but the money spent now was an investment in future incarceration, a reactive measure taken before one was needed and while preventative measures were still possible. During an election year it is critical to fund the campaigns of county commissioners who will listen to the public rather than be swayed by law enforcement unions, candidates who will put schools first. Activists can start by researching incumbents' voting records and comparing them to the promises and backgrounds of candidates. No elected official is untouchable during the election season and supporting a qualified challenger by funding their campaign or volunteering to help raise their profile can make the difference for lesser-known candidates.

Sheriffs
Individually, sheriffs have more power than any other law enforcement personnel in the state within their jurisdiction. County sheriffs, without exception, lack accountability beyond the ballot. You could argue a court or the legislature limits the scope of that power, but the same is true of every public official and it does little to slow down systemic problems that lead to overpolicing, in-custody deaths during arrest and confinement at county jails, or brutality during enforcement. Sheriffs hire and fire deputies at will, retaining officers known for committing crimes under the guise of carrying out their duties and hiding the evidence.[12] North Carolina sheriffs, for example, "shaped [a] new body-camera law that limits who can release footage" and "despite calls for transparency," continue to "hide details on officer killings and serious assaults."[13] Any elected official who pursues less transparency, hides in-custody death records, and evades accountability by restricting what should be public information (the idea that a public official can make any information

about the practices of his or her office private or concealed is inconsistent with serving the public trust) does not belong in office. Sheriffs are beholden to citizens of the county in which they were elected. When deputies in their service harm the people they are sworn to serve, they must be fired and prosecuted. If sheriffs do not hold themselves and their deputies to a higher standard, then they must be replaced at the ballot.

Even on election day sheriffs are not always held accountable for overpolicing minority communities, acts of brutality and homicide carried out by deputies, in-custody deaths that go unchecked in county jails, and other forms of misconduct by law enforcement. Sheriffs are often "hometown heroes" of the entrenched white majority, "good ol' boys" who can do no wrong. Many citizens do not think it is possible to replace county sheriffs with a candidate of their choosing. Like other carceral gatekeepers though, sheriffs are just as susceptible to voters and crowdfunded campaigns of opponents who will work for every citizen.

District Attorneys

District attorneys (DAs) are arguably the most responsible for mass incarceration, with the power to charge a person with a crime, recommend a sentence, and fight postconviction relief. The state conference of district attorneys has substantial power in the legislature and is often able to kill any bill contrary to their interests, which includes pushing back against more funding for public defenders offices. DAs, and the prosecutors working for them, have broad latitude over the degree and type of charge, and what type, if any, of a plea bargain is offered. Though unethical, DAs sometimes influence criminal investigations by directing law enforcement to focus on one person over another, which can lead to wrongful convictions because exculpatory evidence is withheld from the defense. Between 1989 and 2015 out of 1,740 recorded exonerations, official misconduct accounted for nearly half of all wrongful convictions.[14] That misconduct doesn't even include crime scene tampering by law enforcement who collaborate with prosecutors. In addition to seemingly limitless resources, part of what makes DAs so powerful and unassailable is their lack of accountability for wrongful prosecutions, arbitrary charging and plea bargaining, excessive sentences, and overincarceration. The reverse is true of officer-involved homicides and assaults of unarmed citizens. Rarely does a DA prosecute such cases; not because qualified immunity protects law enforcement officers from civil suits, but rather because DAs work hand-in-hand with law enforcement and if they have any ambition, will need the support of police unions and sheriffs' associations to get elected as a judge or attorney general. Vote them out.

Judges

Considering how difficult it is to hold DAs accountable for misconduct, it should be unsurprising that judges are nearly untouchable even when they commit crimes. In an investigation into judicial misconduct across the United States, Reuters news agency found at least 5,206 people directly affected by a judge's misconduct during a twelve-year period.[15] In addition, "reporters identified another 3,613 cases from 2008 through 2018 in which states disciplined wayward judges but kept hidden from the public key details of their offenses—including the identities of the judges themselves."[16] No state tracks how many people were victimized by a judge's misconduct so Reuters had to match state misconduct files with court and jail databases and other records, to track victims of judicial misconduct.[17] Ordinarily it's other judges who review the misconduct of their brethren, and this occurs privately. Without any oversight or accountability, corrupt judges are allowed to operate with impunity even after being reprimanded by the judicial standards committee of a given state. The surest way to remove rogue public officials who believe they are above the law is to organize around their opponent during an election cycle and crowdfund the campaign. Vote them out.

Even state-wide races for judicial seats can be impacted by crowdfunding. The North Carolina Supreme Court had two incumbent justices up for reelection in 2022. The incumbents, both Democrats, were all that stood between Republican efforts to restart executions in the state, overrule precedent-setting cases that uphold previous filings under the Racial Justice Act, and reverse recent court rulings that give parole eligibility to juvenile lifers. The incumbents brought in more small donations than their opponents, with contributions of less than one hundred dollars accounting for an average 9.5 percent of campaign financing. As one candidate stated, "It takes a lot of funds to communicate with voters."[18] Ultimately, the NC Supreme Court flipped to a 5-2 Republican majority.

Voting in every election is critical, but it's no longer enough. Protests in the streets generate energy and attention, and passing along information about public officials in need of removal via social media is essential to organization. Votes harness the power of that organized effort, but it will take supporting candidates who can engineer systemic change in the criminal legal system. Even if you don't have "disposable income" you can still be a sponsor by spreading the word about crowdfunded political campaigns and what exactly the issues are to build local community support.

Crowdfunding local campaigns on such platforms as Indiegogo, Kickstarter, GoFundMe, or Crowdpac is an increasingly popular forms of economic support for would-be public officials. GoFundMe regional spokesperson Jenny Perillo acknowledged the platform's use by some candidates. "Raising money to support a school board and political fundraising is allowed," Perillo told the *Idaho Capital Sun*, but "it is the candidate's responsibility to comply with local election laws."[19] The platform also helps identify donors at the candidate's request.[20]

Bob Phillips, executive director of the government watchdog group Common Cause NC argues money is the biggest factor for helping a candidate establish name recognition, which translates to voters remembering the candidate and attendant policies when they go to the ballot box.[21] While voters might take issue with big money donors because it gives the appearance of "special interests" such as the CCPOA and similar law enforcement organizations, crowdfunding is more akin to public funding where candidates garner support from actual citizens—not organizations, corporations, or unions pursuing self-serving agendas. Ending mass incarceration serves public safety in a way law enforcement fails to do. Disrupting the school-to-prison pipeline is a community-strengthening measure that school boards and county commissions consistently undermine. Where special interest seeks greater power and profit, community interest seeks to build up the world we want to exist by removing those public officials from office who have forgotten they serve the public—not their own careers.

The best part of organized crowdfunding a candidate's campaign for a local office is that it doesn't take a lot of money or experience, just a vested interested in a particular platform. Sometimes the amount needed is a few thousand dollars for school board seats, to twenty or thirty thousand for county commission seats. Timing matters too. A district attorney in North Carolina's western district almost lost to a progressive challenger. Had she entered the race sooner, invested in social media platforms, or had local crowdfunding help her raise more money to spend on ads and outreach, her loss by a few hundred votes could have been changed into a win. Of course, money does not guarantee a win, but in conjunction with voting and disseminating a campaign's platform, organized crowdfunding can make a difference.

Voting is imperative to maintaining democratic freedoms. Before heading to the polls, research policy positions of the candidates. Register with the correct precinct. Take a sick day to vote if necessary. As more lawmakers gerrymander districts, pass restrictive voting laws, and otherwise disenfranchise people who have fought for equal representation since the end of the Civil War, the opposition to our democracy is real. Irresponsible voting has led to an erosion in civil rights gains over the last seventy years. Remember this when selecting candidates to crowdfund. Recall that collective action and misguided thinking created mass incarceration and, like efforts that undermine free and fair elections, can seem insurmountable. That is why now, more than ever, to protect democracy we must participate in it at every level. Use every available means to challenge the gatekeepers of the carceral state. Effective activism is a concerted effort and driving factor of systemic change.

Chapter 31

Reform or Abolish

Taking Steps to Shrink the Carceral State

Ordinarily, "reform" is a neutral term that means to "improve by alteration" or to "correct of errors." In the history of prisons, reforms have begun as good intentions but become ultrapunitive functions and structures of the carceral system. Reformers created the penitentiary. Reformers created the modern supermax. A reformer "improved" capital punishment with the lethal injection. America's prolific use of life without parole (LWOP) is a consequence of penal reform. Similar to how the word "justice" is a euphemism for vengeance, reforming the way crimes are punished has come to mean instituting increasingly draconian measures. Be that as it may, public calls for reform of the criminal legal system are louder than ever.

Students unfamiliar with the penal history of reform have frequently asked what I would do to change the system. If prisons constantly fail, and high rates of recidivism and penal violence are evidence, what can be done to "improve" the way they work? The question echoes one asked by another student: What can be done to fix the death penalty so it works as designed? Both questions maintain a core—prisons in one, the death penalty in the other—without consideration of alternative solutions. The problem with prison reform is that it incorporates *more* punishment in a system of excess. The student who asked me about fixing the death penalty so it "works" wanted to learn about capital punishment, so I did my best to educate him. The death penalty cannot be "fixed" because there is no such thing as humane murder, and because the system from which it extends is fundamentally flawed. Reforming a flawed system does nothing to address the flaw. Better to do away with the whole system. Abolish the death penalty because it is an unnecessary waste of human life and resources, and because it is inhumane, arbitrary, cruel, and disproportionately applied to Black, brown, and Indigenous people of color.

Abolishing the death penalty is one thing though; prison abolition is something altogether different. With over a quarter century of incarceration I have spent the majority of my life in a cell. I wake up to walls that have erased me and millions of others from society and ask: who in their right mind would want to maintain this place? Most people who have experienced the worst prison has to offer wouldn't wish it upon anyone. The student who asked about fixing the death penalty may not have done so if he knew what the weight of a death sentence feels like. Similarly, if all the lawmakers who voted to pass the 1994 Omnibus Crime Bill really understood that they were creating mass incarceration, and not safer communities, it is unlikely the bill would ever have been signed.

Prison is a bad place. It has always been an instrument of classist oppression and torture. After five presidents, five governors, and numerous iterations of Congress and the North Carolina General Assembly during my incarceration, I recognize prison cannot be reformed. Why? Because no elected official has been willing or able to address fundamental flaws within the criminal legal system. Many have tinkered with the edges of mass incarceration, but that is all.

To shrink the carceral state is to cut off the flow of people. To cut off the flow of people into prison is to greatly restrict and regulate the mechanisms at the gate and beyond. Before we can eliminate the need for prisons, incarceration must go from a first resort to a last. What follows are fundamental changes to how crime and punishment is approached. Though not panaceas, these measures can begin the hard work of ending mass incarceration.

First, enforce the Eighth Amendment's prohibition against cruel and unusual punishment by abolishing the death penalty.

Second, reinstate the parole system for federal prisoners and in those states where it was eliminated in the nineties. This also means ending LWOP and virtual life sentences of fifty years and over. There must be a possibility of release for prisoners who demonstrate rehabilitation over time. Similarly, clemency is a critical second-look mechanism that acknowledges the criminal legal system gets it wrong. Parole commissions should not be political positions any more than clemency boards. The further removed from politics these bodies are, the greater the chance for more people to obtain relief after serving their time.

Third, hold prison officials accountable for recidivism in their state. Corrections must coordinate with the parole commission to ensure prisoners have an incentive for participating in rehabilitative and educational programs. This also means investing in restorative justice programs that teach people true accountability for the harm they have caused others. Some states already have close contact between the parole board and prison officials—more must follow.

Fourth, eliminate prosecutor's absolute immunity and hold them accountable for abuses of power while in office. Those abuses of power mean everything from wrongful prosecutions and false imprisonment, to overcharging as a way to leverage guilty pleas from innocent defendants.

Fifth, apportion correctional budgets according to county population and crime rate, capping the number of people a given district can send to prison. This would force district attorneys to reserve costly, long-term sentences for the most serious crimes, and use diversion programs, combination sentences, and restorative justice whenever possible. Nonviolent prisoners should be made to pay restitution, do community service, and engage in community-centered programming rather than be incarcerated.

Sixth, abolish the cash bail system. Multimillion-dollar bails are unreasonable, unattainable, and punitive prior to being convicted of a crime. Court release, home confinement, probation, and postrelease supervision are often associated with fees that make it impossible to pay bills or stay out of what amounts to debtor's prison, which is unconstitutional.

Seventh, eliminate the collateral consequences of incarceration that disenfranchise millions. Allow the incarcerated to vote by absentee ballot as they do in Maine, Vermont, and DC. Expunge all records after a five-year period without reoffense. Limit felony probation and postrelease supervision to two years. Provide tax incentives to companies willing to hire people out of prison.

Eighth, end jail and prison profiteering via the goods and services provided to people in confinement. Companies such as ViaPath (GTL), Securus, JPAY, Keefe, GEO Group, CoreCivic, Wellpath, and others should be strictly regulated by the Federal Trade Commission and Federal Communications Comission to prevent predatory fees, price gouging, and monopolies.

Ninth, create a criminal justice agency that regulates law enforcement, the Bar Association, the judiciary, corrections, and probation, which are directly involved in the apprehension, prosecution, defense, sentencing, incarceration, and supervision of those suspected of or charged with criminal offenses. Central to the function of a criminal justice agency would be ensuring the Constitution is upheld at every stage of the criminal legal proceedings, prevent the expansion of the penal system, hold officials within individual branches of the criminal legal system accountable, and conduct reviews of all related branches.

Tenth, eliminate the exception to slavery in the Thirteenth Amendment. This would most likely require a constitutional amendment that upholds human dignity and prohibits slavery in any form against any person for any reason.

These regulations are not the only possibilities. More, in fact, are needed. Ultimately, significant shifts like these require legislative action. That means voting out of office any elected official unwilling to commit to abandoning the patchwork draconian criminal legal system that maintains mass incarceration.

ભ

Proposing fundamental changes that seek to not only limit but also reduce the size and unchecked power of the criminal legal system is entirely different from carrying them out. After the 2020 George Floyd protests, North Carolina Governor Roy Cooper signed Executive Order 145, creating the Task Force for Racial Equity in Criminal Justice (TREC). It was the job of the task force to develop policy solutions that addressed racial inequities in the criminal justice system. Led by Attorney General Josh Stein and Associate Justice Anita Earls, TREC was divided into four working groups: law enforcement management, policing policies and practices, court-based interventions to end discriminatory criminalization, and advancing racial equity in trials and postconviction.[1] Each group contained "a diverse cross section of leaders" that included advocates, elected officials, judges, prosecutors, public defenders, law enforcement, policy experts, and academics.[2]

The task force met virtually during the pandemic, the meetings livestreamed on the North Carolina Attorney General's YouTube page. Because transparency and public input were important to TREC, numerous academics, specialists, policymakers, advocacy groups, and individuals submitted written material for consideration. As one of those individuals, I submitted four proposals through the Digital Abolitionist, a group that seeks to amplify incarcerated voices. My proposals were:

- Abolish the death penalty.
- Create a second-look mechanism that grants the NC Postrelease Supervision and Parole Commission the authority to review life, virtual life, and life without parole sentences of prisoners who have served a minimum of twenty-five years, providing qualifying prisoners relief where appropriate.
- Establish a rehabilitative mandate throughout North Carolina prisons that ensures implementation of mental health, vocational, and educational programs in every facility.
- Commission an Ombuds office* to oversee conditions of confinement in NC prisons and jails, with the authority to investigate complaints of neglect and abuse, and bring those findings before the court and North Carolina Department of Public Safety (NCDPS) officials for a mediated solution.

My proposals were submitted to attorney Henderson Hill, a leader of TREC, and read aloud during a period of public comments by a member

---

* A neutral or impartial conflict resolution specialist who provides confidential assistance on a variety of concerns.

of the Digital Abolitionist. I participated, to the best of my ability, in the effort to fundamentally change North Carolina's criminal legal system. As someone with a vested interested in that change, a writer and public advocate for the incarcerated, it is the best form of activism I knew to do.

Ultimately, the task force made over 124 recommendations to the governor, all of which were supported by reams of data and expertise, haggling among the groups, and participation by law enforcement. After each recommendation was a description and action step. For example:

> #116. Review All Future Sentences after Twenty Years or Before.
> Requires all future sentences to be reviewed at the twenty-year mark or before by a judge or judicial panel.
> Necessary Action: legislative change.[3]

Most of the recommendations require legislative change, while others required changes in NCDPS, prosecutorial, or judicial policy. A number of bills were submitted to the Republican-controlled General Assembly, which objected to the creation of or need for the task force. No bill stemming from TREC was passed by the General Assembly. Any action came as a result of policy change or executive order, such as creation of the Juvenile Sentence Review Board discussed in Ben Finholt's interview in this collection. When I asked Kerwin Pittman, a member of TREC, who was the most difficult to work with and gave the least ground, his answer was immediate. "Law enforcement. They have too much authority and see no need to listen to anyone else. Them and the Republicans."

The sentiment was expressed by everyone I interviewed or have ever spoken with about the subject of systemic change. To be fair, there are Democrats who are also okay with the bloated and egregiously abusive criminal justice system in America. In fact, there are many elected leaders who believe the system works as it was designed: for them. Change would happen more often and be less urgent if it was easy. That is why we fight and resist and strive with every labored breath for a society that serves and protects all of us. Until that day arrives...

November is coming.

Amber Caron
Interviews Lyle C. May

Amber Caron* (AC): You've said in other interviews that your interest in writing developed through writing letters. I'm fascinated by this idea and would love to hear more about it. Can you describe what lessons you learned through letter writing? And was there a turning point for you when you realized you wanted to shift from the personal audience (family and friends) to a more general audience? What challenges did you face as a writer when you made that shift?

Lyle May (LM): My first letters home were mailed from the Maine Youth Center. They weren't really conversations, just questions. *Can you come visit? Will you send some pictures? Have you talked to my probation officer?* At sixteen, my letters were less about conveying experience and more about gaining information. This changed in the county jail when I was charged with a double murder I did not commit, mainly because the pending capital trial and potential death sentence drove home the imminent possibility of my execution.

By age nineteen I was no more qualified or expert at writing letters, but my desire to be understood grew. My parents and family needed to know I did not kill anyone. But how do you convince people of that when all they hear is the worst from prosecutors and the media? Saying

---

* Amber Caron is a writing instructor at Utah State University and author of the short story collection, *Call Up the Waters* (Milkweed Press, 2023.)

"not me" and proving "not me" left a lot of explanation in between. All I had was a GED and letters. Writing became a practice, a desperate plea for understanding, to listen, help, and not abandon me. Some letters were streams of consciousness that wrestled with anxiety, depression, fear, hopelessness, confusion, and anger—so they held little structure, becoming garbled signals from a distant radio tower. I hoped for responses, and some did. Many did not.

As my grammar improved, I mimicked some of the things I read. Sometimes I wrote down passages that spoke to something as yet undefined in me. This was especially true when I read Viktor Frankl's *Man's Search for Meaning*. Back then my "identity" was undeveloped. I didn't know who I was, only how the state wanted to define me. In the wake of my death sentence, and the execution of friends, the search intensified. Some of the quotes were threads of meaning beyond the reach of immaturity, but I recognized that they held value and wrote them down in a journal even if I didn't understand them. In a way, the most important lessons had already been written, I just had to find a way to make them my own.

The turning point from personal letters to writing for an audience came after several years of running a fantasy-based role-playing game (RPG). The fantasy and science fiction genres played a big role in my incarceration. These books were pure escapism and imagination. The plots, adventures, and characters so vivid that I wanted to recreate or contrive the stories. In the beginning, a few of my friends and I got together and, using half-remembered rules from Advanced Dungeons & Dragons, made up a bootleg version of D&D. Central to the game is storytelling and character development. I genuinely liked, and was good at, world-building, to the point where gaming sessions lasted from after breakfast until the cell doors were closed for the night. It was better than TV, and gave us a modicum of control over our world.

RPGs shifted into writing whenever I prepared extended campaigns by sketching out antagonist backstories and plots. The best ones endured through multiple sessions and were memorable enough to spark conversations, or in my case, nicknames. I fell in love with the longevity of these creative works. One year the NCDAC [North Carolina Department of Adult Corrections] offered a writing contest, so I tried my hand at short stories. I immediately discovered the difference between vocalizing a story and writing one to win a contest or get published. I struggled to write beyond the kind of books I read and learned an important early lesson: Writers are what they read. And yet, I like fantasy and sci-fi. I like writing. This does not necessarily make me a qualified fantasy/sci-fi writer. It was a humbling discovery. It would be some time before I understood writing as a craft and responsibility, or knew what needed to be written.

AC: Most people will probably be surprised to learn that the only technology you have access to is a telephone,* and the telephone only arrived on death row in 2016. How did access to a phone impact your writing and publishing efforts?

LM: I can't overstate how much the phone advanced my writing and publishing efforts. Before June 2016, all of those efforts were slow, with revisions taking months and rejected submissions feeling like major setbacks. Up to that point I had several essays published, which felt like big achievements without the benefit of technology. The phone sped up this process. Research became possible in a fifteen-minute conversation. Faster decisions—about where to submit a manuscript, how it had been revised, troubleshooting delays, and simple adjustments—made more publications possible. Communicating more quickly with editors became possible because I could dictate brief emails to my friend Tara. Maybe most importantly, the phone helped me network and connect directly with my audience.

Connecting with professors and church leaders brought me into the classroom and congregations in a way that writing does not. As a living voice, what I had to say became harder to ignore and sparked conversations after the calls ended. My writing became a hybrid of memoir reporting—activism that would have taken years to develop without the phone. It makes me wonder about those scenes in movies and on TV shows where a bored author sits at a table signing books rather than engaging the audience about the material.

---

* This interview was conducted prior to the arrival of tablets on death row in April, 2022.

Is my advantage that I don't take technology or the audience for granted? Or that I have more to lose by failing to connect? Maybe I'm feeding a stereotype, and most authors do what they can to engage readers. They can actually visit bookstores or go to conferences. The phone, through the technology of Zoom, makes it possible for me. While promoting *Crimson Letters: Voices from Death Row* [renamed *Inside: Voices from Death Row* once republished by Scuppernong Editions] during the pandemic, Tessie Castillo set up Zoom events with private schools, universities, book clubs, and church groups. I or one of the other coauthors called Tessie's phone, she would log into Zoom, and we could talk to the Zoom participants just like a conference call. This supercharged our connection with the public in a way unheard of for death row prisoners. I could, in the course of two or three fifteen-minute phone calls talk to hundreds of people about prison abolition, sentencing policies, and activism around the criminal legal system.

AC: Perhaps on a somewhat similar note: many of your pieces are heavily researched. Can you describe the role research plays in your writing and how you gain access to the necessary books, articles, data, and stories? Or perhaps what challenges you've faced trying to gain access to the necessary materials?

LM: Research is critical to my writing because I want to build upon the work of scholars who came before me, and I want readers to understand my writing through that lens. Researched articles raise the level of credibility of my writing even as I contextualize facts and dispute or support theories. Part of this is my education in the social sciences, and another part of it is my desire to have a solid foundation for my arguments. Plus, there is no need to reinvent topics when, by citing valuable contributions to the study of criminal justice policies, I can expand the conversation with my experience and knowledge.

Outside of scholarly works, I rely a lot on newspaper articles, because they are a primary source of reporting on the criminal legal system. It is also the popular narrative I push back against the most. By using readily available public information, then challenging its many misconceptions and fallacies, I do the sort of basic work taught in college English classes about critical analyses of a source or argument. I respect journalism as a profession and do my best to mimic the process, but prison journalism requires creative sourcing, cobbling together facts in alignment with my experiences and those of my peers, while recognizing there is a thread of advocacy holding it all together. I don't pretend neutrality. Sometimes all I have is experience, but even then I try to think about it critically and use its undiluted form sparingly.

Gaining access to data for an article can be tricky. I do my best to anticipate needed information by collecting newspaper articles on subjects related to the criminal legal system. Prison Legal News and Criminal Legal News are incredibly valuable resources because they essentially do the same thing but from online sources, nonprofits like the Cato Institute, and newspapers around the country. I also get book recommendations from friends, professors, and other professionals. There is no library at Central Prison containing the subject matter I cover, because it's often censored. For a long time, Michelle Alexander's *The New Jim Crow* was on the banned list. So too are books about the history of lynching and influence of southern penalty. *Crimson Letters* is on the banned list and I fully expect *Witness* will be. This is unfortunate, but it brings up another reason why my writing is heavily researched: it's harder for prison officials to retaliate against previously reported facts and agreed-upon truths.

Not having access to the internet for in-depth research can be frustrating. There are times I would have loved to dig into NCDPS [North Carolina Department of Public Safety] archives or file a FOIA [Freedom of Information Act] request for certain public officials' email exchanges, but this could be a blessing in disguise. Digging too deep in a decaying penal system could make the wrong people angry. I have been fortunate this far into my prison journalism not to face any serious backlash. That could easily change if I had access to the same depth of information as an ordinary journalist, simply because it could be construed as a weapon in the hands of a prisoner. Thus, some information is considered a "threat to security."

AC: Can you talk a little more about your actual writing process? You don't have access to a computer and yet you're publishing

regularly in print and online journals, magazines, and newspapers. What does that look like for you? What challenges have you faced along the way?

LM: My first journal publication, "Domesticated," in the *J Journal*, happened because a close friend suggested I submit something. He read another prisoner's essay and believed mine could find a place there too. I wrote and revised an essay, sent it to Tara for typing, and she in turn mailed it to the *J Journal*, located at the John Jay College of Criminal Justice in New York. When an editor replied they wanted to publish the essay, it felt like such a huge accomplishment. When suggested revisions arrived in the mail, they were minimal and made sense. I okayed them, and within six to eight weeks received copies of the journal where my writing appeared. This same process of word-of-mouth submission played out for the *Marshall Project*, PrisonWriters, the *Copper Nickel*, and *Scalawag* magazine. Each publication was a reference by a friend. Every submission a slow process of write, revise, send, wait for a response, edit, and wait for publication. The online publications were a little less satisfying and, like the blog, felt like wishing wells. Not seeing my work published meant trusting that it actually had been. Tara, of course, told me when it appeared though, and she soon became both a critical part of my ability to publish and the bearer of good and bad news alike. She has always been a great friend, but in this she went above and beyond. That stability gave me the confidence to keep trying. Other than this, the publication process is for me, as I imagine it is for other budding writers, one of trial and error. Maybe one thing that is different in all of this—when I write and submit things to publishers, I try to make certain it's not frivolous, to ensure I don't waste her time or mine. In this way, writing became a very intentional activity, whereas publishing was always a team effort, and the customary rules of communication, cooperation, and coordination apply.

Something else readers should consider about my lack of access to technology is that I became a writer without a computer or typewriter. I have never been dependent on technology, so its absence, while limiting, prevents nothing. What has happened is the natural development of networks and publication through vicarious use of technology. Sure, with direct access to a computer, writing and publishing would go quickly, I would do more speaking events to larger audiences, my networking ability would be limitless. Yet, even now, those goals are not impossible from prison. I have proven that much. Hard, yes. Tenuous, absolutely. Frustratingly slow at times, but not impossible. The process of writing and publishing from prison makes certain I don't take success for granted. I will not get lost in the ease of communicating via email, Twitter, or some other method because maintaining contact with the outside world from the inside takes effort. Communicating important information like that contained in *Witness* requires a daily commitment to writing and a firm belief in its value.

AC: Over the last two years, you've had a number of speaking engagements at several colleges, universities, and centers around the country, including UNC-Chapel Hill, Florida Southern College, University of Minnesota, Columbia University, New York University Public Interest Law Center, Ohio University, among others. What are some of the fundamental lessons or ideas that you hope to expose to college students? Why does it feel important to engage students in this way?

LM: This might sound redundant, but I stress students do their due diligence. The criminal legal system is complex, nuanced, and massive, which means accepting a single, mainstream narrative ignores the lived experiences of millions. It also makes you naive. I often end talks by imploring students to dig deeper on a given topic—don't just take my word for it. A holistic understanding of the carceral state is the only way to dissolve it. That cannot be done by relying on one media account, political perspective, public figure, or prisoner for information or direction.

The lesson of narratives is crucial to understanding the carceral state, but that point was driven home in the era of Trump. Propaganda created mass incarceration. In the 1980s and 1990s penal populists convinced Congress and a majority of America that penal experts—the people who manage prisons—failed the public. Populism, fueled by the fear of crime and an inability to manage it, corrupted perceptions about the purpose of prison. Suddenly, higher education in prison, incentives like parole, and basic human decency were thought of as too good for the incarcerated. Torture in confinement became acceptable. The ease with which an entire generation was discarded in prison is frightening in the scope of history. Other groups were similarly devalued, denigrated, oppressed, and exterminated under the false label of "justice," but to the outside world it was often genocide and always wrong. At the root of it all are the catalysts: misinformation, disinformation, and willful ignorance. I am in a position to help disrupt that slippery slope, praying each talk dispels the willful ignorance and blind obedience to a single narrative.

I also do my best to awaken students to their stereotypes and biases about the incarcerated on death row. Not everyone talks, looks, thinks, or acts the same in our environments. People vary. We are multifaceted, ever-evolving, and often misunderstood. This is a basic truth. Prison is a miserable, obscure public institution that fails as a public safety measure because it hides a basic truth about people. We are anything but the static nature of a specific moment in time. Bryan Stevenson says we are all more than our worst mistakes—I do my best to remind students of this in different ways and challenge their understanding of prison by pulling back the curtain.

AC: Looking through this book it's interesting to note the broad range of topics you explore in your writing. You engage and report on many facets of the prison system: law, health care, education, religion, politics, and even food. Can you describe how your interests have evolved over the years as a journalist and activist? And can you describe where your interests are taking you now? In other words, what projects are you most excited about?

LM: There is no shortage of topics to write about the criminal legal system. Sometimes it can feel overwhelming, or as if I can never do enough, or the subject matter is too complex, but these are the same reasons many people shy away from the hard work of holding corrupt systems accountable. I can't ask anyone to engage in that effort if I'm not willing to put in the work too. I don't have the luxury to ignore my environment. But earning an [associate's] degree on death row changed everything. It made me responsible in a way I never expected. Higher education in prison is rare enough, but on death row it's anomalous, so I couldn't help feeling "chosen." Maybe this is where fantasy and faith meet my desire to prove the state wrong: they don't have a right to kill—no one does. Maybe in discovering myself on death row and learning about the prison-industrial complex this crucible of society's ills will always be my front line. In that sense it's essential others in prison are equipped like I have been. My thinking is not special. I am not special. My access to higher education has been special. Thus, my next book, *The Transformative Journey of Higher Education in Prison: A Class of One,* is due to be published by Routledge Academic Press in 2024.

My work as an incarcerated journalist and subsequent public speaking is ongoing. It was at an *Inside: Voices from Death Row* (Scuppernong Editions, 2022) book event I connected with Dr. Robert Johnson of American University. We agreed to coauthor an article comparing congregate death row confinement with solitary death row confinement, focusing on how, regardless of the type, the psychological torture of a death sentence cannot be avoided, and is fundamentally cruel and unusual punishment. This comes at a time when Ohio seems poised to abolish its death penalty and President Biden has claimed a willingness to end the federal government's use of capital punishment. If both were to abolish [the death penalty], it could place capital punishment at a tipping point even the conservative US Supreme Court will struggle to ignore. Whether they ultimately determine a minority of the states maintaining the death penalty violates the "unusual punishment" elements of the Eighth Amendment remains to be seen. Regardless, I will make my voice heard in this fight.

AC: I imagine a lot of people will finish reading this book and want to do something to help put an end to the death penalty. What do you recommend these readers do to help change the criminal justice system? What practical steps can they take to make meaningful change?

LM: The prison-industrial complex is a colossal pile of rubble that has buried millions of people. The effort to excavate those people must be a collective one. Some of it must be organized and address key laws and structures within the criminal legal system, but every effort helps. If you're new to the topics in *Witness*, get educated by reading some of the works cited in this book. Do your own research into a specific topic, learn about it, then look for ways to address the problem. Some basic ways to get involved as a concerned citizen include voting and outreach. Don't simply vote for one party or another; research all of the local races, especially for district attorney, sheriff, and any judicial seat. These are the gatekeepers who determine changes, sentence length, prosecution of police brutality, conditions of jail confinement, whether someone is released from prison, tried for death, fined, sent to drug court, and more. Voting really matters in these local races. Your inaction or failure to vote makes you complicit in the problem. Voting conscientiously is a powerful tool in the hands of the oppressed. Why do you think some public officials try to restrict this constitutional right?

If you're already a conscientious voter familiar with the [prison-industrial complex] make sure everyone in your circle is too. Connect with your family, neighbors, coworkers, and anyone on social media to make them aware and get them involved. Pick a single issue like diversion programs, pretrial detainment, immigration, or probation fees and explain to others why and how it should change. Engaging in activism may involve protests, boycotts of companies or celebrities that invest in private prisons, projects that encourage voting for a particular candidate, encouraging your district's legislator to support a particular reform, or attending city council meetings whenever there is a referendum or discussion that involves an element of the criminal legal system. Get other people to share your enthusiasm or interest in dissolving the carceral state and disrupting the school-to-prison pipeline.

At the end of the day, it's equally important to support someone in prison. Write to him or her on a consistent basis. If you can, send books or a little money for the canteen or phone calls. Visit. You would be surprised at how lonely prison is and the need we all have for someone to just listen and be there. Outside of activism, the human connection with people behind the fence is critical to understanding our plight.

Prisons are public institutions. They belong to tax-paying citizens, which makes them a public responsibility. When they generate greater harms in a community, when they torture, devalue, and kill, this is a consequence of ignoring that responsibility. Transformative justice that works for everyone means engaging the criminal-legal-carceral process in whatever capacity you have to build the world you want to exist. That's all I can ask anyone. It begins now.

AC: This is a potentially unfair question, but I'll ask it anyway: If you had one book to recommend on prison reform or ending the death penalty, what would that book be and why?

LM: Ha. That *is* an unfair question, but not an unfamiliar one. I draw a lot of information and inspiration from Rachel Elise Barkow's *Prisoners of Politics: Breaking the Cycle of Mass Incarceration.* It is essential reading for anyone truly interested in ending mass incarceration and replacing the adversarial criminal legal system with transformative justice. Dr. Barkow's experience as law clerk for Justice Antonin Scalia, as a member of the Manhattan DA's Conviction Integrity Policy Advisory Panel, and a member of the US Sentencing Commission lends substantial weight to what might otherwise be deemed radical reforms. Central to this book is Dr. Barkow's argument for an institutional shift in criminal justice policy toward data and expertise, a criminal justice agency removed from the electorate and politics of crime. It's not just that she presents a grand idea for systemic change; her arguments are detailed examinations of dysfunctional policies, what to replace them with, how to do it, and the impact it will have on the entire system. Saying you want to end mass incarceration or abolish the prison-industrial complex is easy. In the face of the carceral state real change can be overwhelming. Where do you begin? *Prisoners of Politics* is a twenty-first-century map for real justice, nuanced policies, and an end to the corruption of politics in crime control. I envy Dr. Barkow's students at NYU. For the rest of us, her writing is the next best thing.

An essay adapted from Lyle C. May's

The Transformative Journey of Higher Education in Prison: A Class of One

Forthcoming from Routledge Academic Press in 2024

Overlapping conversations drowned out thought amid the dining hall stench: a blend of sour mop and something dead—probably a rat—left to rot. It blunted any appetite for the slop shoved out of the window in a wretched assembly line that fed thousands daily. Small flies fed on juice spilled from the top of yellow Igloo jugs. Other than waking up, standing in the chow line was one of the most hated rituals in prison.

A wide metal door at the front of the dining hall buzzed open, admitting Ms. Y, a middle-aged woman as loud and brash as she was petty and vindictive. She smiled and waved at various people, a folded piece of paper in hand fanning flies. "Lyle May? Lyle May!" she yelled. As an assistant unit manager, Ms. Y drew attention, but also because she was a woman in a male prison. "You hear me? I got something you want." Snickers and a few lewd comments followed, but the assistant unit manager just narrowed her eyes as she walked to the front of the line where I stood. She shoved the paper at me. "Here. This is yours."

I put it in my pocket. Ms. Y said, "Aren't you going to look at it?"

Frowning, I removed the staple and unfolded the paper. It was a

photocopy of my Ohio University associate in arts degree. I had "graduated" the month before and had eagerly awaited the diploma. Staring at the
May 13 date written in cursive script above the university seal, irritation
flashed. "Why can't I have the original?" It had been nearly nine years
since a prison official approved my enrollment in college correspondence
courses. During that time, I never asked for anything beyond a proctor
for exams, receipt and delivery of course materials sent by the university,
and a programs director's signature on registration forms. These were the
original tasks then—associate warden of programs Mr. Mac agreed the Programs Department would handle. Surely they could let me have the original diploma?

Ms. Y rolled her eyes, hand on hip, and spoke as if to a child or dog.
Voice pitched high, she mimicked me. "Why can't I have the original?"
Then she looked over her glasses. "Because you can't have documents like
that. It's against policy. Jeez. You're lucky you got that. Thank me and be
glad I gave you a copy."

Swallowing my anger, I thanked Ms. Y, grabbed a tray, and sat at a
table with some friends. My interactions with staff were limited to avoid
encounters like this one, because some of them acted as if imprisonment
gave people in positions of authority the right to treat the incarcerated as
less than people, as if we were property that could be caged, subjected to
subtle forms of torture, or put to death. Fortunately, I knew the path of
higher education in prison was never intended to be easy.

In the beginning, I had to overcome my aversion to communicating
with staff and request permission from the associate warden of programs
to enroll in a correspondence course. That person happened to be Mr.
Mac, an old-school prison official who was around when the rehabilitative ideal governed prison systems around the country. Mr. Mac was
easygoing and immediately supportive of my request to take college
courses. He cautioned me though, explaining all he could do was provide an "okay," the rest would be up to me.

"It's not like it used to be when Shaw University taught here," the
associate warden of programs told me. "Once the government ended Pell
Grants for you guys it changed the way prisons work. The state funds
very few programs, then expects me to pick up the slack. And if I help

y'all too much, somebody is breathing down my neck about siding with inmates." He shook his head in disgust. "As long as you find someone to pay for the courses, I'll do what I can to help. Just remember everyone you deal with won't be so supportive."

I understood. Having spent time in the Maine Youth Center and juvenile solitary confinement, living on the street as a teen struggling with addiction, these experiences taught me to appreciate small kindnesses in a world of exceptional brutality. Freedom, safety, and now the pursuit of a higher education depended on those kindnesses.

ॐ

Discussion Questions

1. Who were the original anti–death penalty activists? What made their role as such so dangerous?

2. Why doesn't the public get to vote for or against the death penalty?

3. What makes long-term confinement a form of torture?

4. Who holds the most power in the criminal legal system?

5. Why are law enforcement and other public officials held less accountable than citizens?

6. Where is the nearest prison to your house? Is it a private or state-run prison? What's the difference?

7. How many innocent people need to be exonerated from death row before you will contact your local district attorney and demand they stop seeking capital punishment, or speak against its use?

8. How do confirmation bias, political echo chambers, and popular media outlets disseminate misinformation about the criminal legal system?

9. If only 40 percent of crimes are reported and processed through

the criminal legal system, and 60–65 percent of all people who leave prison return within five years, what does this say about the purpose of prison?

10. Why does the United States ignore international standards of torture when it comes to confining its own citizens?

11. What role does religion play in application of the death penalty?

12. How can the Willie Horton effect, the idea that one bad case spoils an otherwise effective program like parole, be prevented from influencing criminal justice policy?

13. What steps can be taken to separate politics from criminal justice policies that reduce crime and recidivism without growing the carceral state? (Hint: think about your response to #8.)

14. Should higher education be a basic right? Why?

15. Can you name the following people for your county, city, district, and state: district attorney, mayor, city council, senior resident superior court judge, district court judge, attorney general, supreme court justices, senate majority leader, house majority leader, and governor? If you can only name a few, google any you don't know. These public officials—all of whom are elected by your vote (or lack thereof) control the carceral state.

Notes

Chapter 1: Learning to Die
Originally published by the *Copper Nickel*.

Chapter 2: Secrecy and the Death Penalty
Originally presented as a lecture, UNC Chapel Hill: POLI 203: "Race, Innocence, and the End of the Death Penalty," February 23, 2020.

1. Seth Kotch, *Lethal State: A History of the Death Penalty in North Carolina* (Chapel Hill: University of North Carolina Press, 2019).
2. Kotch, *Lethal State*.
3. Anthony Ray Hinton with Lara Love Hardin, *The Sun Does Shine* (New York: St. Martin's Griffin, 2018), 166.
4. *State of North Carolina v. Andrew Darrin Ramseur*, NCSC No. 388A10 (June 5, 2020).
5. Danielle Battaglia, "Forsyth Deputies and a Nurse Charged Following Death of an Inmate," *News & Observer*, July 9, 2020, https://www.newsobserver.com/news/state/north-carolina/article244070427.html.

Chapter 3: A Confirmation of Faith
Originally published by *America Magazine*.

Chapter 4: Death Row Phenomenon
1. *Soering v. United Kingdom*, 161 (1989) Eur Court HR (ser A).
2. *Soering*.
3. UN General Assembly, Resolution 39/46, United Nations Convention against Torture and Other Cruel, Inhuman or Degrading Treatment or

Punishment, Article 1 (December 31, 1984).

4. Victor L. Streib, *Death Penalty in a Nutshell*, 4th ed. (St. Paul, MN: Thomson/West, 2013), 289.

5. Streib, *Death Penalty*.

6. Streib, *Death Penalty*, 283.

7. Streib, *Death Penalty*, 285.

8. *Stanford v. Kentucky*, 492 US 361, 109 S. Ct. 2969, 10 L.Ed. 2d 306 (1989).

9. Stuart Grassian and Nancy Friedman, "Effects of Sensory Deprivation in Psychiatric Seclusion and Solitary Confinement," *International Journal of Law and Psychiatry* 8, no. 1 (1986): 4965; Stuart Grassian, "Psychopathological Effects of Solitary Confinement," *American Journal of Psychiatry* 140, no. 11 (November 1983): 1450–54.

10. Sharon Shalev, "A Sourcebook on Solitary Confinement" (London: Mannheim Centre for Criminology, 2008), www.solitaryconfinement.org.

11. Holly A. Miller and Glenn R. Young, "Prison Segregation: Administrative Detention Remedy or Mental Health Problem?," *Criminal Behavior and Mental Health* 85, no. 92 (1997): 7.

Chapter 5: A Tale of Two Henrys

Originally published by *Scalawag* magazine.

Chapter 6: Qualified Immunity

Originally published by *Scalawag* magazine.

1. Andrew Carter, "Sentenced to Death after Being Convicted by a Lie, NC Brothers Still Wait for Justice," *News & Observer*, March 12, 2021, https://www.newsobserver.com/article249376940.html.

2. Carter, "Sentenced to Death."

3. Andrew Carter, "Jury Awards Wrongfully Convicted NC Brothers $75 Million in Federal Civil Rights Case," *News & Observer*, May 15, 2021, https://www.newsobserver.com/article251411148.html.

4. Sam Cabral, "Does a $75m Settlement Make Up for Three Decades in Prison?," *BBC News*, May 23, 2021, https://www.bbc.com/news/world-us-canada-57152860#.

5. Lateshia Beachum, "Two Brothers Were Wrongfully Convicted of Murder and Rape. Decades Later, a Jury Has Awarded Them $75

Million," *Washington Post*, May 16, 2021, https://www.washingtonpost.com/nation/2021/05/16/north-carolina-brothers-exonerated-75million/.

6. Carter, "Jury Awards Wrongfully Convicted."

7. *State v. Lyle May*, 97CRS-60515-16 (Buncombe Co.) Trial Transcript, Vol. 5, Tp. 674-686.

8. *State v. Lyle May*, Tp. 704.

9. Steven A. Drizin and Richard A. Leo, "The Problem of False Confessions in the Post-DNA World," 82 N.C. L. Rev. 891 (2004), https://scholarship.law.unc.edu/nclr/vol82/iss3/3.

10. Matthew Clarke, "Controversial Police Interrogation Technique That Often Results in False Confessions Abandoned by Influential Training Consultant," *Criminal Legal News*, May 2018, https://www.criminallegalnews.org/news/2018/apr/19/controversial-police-interrogation-technique-often-results-false-confessions-abandoned-influential-training-consultant/.

11. California Innocence Project, "False Testimony/Confessions," California Western Law School, https://californiainnocenceproject.org/issues-we-face/false-confessions/.

12. Clarke, "Controversial Police."

13. Jeff Welty, "Recording Interrogations," North Carolina Criminal Law: A UNC School of Government Blog, February 16, 2009, https://nccriminallaw.sog.unc.edu/recording-interrogations/.

14. *State v. May*, Vol IX, Tp. 1203, 1204.

15. Mariame Kaba, *We Do This 'Til We Free Us: Abolitionist Organizing and Transforming Justice* (Chicago: Haymarket Books, 2021), 107, 108.

16. "Chicago Torture Justice Memorials," ChicagoTorture, May 17, 2021, https://chicagotorture.org/.

17. Kaba, *We Do This 'Til We Free Us*.

18. Jay R. Schweikert, "Qualified Immunity: A Legal, Practical, and Moral Failure," Cato Institute, September 14, 2020, https://www.cato.org/policy-analysis/qualified-immunity-legal-practical-moral-failure.

19. Schweikert, "Qualified Immunity."

20. Schweikert, "Qualified Immunity."

21. Schweikert, "Qualified Immunity."

22. Carter, "Sentenced to Death."

23. Frank Baumgartner et al., *Deadly Justice: A Statistical Portrait of the Death Penalty* (New York: Oxford University Press, 2018), 218.

24. Michael Gordon, "What's the Price for Decades of Wrongful Imprisonment? Ronnie Long Sues NC City, Cops," *Charlotte Observer*, May 4, 2021, https://www.charlotteobserver.com/news/local/article251123624.html.

Chapter 7: The Economics of Capital Punishment

Originally delivered as a lecture for Dr. Lisa Carter's Death Penalty in America Criminology class for undergraduates, April 7, 2021.

1. David McCord, "If Capital Punishment Were Subject to Consumer Protection Laws," *Judicature* 89, no. 5 (March–April 2006): 305.

2. Alan Blinder, "Joe Freeman Britt, Called America's 'Deadliest D.A.,' Dies at 80," *New York Times*, April 12, 2019, https://www.nytimes.com/2016/04/13/us/joe-freeman-britt-called-americas-deadliest-da-dies-at-80.html.

3. Anthony Ray Hinton with Lara Love Hardin, *The Sun Does Shine* (New York: St. Martin's Griffin, 2018), 166.

Chapter 8: On Death Row, Eating to Live

Originally published by *Meal Magazine*.

Chapter 9: Life without Parole Is a Silent Execution

Originally published by *Scalawag* magazine.

1. Anne Blythe, "She's Serving a Life Sentence for Killing Her Husband. But She Goes Out to Lunch?" *News & Observer*, September 22, 2017, http://www.newsobserver.com/news/local/article174912241.html.

2. Sentencing Project, "Incarceration Rates in an International Perspective," policy brief, Sentencing Project, June 28, 2017, accessed November 6, 2017, http://www.sentencingproject.org/issues/incarceration/.

3. From the review of Christopher Seeds, *Death by Prison: The Emergence of Life without Parole and Perpetual Confinement* (Berkeley: University of California Press, 2022).

4. Carol S. Steiker and Jordan M. Steiker, *Courting Death: The Supreme Court and Capital Punishment* (Cambridge: Harvard University Press, 2016), 294.

5. Frank Baumgartner et al., *Deadly Justice: A Statistical Portrait of the*

Death Penalty, (New York: Oxford University Press, 2017), 174, 176.

6.   *Jones v. Chappell*, 31 F. Supp. 3d 1050 (C.D. Cal. 2014).

7.   Walter Lomax and Meredith Curtis, *Still Blocking the Exit*, ACLU of Maryland, January 20, 2015, https://www.aclu-md.org/en/publications/still-blocking-exit.

8.   Gordon Haas and Lloyd Fillion, *Life without Parole: A Reconsideration* (Boston: Criminal Justice Policy Coalition, 2010), 37, http://www.cjpc.org/uploads/1/0/4/9/104972649/life-without-parole-a-reconsideration.pdf.

9.   ACLU, *A Living Death: Life without Parole for Nonviolent Offenses* (New York: ACLU, 2013), https://www.aclu.org/report/living-death-life-without-parole-nonviolent- offenses.

10.   Maria Cramer, "Two Life Inmates Plead for Parole," *Boston Globe*, October 27, 2014, at A1, as cited in Haas and Fillion, *Life Without Parole*, 43.

11.   Haas and Fillion, *Life without Parole*, 16.

12.   Danielle Sered, *Accounting for Violence: How to Increase Safety and Break Our Failed Reliance on Mass Incarceration* (New York: Vera Institute of Justice, 2017), https://www.vera.org/publications/accounting-for-violence.

13.   Sered, *Accounting for Violence*.

Chapter 10: Beyond the Wall
Originally published by *Scalawag* magazine.

Chapter 11: Death by Incarceration
Originally delivered as a lecture at UNC Chapel Hill for the course taught by professor Frank Baumgartner, POLI 203: "Race, Innocence, and the End of the Death Penalty," February 24, 2020.

1.   Ben Miller and Daniel S. Harawa, "Democrats Should Stop Saying Some People Should Die in Prison," *Slate*, January 22, 2020, https://slate.com/news-and-politics/2020/01/elizabeth-warren-life-without-parole-death-penalty.html#:~:text=Scalia%20explained%20that%20the%20same,sentenced%20to%20life%20without%20parole.

2.   Ashley Nellis, "Still Life: America's Increasing Use of Life and Long-Term Sentences," *The Sentencing Project*, May 3, 2017, https://www.sentencingproject.org/app/uploads/2022/10/Still-Life.pdf.

3.   Dirk van Zyl Smit and Catherine Appleton, *Life Imprisonment: A Global*

Human Rights Analysis (Cambridge, MA: Harvard University Press, 2018).

4.   Catherine Appleton and Dirk van Zyl Smit, Challengng Life Imprisonment   (2018),   https://www.compen.crim.cam.ac.uk/Blog/ blog-pages-full-versions/guest-blog-on-challenging-life-imprisonment.

Chcpater 12: The Myth of Deterrence

1.   Marie Gottschalk, Caught: The Prison State and the Lockdown of American Politics. Princeton Universiy Press. (2015) p 102; p.329, n.35.

2.   Martha Henderson Hurley, *Aging in Prison: The Integration of Research and Practice*. (United States: Carolina Academic Press, 2017), 123.

Chapter 13: Paroling Michael Pinch

Originally published by *Scalawag* magazine.

1.   Stan Swofford, "In 1979, 20-Year-Old Michael Edward Pinch Killed Two Men at a Bikers Clubhouse in Greensboro. In His 22 Years on Death Row, Many Who Have Met Him Say Pinch Has Found Life after Death," *News & Record*, January 18, 2003, https://greensboro.com/ in-1979-20-year-old-michael-edward-pinch-killed-two-men-at-a-bikers-clubhouse/article_7e4bc9b0-cf0e-5dcd-8ca9-bac3498a6ef7.html.

2.   Swofford, "In 1979."

3.   Robert Weisberg, Debbie A. Mukamal, and Jordan D. Segall, "Life in Limbo: An Examination of Parole Release for Prisoners Serving Life Sentences with the Possibility of Parole in California," Stanford Criminal Justice Center, September 2011, https://law.stanford.edu/ index.php?webauth-document=child-page/164096/doc/slspublic/SCJC_ report_Parole_Release_for_Lifers.pdf.

Chapter 14: Mob Mentality in Politics

1.   Frank Baumgartner et al., *Deadly Justice: A Statistical Portrait of the Death Penalty* (New York: Oxford University Press, 2018), 208.

2.   "Innocence by the Numbers," Death Penalty Information Center, https://deathpenaltyinfo.org/policy-issues/innocence/innocence-by -the-numbers

Chapter 15: Freeing the Press in Prisons

Originally published by *Scalawag* magazine.

1.　　E. Fuller Torrey et al., "The Treatment of Persons with Mental Illness in Prisons and Jails: A State Survey," Treatment Advocacy Center and the National Sheriffs' Association, April 8, 2014, https://www.treatmentadvocacycenter.org/storage/documents/treatment-behind-bars/treatment-behind-bars.pdf.

2.　　Ames Alexander and Gavin Off, "Wrong Side of the Bars?," *Charlotte Observer*, June 2, 2017, https://www.charlotteobserver.com/news/special-reports/article153975449.html.

Chapter 16: Prison Journalism

1.　　*Houchins v. KQED*, Inc., 438 U.S. 1 (1978), No. 76-1310.

Chapter 17: Developing a Career from Prison

Originally published by *Scalawag* magazine.

Chapter 18: On Retaliation against Incarcerated Writers

Originally published by *Scalawag* magazine.

1.　　See, for example: *Pell v. Procunier*, 417 U.S. 817 (S. Ct. 1974) No. 73-918; *Saxbe v. Washington Post Co.*, 417 U.S. 843 (S. Ct. 1974), No. 73-1265; *Houchins v. KQED, Inc.*, 438 U.S. 1 (S. Ct. 1978), No. 76-1310; *Turner v. Safley*, 482 U.S. 78 (S. Ct. 1987), No. 85-1384.

2.　　George Orwell, *1984* (New York: Penguin Books, 2013), 6.

Chapter 19: Keeping the People Ignorant

1.　　*Thomas v. Evans*, 880 F.2d 1235 (11th Cir. 1989).

2.　　*Crawford-El v. Britton*, 523 U.S. 574 (1998), No. 96-827.

3.　　*N.C. State Conference of NAACP v. Cooper*, 1:18CV1034 (M.D.N.C. Aug. 17, 2021).

4.　　*Buffkin v. Hooks*, 1:18CV502 (M.D.N.C. Mar. 20, 2019).

Chapter 20: "A Modernized, Streamlined Incarceration Experience."

Originally published by *Scalawag* magazine.

1.　　Lyle C. May, "New, Multimillion-Dollar Jail Is No Panacea for Juvenile

Offenders," *Youth Today*, May 26, 2022, https://youthtoday.org/2022/05/new-multimillion-dollar-jail-is-no-panacea-for-juvenile-offenders/.

2. Mark Schultz, "Durham County Has a New Budget. What's in It for Schools, Taxpayers, and New Mothers?," *News & Observer*, June 14, 2022, https://www.newsobserver.com/news/local/counties/durham-county/article262490292.html.

3. State of North Carolina Department of Public Safety, "Social Media Policy," Communications Office, August 13, 2013, https://files.nc.gov/ncdps/emp/Policies/Communications/SocialMediaPolicy_08132013.pdf.

4. *Turner v. Safley*, 78, 89, 107.

5. Danielle Battaglia, "Judge Quietly Seals Death Records of North Carolina Man That Deputies Are Accused of Killing," *News & Observer*, February 8, 2021, https://www.newsobserver.com/news/local/crime/article248958704.html.

6. Lucille Sherman, "While You Were Sleeping: North Carolina Legislators Restricts Access to Public Records," *News & Observer*, December 29, 2020, https://www.newsobserver.com/news/politics-government/article243837792.html.

7. David M. Reutter, "Graphic Violence, Deaths in Alabama Prison Shown in Leaked Photos," *Prison Legal News* 31, no. 2 (February 2020): 28, 29.

8. Reutter, "Graphic Violence."

9. Reutter, "Graphic Violence."

10. Reutter, "Graphic Violence."

11. Salman Rushdie, "PEN vs. Sword," remarks delivered at *PEN America Emergency World Voices Congress of Writers*, New York, United Nations, May 2022, harpers.org/archive/2022/08/pen-america-emergency-world-voices-united-nations-ukraine, as cited in Mary Rasenberger, *The Authors Guild Bulletin* (Summer-Fall 2022): 3.

Chapter 21: Draconian Ideals

Originally published in *Scalawag* magazine.

1. Paul Guerino, Paige M. Harrison, and William J. Sabol, *Prisoners in 2010*, U.S. Department of Justice, December 2011, https://bjs.ojp.gov/content/pub/pdf/p10.pdf.

2. David Garland, "Foucault's *Discipline and Punish*: An Exposition and

Critique," *American Bar Foundation Research Journal* 11, no. 4 (1986): 847–80.

3. Caitlin Saunders, Joel Rosch, Susan Katzenelson, Michelle Li, and Sydney Curtis, *Improving Staffing and Security in North Carolina Prisons: A Review of Nationwide Prison Management Practices*, Duke University Sanford School of Public Policy, December 7, 2017, https://files.nc.gov/ncdps/documents/files/17.12.07%20FINAL_Crime%20Commission%20Prison%20Report.pdf.

4. Prison Reform Advisory Board, "Meeting Minutes," Reports and Recommendations, June 19, 2018, https://files.nc.gov/ncdps/documents/files/PRAB_2019ReportFINAL-oct2219.pdf.

5. Lauren Gill, "Federal Prisons' Switch to Scanning Mail Is a Surveillance Nightmare," *Intercept*, September 26, 2021, https://theintercept.com/2021/09/26/surveillance-privacy-prisons-mail-scan/.

6. Gill, "Federal Prisons' Switch."

Chapter 22: Science vs. Anti-Intellectualism and the Death Penalty

1. Alexandra O. Cohen et al., "When Is an Adolescent an Adult? Assessing Cognitive Control in Emotional and Nonemotional Contexts," *Psychological Science*, 27, no. 4, (2016): 549–62, https://doi.org/10.1177/0956797615627625.

2. American Bar Association, "Death Penalty Due Process Review Project Section of Civil Rights and Social Justice," Report to the 111th House of Delegates, https://www.ca1.uscourts.gov/sites/ca1/files/citations/ABA%20Death%20Penalty%20DP%20Review%20Project.pdf.

Chapter 24: Inside the Tinder Box

Originally published by *Scalawag* magazine.

1. Molly Gill, letter to Representatives John Bell, David Lewis, and Darren Jackson, FAMM.org, March 25, 2020, https://famm.org/wp-content/uploads/FAMM-Public-Comment-North-Carolina-COVID_19-Working-Group.pdf.

2. North Carolina Conference of the NAACP et al., Emergency Original Petition for Writ of Mandamus, https://www.acluofnorthcarolina.org/

sites/default/files/nc_naacp_v._cooper_covid-19_pwm_exs_tofile.pdf.

3.   Ames Alexander, "'It's Ground Zero.' How Fear Gripped a North Carolina Prison as COVID-19 Infected Hundreds," *Charlotte Observer*, April 28, 2020, https://www.charlotteobserver.com/news/coronavirus/article242109076.html.

4.   Alexander, "'Its Ground Zero.'"

5.   Joseph Neff and Keri Blakinger, "Few Federal Prisoners Released under COVID-19 Emergency Policies," Marshall Project, April 25, 2020, https://www.themarshallproject.org/2020/04/25/few-federal-prisoners-released-under-covid-19-emergency-policies.

Chapter 26: Executing Illness

1.   Richard C. Dieter, *Battle Scars: Military Veterans and the Death Penalty*, Death Penalty Information Center, November 11, 2015, https://dpic-cdn.org/production/legacy/BattleScars.pdf.

2.   Dieter, *Battle Scars*, 9.

3.   Dieter, *Battle Scars*, 17.

Chapter 27: Jesus as a Man on Death Row

Originally presented as a lecture given at St. Paul's Lutheran Church, Durham, NC, 2018.

1.   Donald Senior and John J. Collins, eds., *The Catholic Study Bible*, 2nd Ed., New American Revised Edition (New York: Oxford University Press, 2011).

2.   Lori Brandt Hale and Reggie L. Williams, "Is This a Bonhoeffer Moment? Lessons for American Christians from the Confessing Church in Germany," *Sojourners Magazine* 47, no. 2 (February 2018).

Chapter 28: The Hole

1.   Brian Jarvis, *Cruel and Unusual: Punishment and US Culture* (London: Pluto Press, 2004), 35.

2.   Jarvis, *Cruel and Unusual*, 35.

3.   Jarvis, *Cruel and Unusual*, 36.

4.   Mary Hawthorne, "Dept. of Amplification: Charles Dickens on Solitary Confinement," *New Yorker*, March 23, 2009, https://www.newyorker.com/books/page-turner/

dept-of-amplification-charles-dickens-on-solitary-confinement, as cited in Philip Goodman, Joshua Page, and Michelle Phelps, *Breaking the Pendulum: The Long Struggle Over Criminal Justice* (New York: Oxford University Press, 2017), 30–31; N.52.

5.   Terry A. Kupers, "Who's in SHU? A Survey of Solitary Confinement," *Prison Legal News* 31, no. 7 (July 2020) 28–29.

6.   Gabrielle Corona, "Food, Punishment, and the Angola Three's Struggle for Freedom, 1971–2019," *Southern Cultures* 27, no.3 (Fall 2021): 77.

7.   Corona, "Food, Punishment," 79.

8.   Corona, "Food, Punishment," 79.

9.   Corona, "Food, Punishment," 80.

10.   Corona, "Food, Punishment," 91.

11.   Corona, "Food, Punishment," 91.

12.   Wilbert Rideau and Billy Sinclair, "Prisoner Litigation: How It Began in Louisiana," *Louisiana Law Review* 45, no. 5 (May 1985): 1061–76, as cited in Corona, "Food, Punishment."

13.   Patrick Alexander and Albert Woodfox, "Opening Keynote" (Making and Unmaking Mass Incarceration Conference, Oxford, MS, December 4, 2019), cited Corona, "Food, Punishment," 91.

14.   Gregory S. Taylor, *Central Prison: A History of North Carolina's State Penitentiary* (Baton Rouge: Louisiana State University Press, 2021), 239.

15.   Taylor, *Central Prison*, 240.

16.   Taylor, *Central Prison*, 244.

17.   Taylor, *Central Prison*, 245.

18.   Taylor, *Central Prison*, 246.

19.   Taylor, *Central Prison*, 247.

Chapter 29: The Fury of Our Resistance

1.   V. L. Bounds, "Riot at Central Prison," Report of Commissioner of Prisons (Raleigh, NC: NP, 1968), cited in Gregory S. Taylor, *Central Prison: A History of North Carolina's State Penitentiary* (Baton Rouge: Louisiana State University Press, 2021), 168, 276, 285.

2.   North Carolina Department of Public Safety: Prisons, "Offender Disciplinary Procedures," Chapter: B, Section: .0200, Policy and Procedure, issued January 19, 2022.

3. North Carolina Department of Public Safety, "Disapproved Publications Report" (Bulletin Board Posting) February 1, 2022, https://prisonbooks. info/img/resource-banned-books-2022.pdf.

4. Malcolm M. Feeley and Edward L. Rubin, *Judicial Policy Making and the Modern State: How the Courts Reformed America's Prisons* (New York: Cambridge University Press, 1998), 13.

5. Joshua Page, *The Toughest Beat: Politics, Punishment, and the Prison Officers Union in California* (New York: Oxford University Press, 2013), 21, 237n31.

6. John Irwin, *Prisons in Turmoil* (Boston: Little, Brown and Co, 1980), 69–70, as cited in Page, *Toughest Beat*, 21, 237n29.

7. Robert Johnson, Ann Marie Rocheleau, and Alison B. Martin, *Hard Time: A Fresh Look at Understanding and Reforming the Prison System*, 4th ed. (Hoboken, NJ: Wiley-Blackwell, 2017).

8. Page, *Toughest Beat*, 21, 237n33.

9. Taylor, *Central Prison*, 166, 276n7, 276n8.

10. Taylor, *Central Prison*, 166.

11. Taylor, *Central Prison*, 167.

12. Taylor, *Central Prison*, 168.

13. Taylor, *Central Prison*, 169.

14. Taylor, *Central Prison*, 169, 267n15.

15. Taylor, *Central Prison*, 169, 276n18.

16. Page, *Toughest Beat*, 22–24, 238n38, 238n39, 238n42.

17. Heather Ann Thompson, "Behind the Wall: Half a Century after Attica, Prisoners Are Still Rising Up against Brutal Conditions," *Time*, September 13, 2021, 54–59.

18. Thompson, "Behind the Wall," 58.

19. Thompson, "Behind the Wall," 58.

20. Thompson, "Behind the Wall," 58.

21. Taylor, *Central Prison*, 174.

22. Taylor, *Central Prison*, 174.

23. Taylor, *Central Prison*, 175.

24. Taylor, *Central Prison*, 175.

25. Taylor, *Central Prison*, 176.

26. Taylor, *Central Prison*, 176.

27. Angela Y. Davis, *Are Prisons Obsolete?* (New York: Seven Stories Press,

2003), 127.

28. Mike Hannigan and Tony Platt, "Interview with Angela Davis," *Crime and Social Justice*, no. 3 (Summer 1975): 30, as cited in Seth Kotch, *Lethal State: A History of North Carolina's Death Penalty* (Chapel Hill: University of North Carolina Press, 2019), 167n96.

29. Ginny Carroll, "4,000 March Here in Peaceful Protest," *News & Observer*, July 5, 1975, as cited by Kotch, *Lethal State*, 167n97.

30. Genna Rae McNeil, "The Body, Sexuality, and Self-Defense in *State v. Joan Little*, 1974–1975," *Journal of African American History* 93, no. 2 (Spring 2008): 251, 252, as cited by Kotch, *Lethal State*, 168n102.

31. Kotch, *Lethal State*, 168.

32. Angela Y. Davis, *Women, Race, and Class* (London: Women's Press, 1981), 175, 183, as cited in Brian Jarvis, *Cruel and Unusual: Punishment and US Culture* (London: Pluto Press, 2004), 101.

33. Kotch, *Lethal State*, 168.

34. Taylor, *Central Prison*, 175.

35. Taylor, *Central Prison*, 176.

36. Jonathan Wilson-Hartgrove, phone interview by Lyle C. May at Central Prison, Unit-3 Death Row, March 16 and 17, 2022.

37. Hartgrove, interview.

38. Hartgrove, interview.

39. Hartgrove, interview.

Chapter 30: Attention, Activists, and Election Cynics

1. Joshua Page, *The Toughest Beat: Politics, Punishment, and the Prison Officers Union in California* (New York: Oxford University Press, 2013), 4.

2. Page, *Toughest Beat*, 5.

3. Page, *Toughest Beat*, 48.

4. Page, *Toughest Beat*, 4.

5. Page, *Toughest Beat*, 48.

6. Carol J. Williams, "Justice Kennedy Laments State of Prisons in California, US," *Los Angeles Times*, February 4, 2010, https://www.latimes.com/archives/la-xpm-2010-feb-04-la-me-kennedy4-2010feb04-story.html, as cited in Page, *Toughest Beat*, 5.

7. Keisha N. Blain, "Whitewashing Slavery Isn't Education; It's Propaganda,"

MSNBC.com, July 6, 2022, https://www.msnbc.com/opinion/msnbc-opinion/texas-students-may-get-whitewashed-version-slavery-n1296842.

8. Racheal Pesta, "Labeling and the Differential Impact of School Discipline on Negative Life Outcomes: Assessing Ethno-Racial Variation in the School-to-Prison Pipeline," *Crime and Delinquency* 64, no. 11 (2018):1489–1512, https://doi.org/10.1177/0011128717749223.

9. Pesta, "Labeling and the Differential."

10. Pesta, "Labeling and the Differential."

11. Mark Schultz, "Durham County Has a New Budget. What's in It for Schools, Taxpayers, and New Mothers?" *News & Observer*, June 15, 2022, https://www.newsobserver.com/news/local/counties/durham-county/article262490292.html; Danielle Battalia, "What a Discussion in Durham Reveals on the Nuance of Incarceration," *News & Observer*, 2022.

12. Mandy Locke, "North Carolina Sheriffs Carry Clout When Defending Officers at Risk of Losing Their Badges," *News & Observer*, June 30, 2022, https://www.newsobserver.com/news/state/north-carolina/article262896278.html.

13. Locke, "North Carolina Sheriffs."

14. Frank Baumgartner et al., *Deadly Justice: A Statistical Portrait of the Death Penalty* (Cambridge: Oxford University Press, 2016), 218.

15. John Shiffman and Michael Berens, "The Long Quest to Stop a 'Sugar Daddy' Judge Accused of Preying on Women," Part 3 of Exploring the Bench, Reuters, July 14, 2020.

16. Shiffman and Berens, "Long Quest."

17. Shiffman and Berens, "Long Quest."

18. Kyle Ingram, "Democrats Lead Fundraising for NC Supreme Court. See Who's Giving to the Candidates," *News & Observer*, July 27, 2022.

19. Clark Corbin, "Local Idaho Candidates Begin Using GoFundMe to Raise Campaign Money," *Idaho Capital Sun*, September 27, 2021, https://idahocapitalsun.com/2021/09/27/local-idaho-candidates-begin-using-gofundme-to-raise-campaign-money/.

20. Corbin, "Local Idaho Candidates."

21. Lena Geller, "Money in Politics: A Q&A with Bob Phillips of CommonCause," *Indy Week*, May 25, 2022, https://indyweek.com/news/northcarolina/pac-money-bob-phillips-common-cause/.

Chapter 31: Reform or Abolish

1.   "Task Force Roster and Structure," North Carolina Department of Justice, https://ncdoj.gov/trec/roster/.

2.   "Task Force Roster and Structure."

3.   "Racial Equity and Law Enforcement Recomendations Chart," North Carolina Department of Justice, https://ncdoj.gov/wp-content/uploads/2021/02/TREC_Recommendations_02262021.pdf.

Acknowledgments

Writing and publishing a book is hard work, an extensive process that involves a number of different people and challenges along the way. This is especially true for incarcerated writers, who have to overcome additional obstacles specific to confinement. I am blessed with numerous friends who have helped me overcome each one of those obstacles to make publication of *Witness* a reality. Thank you for all of the love, support, and investment of your time in this project. Your contributions are what make changing the criminal legal system possible.

Thank you Danielle Purifoy for writing the foreword and sharing what it is like to have a loved one on the inside. Your collaboration and willingness to give me a chance at *Scalawag* magazine helped me more effectively express carceral experience through illustrative stories that make sense of public policy.

Thank you Amber Caron, for helping me bring the vision of *Witness* into a manageable shape, turning a collection of miscellaneous essays into a meaningful book. Your ability to troubleshoot structure, and guide me through the publication process as an experienced author, is why I will be able to finally celebrate my successes.

Thank you Lovey Cooper, for editing many of the articles that became chapters in this book, and for holistic revisions that brought us closer to the finish line.

Thank you Julia Udell for reaching out to Haymarket Books on my behalf and being unwilling to take no for an answer, encouraging me to do the same, and teaching me about abolition. Thank you Tara Kumar, for being a steady presence in my life for over two decades, but also helping organize communication, relay messages, and handle many of the tasks I cannot. You give me the confidence to reach beyond the wall.

Thank you professors Frank Baumgartner—UNC Chapel Hill, Amanda Cox—Ohio University, Lisa Carter—Florida Southern College, and Robert Johnson—American University, for inviting me to speak with your students on multiple occasions and experience the joys of teaching people about the criminal legal system. Thank you Emily Baxter for connecting me to Ally Traznick and St. Paul›s Lutheran Church in Durham. Thank you Tessie Castillo, Ben Finholt, Kerwin Pittman, Kathy Williams, Marsha Owen, and Jonathan Wilson Hartgrove for your advocacy, activism, and agreeing to be interviewed for *Witness*.

Thank you to Haymarket Books for helping me reach the public with my writing, and for the hard work of Eric Kerl, Rory, Maria Carlos, and staff. Finally, thank you Mom and Dad for raising me with the belief that I can achieve anything with hard work and dedication.

About the Authors

LYLE C. MAY is a prison journalist and Ohio University alum. He is currently finishing a bachelor's program in interdisciplinary studies through Adams State University. He is a member of the Alpha Sigma Lambda Honor Society and the Author's Guild. Lyle's writings have appeared in *Scalawag* magazine, *Perspectives on Politics*, the *Intercept*, *America* magazine, *Inside Higher Ed*, and elsewhere. Lyle is also a coauthor of *Inside: Voices from Death Row* (Scuppernong Editions, 2022) and contributor to *Right Here, Right Now: Life Stories from America's Death Row* (Duke

University Press, 2021). He routinely lectures to high school and university students, church groups, and community organizations on the politics, policies, and experiences of mass incarceration. As he pursues every legal avenue to overturn his wrongful conviction and death sentence, Lyle advocates for greater access to higher education in prison.

DANIELLE PURIFOY, JD, Ph.D, is an assistant professor of Geography and Environment at the University of North Carolina at Chapel Hill, where she also serves as a faculty project lead for the UNC Environmental Justice Action Research Clinic. Danielle is the former Race and Place editor of *Scalawag*, a media organization devoted to Southern storytelling, journalism, and the arts. You can also find her work in *Society and Space*, *Inside Higher Ed*, *Environmental Sociology*, *Southeastern Geographer*, *Southern Cultures*, and *Transactions of the Institute of British Geographers*, among other publications.

About Haymarket Books

Haymarket Books is a radical, independent, nonprofit book publisher based in Chicago. Our mission is to publish books that contribute to struggles for social and economic justice. We strive to make our books a vibrant and organic part of social movements and the education and development of a critical, engaged, and internationalist Left.

We take inspiration and courage from our namesakes, the Haymarket Martyrs, who gave their lives fighting for a better world. Their 1886 struggle for the eight-hour day—which gave us May Day, the international workers' holiday—reminds workers around the world that ordinary people can organize and struggle for their own liberation. These struggles—against oppression, exploitation, environmental devastation, and war—continue today across the globe.

Since our founding in 2001, Haymarket has published more than nine hundred titles. Radically independent, we seek to drive a wedge into the risk-averse world of corporate book publishing. Our authors include Angela Y. Davis, Arundhati Roy, Keeanga-Yamahtta Taylor, Eve Ewing, Aja Monet, Mariame Kaba, Naomi Klein, Rebecca Solnit, Olúfẹ́mi O. Táíwò, Mohammed El-Kurd, José Olivarez, Noam Chomsky, Winona LaDuke, Robyn Maynard, Leanne Betasamosake Simpson, Howard Zinn, Mike Davis, Marc Lamont Hill, Dave Zirin, Astra Taylor, and Amy Goodman, among many other leading writers of our time. We are also the trade publishers of the acclaimed Historical Materialism Book Series.

Haymarket also manages a vibrant community organizing and event space in Chicago, Haymarket House, the popular Haymarket Books Live event series and podcast, and the annual Socialism Conference.

Also Available from Haymarket Books

Abolition: Politics, Practices, Promises, Vol. 1
by Angela Y. Davis

Abolition for the People
The Movement For a Future without Policing and Prisons
Edited by Colin Kaepernick

American Inmate
by Justin Rovillos Monson

The Sentences That Create Us: Crafting A Writer's Life in Prison
by PEN America, edited by Caits Meissner

A Time to Die: The Attica Prison Revolt
by Tom Wicker

The Long Term: Resisting Life Sentences Working Toward Freedom
Edited by Alice Kim, Erica Meiners, Jill Petty, Audrey Petty,
Beth E. Richie, and Sarah Ross

How to Abolish Prisons: Lessons from the Movement against Imprisonment
by Rachel Herzing and Justin Piché
Foreword by Mariame Kaba